Dictionary of Long-Term Care and
Related Terms

介護福祉用語
和英・英和辞典

中央法規

澤田 如・住居広士 |著|

Yuki Sawada | Hiroshi Sumii

はしがき

　世界に例をみない速さで急速に進む高齢化や2000年に創設された介護保険制度の定着に伴い，「介護福祉」は国民の日常生活を支えるという重要な役割を果たしている．

　その介護福祉の役割はそれを取り巻く環境とともに徐々に変化してきている．たとえば，1987（昭和62）年制定の「社会福祉士及び介護福祉士法」が2007（平成19）年に改正されたことにより，介護福祉を担う介護福祉士の定義や義務規定，資格取得方法が改正された．2011（平成23）年の改正では，介護福祉士を含む介護職員等でも一定条件を満たせば，たん吸引・経管栄養が可能となった．2012（平成24）年からは，新教育カリキュラムに応じた介護福祉士国家試験が開始され，2016（平成28）年度の国家試験からは受験資格の改正により，実務経験者は実務経験3年以上に加えて，実務者研修の修了が義務付けられた．

　さらに，原則として他国から労働者を受け入れてこなかった看護・介護現場において，日本とインドネシア，フィリピンおよびベトナムとの間で締結された経済連携協定（EPA）や「外国人の技能実習の適正な実施及び技能実習生の保護に関する法律」において技能実習制度の対象職種の一つとして介護職種が追加されたことにより，外国人看護師・介護福祉士候補者および技能実習生の受け入れが可能となった．

　このように，介護福祉にかかわる人々には今後，専門技術や幅広い知識が求められると同時に，国際的にも交流を展開していくことが求められる．

　そこで本辞典では，介護福祉関連の近年の動向を反映していると評価されている中央法規出版編集部編『七訂 介護福祉用語辞典』（中央法規出版，2015）に収載されている約3,600用語に加え，過去3回の介護福祉士国家試験において出題された用語を抽出し，翻訳・校閲した．国外で刊行された文献等からも高齢者福祉や医療，看護，リハビリテーション，心理学等，多領域における用語を包括的に検証したうえで抽出し，翻訳・校閲した．

　また，日本の看護・介護国家資格の取得を目指す外国人が学べるよう，さらに，介護福祉現場の専門職や教育・研修関係者および研究職の人々の国際的な交流に役立つよう，約500語を抽出し，英語にて概説した．

　医療・介護福祉用語や制度，法令，報告書等の翻訳については，日本において定訳化しつつある既存のものをできる限り参照しながら検証し，翻訳・校閲した．しかし，それらは公定訳ではなく，あくまで読者の皆様に理解を深めていただくために独自に翻訳した参考翻訳である．そのため，本辞典に収載されている和訳・英訳の適用については読者の皆様の判断にゆだねるとともに，引き続き検証し，最善の翻訳になるよう尽力していきたい．

　本辞典の出版にあたりご指導・ご協力を賜った社会福祉法人浴風会 京極髙宣理事長をはじめ，関係者の皆様に心からお礼申し上げる．

また，今回の出版にご尽力頂いた中央法規出版の日高雄一郎氏ならびに膨大なデータ収集・編集等の作業を助けてくださった野池隆幸氏，須貝牧子氏をはじめとする編集部の皆様に心から感謝申し上げる．

本辞典が介護福祉にかかわる皆様にとって良きものとなれば幸いである．

2017年8月吉日

澤田 如
住居広士

Preface

Since the long-term care insurance system was implemented in Japan in 2000, many changes have taken place including changes in the Social Workers and Care Workers Act of 1987 which altered the role and responsibility of long-term care professionals, modifications to the academic requirements for certification, and the acceptance of foreign nurse and care worker candidates. In a new era of long-term care, professional caregivers are required to build their skills and increase their professionalism.

In order to increase academic knowledge and understanding of the basics of long-term care and to expand Japan's academic exchange with other countries, a linguistic common ground needs to be created. With this publication, we hope to build a linguistic bridge that links several specialized fields and enable further exchange and collaboration among long-term care professionals and academics from around the world.

The features and structure of this dictionary are as follows.

For the Japanese-English section (Part 1), we included terms relevant to long-term care and related services found in works such as the Dictionary of Care and Welfare, 7th Edition (Chuohoki Publishing, 2015) and questions from last three years of National Certification Examination for Care Workers. We also included terms from numerous published works in the fields of elder care, medicine, nursing, long-term care, social services, rehabilitation and childcare. In total, about 7,000 terms were included.

For the English-Japanese section (Part 2), we included approximately 5,300 relevant, long-term care terms from a number of internationally published works in addition to the works and fields mentioned above.

In Part 3, for those native speakers of English or other languages trying to learn about long-term care and related terms in Japan, 500 of the 7,000 terms included in the Japanese-English section are explained in English as a noun phrase in a sentence.

Please be advised that the English translations in this dictionary are furnished for information purposes only since they are not official, but approximations and may be changed once a reliable and/or official source of English translation is found. Efforts to make as perfect translations as possible and revisions will continue in updated future editions of this dictionary.

Also, we may have inadvertently excluded some terms that may be included in this dictionary. We would like to ask all our colleagues and readers to provide us with their support and guidance.

This dictionary would not have been published without the support of many individuals who contributed to our understanding of terms and important concepts presented in this book. We would like to express our gratitude to Dr. Takanobu Kyogoku of Yokufukai for enabling us to publish this dictionary. We would also like to thank Yuichiro Hidaka, Takayuki Noike and Makiko Sugai of Chuohoki Publishing for helping us in the process of selection, editing and proofreading.

August 2017

Yuki Sawada and Hiroshi Sumii
Authors

本辞典の特徴と構成

第1部：和英

中央法規出版編集部編『七訂 介護福祉用語辞典』(中央法規出版，2015) に収載されている約3,600用語と過去3回の介護福祉士国家試験で出題された用語を中心に用語を抽出し，英訳・校閲した．また，国内外で刊行された文献から高齢者福祉，医療，看護，リハビリテーション，心理学等の多領域における用語についても検証・抽出し，翻訳・校閲した．用語総数は約7,000である．

第2部：英和

中央法規出版編集部編『七訂 介護福祉用語辞典』(中央法規出版，2015) と過去3回の介護福祉士国家試験で出題された用語に加え，国外で刊行された Encyclopedia of Elder Care や Encyclopedia of Social Work 等の文献から高齢者福祉，医療，看護，リハビリテーション，心理学等に関連する用語を抽出し，翻訳・校閲した．用語総数は約5,300である．

第3部：英文用語解説

第1部の「和英」に収載した用語の中から約500語について，可能な限り簡約な英文にて概説した．

凡例

第1部：和英

1．人名，医学用語などの専門用語を除いて，常用漢字，現代かなづかいとして，五十音（あいうえお）順に配列した．
2．拗音(ようおん)・促音(そくおん)などを表す小字(ぁ，ぃ，ぅ，ぇ，ぉ，ゃ，ゅ，ょ，っ)は，直音と同様に扱った．
　　　例：「認知症」→「ニンチショウ」

3．清音，濁音，半濁音の配列については同格に扱った．
4．長音記号(ー)は，直前文字の母音として読み取って配列した．
　　　例：「ショートステイ」→「シヨオトステイ」

5. 用語内にカッコ（「　」など），ハイフン（−），中黒記号（・）などを使用した場合は，それらを配列上無視した．

6. アルファベットやギリシャ文字は，A（エイ），B（ビイ），C（シイ），α（アルフア），β（ベエタ）と，直前文字の母音として読み取って配列した．

　　　　例：「B型肝炎」→「ビイガタカンエン」

　ただし，PET（ペット），WAM NET（ワムネツト）と一般名で読んで配列したものもある．

7. 日本人名は，姓・名の順で表記した．

8. 外国人名の日本語表記は，カタカナでフルスペルした姓と，名のイニシャル（頭文字）の順で表記した．ミドルネームがある場合は，カタカナでフルスペルした姓と，名とミドルネームそれぞれのイニシャルの順で表記した．原語では，名，ミドルネーム，姓の順で表記した．

　　　　例：「マズロー, A. H.」（日本語表記）
　　　　　　「Abraham Harold Maslow」（原語表記）

　ミドルネームの原語でのフルスペルが不明なものについては，名のあとにミドルネームのイニシャルを続け，ピリオド（．）をうって表記した．

　　　　例：「バルテス, P. B.」（日本語表記）
　　　　　　「Paul B. Baltes」（原語表記）

　原語で名，ミドルネーム，姓の順を入れ替えて表記する場合や名とミドルネームをイニシャルで表記する場合は，以下のような改変が必要である．

● 姓，名，ミドルネームの順で表記する場合には，姓のあとにコンマ（，）をうって名とミドルネームを続けて表記する．

　　　　例：「Abraham Harold Maslow」→「Maslow, Abraham Harold」

● 姓，名の後にミドルネームをイニシャルで表記する場合は，姓のあとにコンマ（，）をうって名を続け，その後ミドルネームのイニシャルにピリオド（．）をうって表記する．

　　　　例：「Abraham Harold Maslow」→「Maslow, Abraham H.」

● 姓の後に名とミドルネームの両方をイニシャルで表記する場合は，姓のあとにコンマ（，）をうち，名とミドルネームのイニシャルの後にそれぞれピリオド（．）をうって表記する．

　　　　例：「Abraham Harold Maslow」→「Maslow, A. H.」

9. 団体・組織名等は，自称の一般名称で表記し，略称は，コロン（：）の後に示した．

10. 一つの用語に対し名称・翻訳等を二つ以上記載する場合は，セミコロン（；）の後に示した．

11. （　）を付した用語は，略語や（　）内の用法でも同様に使われる場合などを示す．

12. ［　］は，簡約の説明を表記した．

13. *を付した用語は，第3部に英文の解説があることを示す．

第2部：英和

1. 基本的には米式綴りを採用し，アルファベット（ABC）順に配列した．本辞典に収載されている用語で英式の綴りを採用する用語の場合には，以下のような一部改変が必要である．

        例）　　米式　　　英式
              labor　　labour
              aging　　ageing

2. 用語内にスペース，ハイフン（－），コンマ（，），アポストロフィ（'）などを使用した場合は，それらを配列上無視した．

3. 団体・組織名等は自称の一般名称で表記し，略称は，コロン（：）の後に示した．

4. 欧文略語の省略記号のピリオド（．）は省いた．

5. 一つの用語に対し名称・翻訳等を二つ以上記載する場合は，セミコロン（；）の後に示した．

第3部：英文用語解説

1. 人名，医学用語などの専門用語を除いて，常用漢字，現代かなづかいとして，五十音（あいうえお）順に配列した．

2. 拗音（ようおん）・促音（そくおん）などを表す小字（ぁ，ぃ，ぅ，ぇ，ぉ，ゃ，ゅ，ょ，っ）は，直音と同様に扱い，長音記号（ー）は，直前文字の母音として読み取って配列した．
        例：「パーキンソン病」→「パアキンソンビョウ」

3. 清音，濁音，半濁音の配列については同格に扱った．

4. 名称等の略称は，コロン（：）の後に示した．

5. 項目にカッコ（「　」等），ハイフン（－），中黒記号（・）などを使用した場合は，それらを配列上無視した．

6. 英文解説内で（　）を付している場合は，略語や法令・通知等の根拠条数，または簡約の説明，（　）内の用法でも同様に使われる場合などを示す．

7. 暦年には，西暦を用いた．

第 1 部 ― 和英

あ

アイコンタクト　eye contact
愛着理論　attachment theory
アイデンティティ　identity
愛の手帳　disability handbook
あえ物　dressed food ; dressed dish
アカウンタビリティー　accountability
アカシジア　akathisia
アキレス腱　Achilles tendon ; calcaneal tendon ; heel cord
悪質商法　fraudulent and unethical sales practices ; fraudulent trading strategy
アクション・リサーチ　action research
悪性関節リウマチ　malignant rheumatoid arthritis
悪性腫瘍　malignant tumor ; cancerous growth
悪性新生物　malignant neoplasm
悪性貧血　pernicious anemia
アクセシビリティ　accessibility
アクセス・フリー　access free
*アクティビティ　activity
アクティビティ・サービス　activity services
あく抜き　removing the bitterness from food
握力　grip strength
アクリル　acrylic
アグレッシブ・ケースワーク　aggressive casework
揚げ物　deep fried food
麻　hemp
朝日訴訟　Asahi litigation
アシドーシス　acidosis
味の相互作用　flavor interactions in foods
足白癬　tinea pedis ; athlete's foot
足病学　podiatry
アシュワース尺度　Ashworth Scale
アスピリン療法　aspirin therapy
アスペルガー症候群　Asperger's syndrome : AS
アスペルギルス症　aspergillosis
*アセスメント　assessment
アセテート　acetate fabric

あせも　heat rash
遊び　play
遊びリテーション　rehabilitation play
亜脱臼　subluxation
アダムス, J.　Jane Addams
圧搾　compression
圧縮記録　compressed recording
圧迫　pressure ; compression
圧迫潰瘍　pressure ulcer
圧迫骨折　compression fracture
アディソン病　Addison's disease
*アテトーゼ　athetosis
アテトーゼ型　athetoid
アトピー　atopy
アトピー咳嗽　atopic cough
アトピー性皮膚炎　atopic dermatitis
*アドボカシー　advocacy
アドボケーター　advocator
アドミニストレーション　administration
アドレナリン　adrenalin ; adrenaline ; epinephrine
アナフィラキシーショック　anaphylactic shock
アニサキス　Anisakis ; herring worm
アニマル・セラピー　animal assisted therapy : AAT
アフターケア　aftercare
油焼け　oil burn
アポクリン腺　apocrine sweat gland
亜麻　Linum usitatissimum ; flax
アミトロ　amyotrophic lateral sclerosis : ALS ; Lou Gehrig's disease
アミノ酸　amino acid
編物　knitting
アミラーゼ　amylase
アミロイドーシス　amyloidosis
アメニティ　amenity
アメリカ精神遅滞協会　American Association on Mental Retardation : AAMR
「新たな高齢者医療制度のあり方について」　Opinion Statement regarding the Reform of the Medical Care System for the Elderly
「新たな高齢者介護システムの確立について」　Mid-Term Report on the Long-Term Care

System for the Elderly

アルカローシス　alkalosis

アルコール依存症　alcoholism

アルコール飲料　alcoholic beverage ; alcoholic drink

アルコール幻覚症　alcoholic hallucinosis ; alcohol-related psychosis

アルコール性肝炎　alcoholic hepatitis

アルコール性肝障害　alcoholic liver disease ; alcohol-induced liver injury ; alcoholic hepatopathy

アルコール精神病　alcoholic psychosis ; alcohol-related psychosis

アルコール性認知症　alcoholic dementia ; alcohol-related dementia

アルコール性脳障害　alcoholic encephalopathy ; alcohol-induced encephalopathy

アルコール中毒　alcoholic

アルコホリックス・アノニマス　Alcoholics Anonymous : AA

*アルツハイマー型認知症　dementia of the Alzheimer's type : DAT

アルツハイマー型認知症不快評価尺度 Discomfort Scale for Dementia of the Alzheimer's Type : DS-DAT

*アルツハイマー病　Alzheimer's disease

α-でんぷん　alpha-starch

アルブミン　albumin

アルマ・アタ宣言　Declaration of Alma-Ata ; Alma-Ata Declaration

アレルギー　allergy

アレルギー性気管支炎　allergic bronchitis

アレルギー性掻痒症　allergic pruritus

アレルギー性鼻炎　allergic rhinitis ; hay fever

アレルギー性皮膚炎　allergic contact dermatitis

アレルギー反応　allergic reaction

アレルギー表示　food allergen labeling

アレルギー様食中毒　allergy-like food poisoning

アンケート　questionnaire ; survey

暗順応　dark adaptation

安静時エネルギー消費量　resting energy

expenditure : REE

安静時狭心症　angina at rest ; rest angina

安静時振戦　resting tremor

安全管理（システム）　safety management (system)

安全指導　safety guidance ; safety education

安全の欲求　safety needs

アントシアニン　anthocyanin

アンドロゲン　androgen

安否確認（システム）　safety confirmation (system)

アンビバレンス　ambivalence

アンフェタミン　amphetamine

*あん法　fomentation

あん摩　Anma massage therapy

あん摩師　Anma massage therapist ; masseur［男性］; masseuse［女性］

あん摩マッサージ指圧師、はり師、きゅう師等に関する法律　Anma Massage and Finger Pressure Practitioners, Acupuncturists and Moxibustion Practitioners Act

安眠　quiet sleep

安眠援助　sleep aid

アンモニア　ammonia

アンモニア解毒　ammonia detoxification

安楽　comfort

安楽いす型　rocking chair

安楽死　euthanasia

い

E型肝炎（ウイルス）　hepatitis E (virus)

胃液　gastric juice

胃炎　gastritis

胃潰瘍　gastric ulcer

医学指示拒否　against medical advice : AMA

医学的判定　medical assessment

医学的リハビリテーション　medical rehabilitation

医学モデル　medical model

怒り　anger ; rage

胃がん　stomach cancer ; gastric cancer

易感染患者　compromised patient

易感染宿主　compromised host

生きがい motivation in life

生きがい保障 assurance of motivation in life

息切れ shortness of breath

息こらえ嚥下 supraglottic swallow

閾値 threshold

異議申し立て appeal

医業 medical practice

医業類似行為 quasi-medical practice

育児・介護休業法 Child Rearing and Family Caregiving Leave Act

育児休業 child care leave ; parental leave ; child rearing leave

育児休業、介護休業等育児又は家族介護を行う労働者の福祉に関する法律 Child Rearing and Family Caregiving Leave Act

育児休業制度 child care leave system ; parental leave system ; child rearing leave system

育児休業手当金 child care leave allowance ; parental leave allowance

育児給付 child care benefit

育児手当 child care allowance

育児ノイローゼ maternity neurosis

育児放棄 child neglect

育成医療 medical treatment for children with disabilities

医原性 iatrogenic

医原病 iatrogenesis

医行為 medical practice

移行期ケア transitional care

遺言 will ; testament

椅座位 seating position

遺産税 estate tax

医師 medical doctor ; physician

意識 consciousness

意識混濁 clouding of consciousness ; brain fog ; mental fog

＊意識障害 disturbance of consciousness

意識消失発作 presyncope

意識喪失 syncope

意識調査 opinion survey

意識変容 altered states of consciousness

維持期リハビリテーション maintenance phase of rehabilitation ; late phase rehabilitation

意識レベル level of consciousness

意思決定 decision-making

意思決定代理者 proxy decision maker

医師自殺幇助 physician-assisted suicide

医師紹介サービス physician referral services ; doctor referral services

意思疎通支援 communication support

意思疎通支援事業 communication support services

意思伝達装置 communication aid

医師登録法 Medical Practitioners Registration Act

意思能力評価 mental capacity assessment

意思の伝達 expressions of desires

医師法 Medical Practitioners Act

いじめ bullying

医事問題 medical issue

医者 medical doctor ; physician

胃・十二指腸潰瘍 gastroduodenal ulcer

萎縮 atrophy

萎縮性胃炎 atrophic gastritis

萎縮性膣炎 atrophic vaginitis

移乗・移動 transfer and mobility

移乗・移動介助 assistance with transfer and mobility

移乗介助 assistance with transfer

異常行動 abnormal behavior

異常姿勢 abnormal posture

異常知覚 dysesthesia

＊移乗動作 transfer motion ; transfer movement

移乗動作訓練 transfer training

異常不随意運動評価尺度 Abnormal Involuntary Movement Scale : AIMS

異常歩行 abnormal gait

移乗補助具 transfer aid

異食 abnormal eating ; eating abnormality

異食行為 abnormal eating habit

胃食道逆流症 gastroesophageal reflex disease : GERD

胃切除術 gastrectomy

胃洗浄　gastric lavage

移送サービス　transportation services

•遺族基礎年金　Survivors' Basic Pension

遺族給付　survivors' benefit

遺族年金　survivors' pension

遺族の心理　psychological and emotional state of bereaved family

依存症　addiction ; dependence

依存性薬物　addictive drug

遺体安置所　morgue

委託　outsourcing ; subcontracting ; contracting out

炒め物　stir-fry

1型糖尿病　type 1 diabetes mellitus ; type 1 diabetes

1ケア1手洗い　hand washing before and after seeing each patient

一次過程　primary process

一時雇用　temporary employment

一次障害　primary impairment

一時性　temporary

一次性(本態性)てんかん　idiopathic generalized epilepsy

一次的動機　primary motive ; motivation

一次的欲求　basic needs ; deficiency needs

一次的老化　primary aging

一次判定　initial assessment

一次妄想　primary delusion

一次予防　primary prevention

一日許容摂取量　acceptable daily intake : ADI

一部介助　limited assistance

一部負担金　co-payment

一類感染症　category I infection ; 1st-category infection

一過性細菌叢　transient flora

一過性脳虚血発作　transient ischemic attack : TIA

一酸化炭素　carbon monoxide

一酸化炭素中毒　carbon monoxide poisoning

逸脱　deviation

逸脱行動　deviant behavior

一般医　general practitioner : GP

一般健康教育　general health education

一般診療所　general medical clinic

一般世帯調査　general household survey : GHS

一般相談支援事業　general consultation and support services

一般病院　general hospital

一般病床　general bed

溢流性尿失禁　overflow incontinence

遺伝子　gene

遺伝子組み換え食品　genetically modified organism : GMO

遺伝子検査　genetic testing

遺伝子診断　genetic diagnosis

遺伝子の突然変異　gene mutation

遺伝(子)病　genetic disorder

移転所得　transfer income

イド　id

•移動介助　assistance with mobility

移動支援事業　transportation services

移動性　mobility

移動動作　locomotor movements

移動用リフト　transfer lift

意図的自己放任　active self-neglect

意図的な感情表現　purposeful expression of feelings

意図的徘徊　purposeful wandering

遺尿症　enuresis

胃の蠕動運動　peristalsis in the stomach

いびき　snoring

易疲労性　easy fatigability

衣服　clothe ; clothing ; garment

衣服圧　clothing pressure

衣服気候　microclimate of clothing

衣服の修繕　clothing repair

衣服の着脱　dressing and undressing

衣服の保温性　warmth of cloth

異物収集　hoarding

意味記憶　semantic memory

意味性認知症　semantic dementia : SD

医薬品、医療機器等の品質、有効性及び安全性の確保等に関する法律　Safety Assurance and Quality Improvement of Pharmaceutical Products and Medical Devices Act : Pharmaceutical Affairs Act

医薬品副作用被害救済制度　adverse drug reaction compensation system ; adverse drug reaction relief system

意欲　motivation

意欲障害　volitional disorder

意欲低下　decline of motivation

イリゲーション　irrigation

遺留分　distributive share

医療　medical care ; health care

医療委任状　health-care proxy

医療・介護関係事業者における個人情報の適切な取扱いのためのガイドライン　Guidelines for the Appropriate Handling of Personal Information for Medical and Healthcare Professionals

医療介護総合確保方針　Comprehensive Assurance Plan for Health and Long-Term Care Services

医療過誤　medical malpractice

医療過誤補償保険　medical malpractice liability insurance

医療過疎地域　medically underserved area

医療型障害児入所施設　health facility for children with disabilities

医療関係者　medical professional

医療関連サービス　health-related services

医療機器（分類）　(classification of) medical devices

医療給付　medical benefit

医療記録　medical records

医療圏　health service area

医療行為　medical practice

医療資源　medical resources

医療事故　medical error

医療従事者　medical personnel ; health care personnel

医療受給者証　medical insurance card

＊衣料障害　clothing-related skin irritation

医療政策　health policy

医療制度改革　health care reform

医療制度改革大綱　comprehensive health care reform

医療専門職　medical professional ; health professional

医療専門職不足地域　health professional shortage areas : HPSAs

＊医療ソーシャルワーカー　medical social worker : MSW

医療大麻　medical marijuana

医療提供施設　medical facility

医療的ケア　medical care

医療の基準　standards of medical practice

医療の質　quality of medical care

医療廃棄物　medical waste

医療費　medical expenses

医療費控除　tax deduction for medical expenses

医療費抑制策　health care cost containment

医療複合体　integrated health care delivery system

医療福祉　healthcare and welfare ; medicine and welfare

医療扶助　medical aid

医療法　Medical Care Act

医療法人　medical corporation

＊医療保険　medical insurance ; health insurance

医療保険加入者　enrollees of health insurance

医療保険者　health insurer

医療保護入院　involuntary psychiatric hospitalization

衣料用防虫剤　pyrethroid insecticide for clothes ; synthetic pyrethroid

医療倫理　health care ethics ; medical ethics

医療倫理の四原則　four principles of health care ethics ; four principles of medical ethics

イレウス　ileus

イレオストミー　ileostomy

入れ歯　denture

胃ろう　gastrostomy

胃ろう経管栄養　gastric tube feeding

胃ろうチューブ gastrostomy tube
陰圧性肺水腫 negative pressure pulmonary edema
インクルージョン inclusion
インシデント報告書 incident report
インスタント食品 convenience food ; tertiary processed food
・インスリン（インシュリン） insulin
インスリン依存性糖尿病 insulin-dependent diabetes mellitus : IDDM ; type 1 diabetes
インスリン自己注射 insulin self-injection
インスリン非依存性糖尿病 non-insulin-dependent diabetes mellitus : NIDDM
陰性症状 negative symptom
インターネット通販 online shopping
インターベンション intervention
引退 retirement
・インテーク intake
インテグレーション integration
咽頭 pharynx
咽頭相 pharyngeal phase
院内感染 hospital-acquired infection ; nosocomial infection
・インフォーマル・ケア informal care
インフォーマル資源 informal resources
インフォームド・コンセント informed consent : IC
インフォームド・チョイス informed choice
インフォメーション・サービス information services
陰部潰瘍 genital ulcer
陰部清拭 peri care ; perineal care
陰部洗浄 genital hygiene ; genital washing
インフルエンザ influenza ; flu
インフルエンザウイルス influenza virus ; flu virus
インフルエンザワクチン influenza vaccine ; flu shot
・インペアメント impairment

う

ウイルス virus

ウイルス肝炎 viral hepatitis
ウイルス感染後疲労症候群 post-viral fatigue syndrome
ウイルス感染症 viral infection
ウイルス性肝炎 viral hepatitis
ウイルソン病 Wilson's disease
ウール wool
ウェアリングオフ現象 wearing-off phenomenon
ウェクスラー児童知能検査 Wechsler Intelligence Scale for Children : WISC
ウェクスラー成人知能検査 Wechsler Adult Intelligence Scale : WAIS
ウェクスラー知能検査 Wechsler Intelligence Scale
ウェクスラー・ベルビュー知能検査 Wechsler-Bellevue Intelligence Scale
ウェクスラー幼児知能検査 Wechsler Preschool and Primary Scale of Intelligence : WPPSI
植込み型除細動器 implantable cardioverter defibrillator : ICD
ウェッブ，シドニー Sidney James Webb
ウェッブ，ベアトリス Beatrice Webb
ウエルシュ菌 Clostridium perfringens ; Clostridium welchii
ウェルナー症候群 Werner syndrome : WS
ウェルニッケ・コルサコフ症候群 Wernicke-Korsakoff syndrome
ウェルニッケ失語 Wernicke's aphasia
ウェルニッケ脳症 Wernicke's encephalopathy
ウェルニッケ野 Wernicke's area
ウェルビーイング well-being
ウォーカーケイン pyramid cane ; hemi walker
ウォームアップ warm up
ヴォルフェンスベルガー，W. Wolf Wolfensberger
うがい gargling ; gargle
右心室 right ventricle
右心房 right atrium
内開き戸 hinged door
うつ depression
うっ血 congestion
うっ血性心不全 congestive heart failure

うつ状態　depressive state ; state of depressed mood

うつ滞性皮膚炎　stasis dermatitis

うつ熱　heat retention

•うつ病　depression

うま味　umami ; umami taste

うま味成分　umami taste component

埋込式ペースメーカー　implanted pacemaker

羽毛アレルギー　down feather allergy

羽毛布団　feather down comforter

うらごし　pureeing

ウレタンフォーム　urethane foam

ウロストミー　urostomy

上乗せ給付　supplemental benefit

上乗せサービス　supplemental service

•運営適正化委員会　Complaints Resolution Committee

運動　exercise ; movement ; motion

運動維持困難症　motor impersistence

運動覚　kinesthetic sense

運動学習　motor learning

運動学的分析　kinematic analysis

運動感覚　kinesthesia

運動器症候群　locomotive syndrome

運動機能　motor function

運動技能　motor skill

運動技能・プロセス技能評価　Assessment of Motor and Process Skills : AMPS

運動強度　exercise strength

運動許容量　exercise capacity

運動工学　sports engineering

運動亢進　hyperkinesia

運動失行　motor apraxia

•運動失調症　ataxia

運動障害　motor impairment

運動処方　exercise prescription

運動神経　motor nerve ; motoneuron

運動制御　motion control ; motor control

運動制限　movement-related functional limitation ; restricted mobility

運動性失語（症）　motor aphasia

運動耐容能　exercise capacity

運動低下　hypokinesis ; hypokinesia

運動ニューロン疾患　motor neuron disease

運動年齢　motor age

運動年齢検査　motor-age test

運動発達　motor development

運動発達評価　motor developmental evaluation

運動評価　motor assessment

運動負荷　exercise load

運動負荷テスト　exercise tolerance test : ETT

運動分析　movement analysis

運動麻痺　motor paralysis

•運動療法　therapeutic exercise

え

エアマット　air mattress

A型肝炎（ウイルス）　hepatitis A (virus)

エイコサペンタエン酸　eicosapentaenoic acid : EPA

A/G比　albumin/globulin ratio : A/G ratio

•エイジズム　agism ; ageism

•エイズ　acquired immune deficiency syndrome : AIDS

衛生　hygiene

衛生学　hygienics

衛生教育　health education

•栄養　nutrition

栄養価　nutritive value of foods

栄養改善　nutrition improvement

栄養改善法　Nutrition Improvement Act

栄養管理　nutrition management ; nutritional management

栄養機能食品　nutrient function claims

栄養ケア計画　nutrition care plan

栄養ケアマネジメント　nutrition care management

栄養剤　dietary supplement ; nutritional supplements

栄養サポートチーム　nutrition support team : NST

•栄養士　nutritionist

栄養失調　malnutrition

栄養指導　nutritional education

栄養士法　Dietitians Act

栄養障害　nutrition disorder ; nutritional disorder

栄養状態　nutritional status

•栄養所要量　recommended dietary allowance : RDA

栄養スクリーニング　nutritional screening ; nutrition screening

栄養摂取量　nutrient intake

•栄養素　nutrient

栄養必要量　nutritional requirement

栄養評価　nutritional assessment

栄養表示　nutrition fact label ; nutrition claim

栄養表示基準　nutrition labeling standards ; food labeling standards

栄養不良　malnutrition

栄養補助食品　dietary supplement

営利団体　for-profit organization

鋭利物損傷　sharps injury

腋窩　axilla

腋窩温　axillary temperature

•腋窩検温　axillary temperature measurement

腋窩支持クラッチ　axillary crutch ; underarm crutch

腋窩動脈　axillary artery

腋臭　axillary osmidrosis

腋毛　axillary hair ; under arm hair

エクリン腺　eccrine gland

エゴ　ego

エコマップ　ecomap

エコロジカル・アプローチ　ecological approach

•壊死　necrosis

エス　es

S状結腸　sigmoid colon ; pelvic colon

S状結腸鏡検査　sigmoidoscopy

エストロゲン　estrogen

エストロゲン補充療法　estrogen replacement therapy : ERT

エスニシティ　ethnicity

壊疽　gangrene

エタノール消毒液　ethanol disinfectant

X線　X-ray

X線検査　radiology test

X線撮影　radiography

X線動画撮影　cineradiography

X線透視検査　fluoroscopy

X連鎖優性遺伝　X-linked dominant inheritance

エディプス期　Oedipus phase

エディプス・コンプレックス　Oedipus complex

N式精神機能検査　Nishimura Dementia Scale : NMS

NPO法　NPO Act ; Promotion of Activities by Specified Nonprofit Organizations Act

NPO法人　nonprofit corporation

エネルギー　energy

エネルギー消費　energy expenditure

エネルギー代謝　energy metabolism

エネルギー代謝率　relative metabolic rate : RMR

エネルギー必要量　energy requirement

エバリュエーション　evaluation

エピソード記憶　episodic memory

エビデンス　evidence

エピネフリン　epinephrine

エリクソン，E. H.　Erik Homburger Erikson

エリザベス救貧法　Elizabethan Poor Law

L字手すり　L-shaped grab bar ; L-shaped handrail

エルボークラッチ　forearm crutch

エレクトラ・コンプレックス　Electra complex

遠隔医療　remote medicine ; telemedicine

遠隔医療システム　remote health care system ; telemedicine system

遠隔学習　distance learning

遠隔記憶　remote memory

遠隔教育　distance education

遠隔ケア　remote care ; telecare

遠距離医療　long-distance medicine

遠距離介護　long-distance care ; long-distance caregiving

•嚥下　swallowing

園芸療法　horticultural therapy

嚥下運動　movement during swallowing

嚥下機能　swallowing function

嚥下機能障害 dysphagia of swallowing function

嚥下訓練 swallowing training

嚥下困難 swallowing difficulty

嚥下困難者用食品 consistency modified diet for people with swallowing difficulties ; consistency modified diet for dysphagia ; dysphagia diet

嚥下障害 dysphagia ; swallowing disorder ; deglutition disorder

*嚥下性肺炎 aspiration pneumonia ; deglutition pneumonia

嚥下造影検査 videofluorography : VF

嚥下痛 odynophagia

嚥下反射 swallowing reflex

嚥下補助剤 thickening agent

エンゲル係数 Engel's coefficient

エンゲルの法則 Engel's law

援護 protection ; relief

円座 circle mat

遠視 hyperopia ; farsightedness

円熟型 mature

援助 assistance ; support

炎症 inflammation

援助関係 therapeutic relationship

援助者 assistant

援助付き雇用 supported employment

遠心性収縮 eccentric contraction

延髄 medulla oblongata

エンゼルケア mortuary practice

エンゼルメイク funeral makeup

塩蔵 salt-preserving

塩素系漂白剤 chlorine bleach

エンテロウイルス enterovirus

エンテロトキシン enterotoxin

エンド・オブ・ライフケア end-of-life care

円背 kyphosis ; roundback ; hunchback

*エンパワメント empowerment

エンパワメントアプローチ empowerment approach

塩分摂取 sodium intake

延命医療 life-sustaining medical treatment

延命治療 life-sustaining treatment ; life-prolonging treatment

お

O157 Escherichia coli O157:H7 : E. coli O157:H7

応益原則 benefit principle

*応益負担 benefit-received principle

横隔膜 diaphragm

嘔気 nausea

*応急手当 first aid

応急入院 involuntary psychiatric hold

黄色ブドウ球菌 Staphylococcus aureus

黄体ホルモン progesterone

黄疸 jaundice

黄斑変性症 macular degeneration

*嘔吐 vomiting ; emesis ; throwing up

*応能負担 ability-to-pay principle

黄斑部変性症 macular degeneration

オーダーメイド made-to-order ; custom-made

オーディトリーバーバル法 auditory-verbal therapy : AVT

オーバーベッドテーブル overbed table

大振り歩行 swing-through gait

オーブン oven

オールド・オールド old-old

悪寒 chill

置き換え displacement

オストメイト ostomate

汚染 contamination

汚染区域 contaminated area

汚染創 contaminated wound

オゾン ozone

おたふくかぜ mumps

オタワ憲章 Ottawa Charter for Health Promotion

音環境 auditory environment ; environmental noise

落としぶた drop lid

Off-JT off-the-job training

オプタコン Optacon ; optical-to-tactile converter

オプチスコープ magnification device ; optical

device
汚物室　dirty utility room
オペラント条件づけ　operant conditioning
おむつ　diaper
*おむつカバー　diaper cover
親孝行　filial piety
親子関係　parent-child relationship
親の会　parent group
オリエンテーション　orientation
折りたたみ前輪歩行器　front wheel folding walker
織物組織　fabric weave ; textile weave
オレンジプラン　Orange Plan
おろし器　grater
温あん法　hot compress ; hot fomentation
音楽療法　music therapy
恩給　pension
音響外傷　acoustic trauma
温湿布　hot compress
音声案内　voice guidance
音声器官　speech organ
音声（機能）障害　speech disorder ; speech impairment
音声増幅器　sound amplifier
温泉療法　balneotherapy
温痛覚過敏　hyperalgesia
温熱環境　thermal environment
温熱作用　thermal effect
温熱療法　thermotherapy ; heat therapy
オンブズパーソン　ombudsperson
オンブズマン　ombudsman
温冷交代浴　contrast bath ; hot/cold immersion therapy

か

ガーゼ　gauze
*臥位　lying position
外因型喘息　extrinsic asthma ; atopic asthma ; allergic asthma
外因性　exogenous
外因性感染　exogenous infection
外因性精神障害　exogenous psychosis

外因性ホルモン　exogenous hormone
下位運動ニューロン　lower motor neuron
開運動連鎖　open kinetic chain : OKC
回外　supination
階級社会　hierarchical society
解決志向的アプローチ　solution-focused approach
解雇　termination of employment
*介護　care ; long-term care ; caregiving
外向性　extraversion
介護オンブズマン　long-term care ombudsman
介護過誤　nursing malpractice
*介護過程　process of care ; care process ; caregiving process
介護技術　nursing care skills
介護技術講習（会）　practical skills training program for care work certification candidates
外呼吸　external respiration
介護休業　family caregiving leave
*介護休業制度　family caregiving leave system
介護休業法　Child Rearing and Family Caregiving Leave Act
*介護給付　long-term care insurance benefit
介護給付等費用適正化事業　rationalization program for long-term care expenses
介護給付費　long-term care benefits and expenses
介護給付費・地域支援事業支援納付金　contributions for long-term care benefits and community support programs
介護給付費等審査委員会　Review Committee for Long-Term Care Benefits and Expenses
介護給付費納付金　contributions for long-term care benefits
介護記録　nursing progress notes
介護研究　long-term care study
介護行為　nursing care practice
介護サービス　long-term care services
*介護サービス計画　care plan
介護サービス情報　long-term care information and resources

和英

あ
か
さ
た
な
は
ま
や
ら
わ

介護サービス情報の公表　public reporting of long-term care services

介護サービス調査票　qualification assessment forms for long-term care insurance benefits

介護サービス提供票　long-term care provider's report

介護支援サービス　care management services

*介護支援専門員　care manager

介護支援専門員資質向上事業　program for improving the quality of care managers

介護支援専門員実務研修　care manager certification course

介護支援専門員実務研修受講試験　enrollment exam for care manager certification course

介護施設　long-term care facility ; nursing facility

介護実習　practical care training

介護実習・普及センター　practice and promotion center for long-term care

介護者　caregiver

介護者ストレス　caregiver stress

介護者の権利　caregivers' rights

介護者の燃え尽き症候群　caregiver burnout

介護者負担　caregiver burden

介護者負担指標　Caregiver Strain Index : CSI

*介護従事者　direct care personnel

介護職員　direct care staff

介護職員初任者研修　training program for entry-level non-certified care workers

介護相談員　long-term care counselor

介護相談員派遣等事業　long-term care counselor's visitation services

介護付有料老人ホーム　private care home

介護手当　long-term care allowance

介護手順　nursing procedures

介護ニーズ　long-term care needs

介護日誌　nursing notes

*介護認定審査会　Long-Term Care Certification Committee

介護認定調査員　long-term care insurance qualification assessor

介護の基準　standards of care

介護の質　quality of care

介護の社会化　socialization of care

介護の倫理　ethics of care

介護費用　long-term care expenses

介護服　adaptive clothing

*介護福祉士　certified care worker : CCW

*介護福祉士国家試験　National Certification Examination for Care Workers

介護福祉士登録　Certified Care Worker Registry

*介護福祉士登録証　care worker certificate

介護福祉士養成施設　school of care worker training

介護扶助　long-term care aid

介護負担　caregiver burden

介護負担質問票　Caregiver Burden Interview

介護負担尺度　Caregiver Burden Scale

介護放棄　neglect

*介護報酬　long-term care insurance reimbursement

*介護保険　Long-Term Care Insurance : LTCI

介護保険サービス　long-term care insurance services

*介護保険事業計画　long-term care insurance planning

介護保険事業計画基本指針　Basic Guidelines for Ensuring Smooth Delivery of Long-Term Care Insurance Benefits

介護保険事業に係る保険給付の円滑な実施を確保するための基本的な指針　Basic Guidelines for Ensuring Smooth Delivery of Long-Term Care Insurance Benefits

介護保険施設　long-term-care facility for the elderly

介護保険指定事業者　long-term care insurance-certified provider

介護保険条例　municipal regulations for long-term care insurance

*介護保険審査会　Review Committee on Long-Term Care Insurance

介護保険特別会計　municipal special accounting for long-term care insurance

介護保険認定調査　long-term care insurance qualification assessment ; long-term care insurance eligibility assessment

介護保険の被保険者　beneficiaries of long-term care insurance ; insured persons of long-term care insurance

*介護保険法　Long-Term Care Insurance Act

介護保険法施行法　Enactment Act of the Long-Term Care Insurance Act

介護保険料　long-term care insurance premium

介護保険料減免　long-term care insurance premium deduction

介護保険料率　long-term care insurance premium rate

介護満足感　caregiving satisfaction

介護マンパワー　long-term care-related manpower

*介護目標　goal of care

介護モデル　long-term care model

介護用具　care equipment

介護用品　care supply

*介護予防　disability prevention services for long-term care insurance beneficiaries

介護予防ケアマネジメント　preventive care management

介護予防サービス　preventive care services

介護予防サービス計画　preventive care services plan

介護予防サービス費　reimbursement for preventive care services

介護予防支援　preventive care services

介護予防支援事業　preventive care services program

介護予防短期入所生活介護　short-term preventive stay for personal care

介護予防通所介護　preventive adult day care services

介護予防通所リハビリテーション　preventive day care rehabilitation

介護予防・日常生活支援総合事業　comprehensive disability prevention and assistance program for independent living

介護予防福祉用具貸与　disability prevention adaptive equipment rental services

介護予防訪問介護　preventive home care services

介護予防訪問入浴介護　preventive home bathing services

介護理念　philosophy of long-term care ; morality of long-term care

*介護療養型医療施設　designated long-term care hospital

*介護老人福祉施設　welfare facility for the elderly

*介護老人保健施設　health facility for the elderly

介護労働安定センター　Care Work Foundation : CWF

介護労働者の雇用管理の改善等に関する法律　Improvement of Human Resources Management for Care Workers Act

概日リズム　circadian rhythm

外出介護員　escort

外出支援　escort services

*介助　assistance

外傷　trauma

外傷後ストレス障害　post-traumatic stress disorder : PTSD

外傷神経症　post-traumatic neurosis

外傷性損傷　traumatic injury

外傷性脳損傷　traumatic brain injury : TBI

介助訓練　assistive exercise

介助犬　assistance dog ; partner dog ; service dog

介助バー　bedside rail

介助用車いす　attendant-propelled wheelchair ; attendant-controlled wheelchair

回診　physician rounds

*疥癬　scabies

外旋　external rotation

回想　life review ; reminiscence

咳嗽介助　assisted coughing

*回想法　reminiscence therapy

階段昇降　scaling stairs

階段昇降機　stair lift

回腸人工肛門　ileostomy

回腸導管　ileal conduit urinary diversion

改訂バーセル指数　modified Barthel index

改訂長谷川式簡易知能評価スケール　Revised Hasegawa's Dementia Scale：HDS-R

改定版ウェクスラー記憶検査　Revised Wechsler Memory Scale：WMS-R

改定版ウェクスラー成人知能検査　Revised Wechsler Adult Intelligence Scale：WAIS-R

改訂水飲みテスト　Modified Water Swallow Test

外的適応　adaptation

外転　abduction

外転歩行　abduction gait

解凍（法）　defrosting；thawing

ガイドヘルパー　escort

回内　pronation

介入　intervention

灰白髄炎　poliomyelitis

外罰型　angry men

外反足　talipes valgus

外反母趾　hallux valgus

外皮　integumentary

回避学習　avoidance learning

外皮系　integumentary system

回避条件づけ　avoidance conditioning

回復期施設　convalescent home

回復期保菌者　convalescent carrier

*回復期リハビリテーション　recovery-phase rehabilitation

外部サービス利用型特定施設入居者生活介護　in-home care services for specified long-term care facility residents

開放骨折　open fracture；compound fracture

開放施設　open facility

開放性損傷　open wound

界面活性剤　surfactant

界面反射　interface reflection

*潰瘍　ulcer

潰瘍形成　ulceration

潰瘍性大腸炎　ulcerative colitis

外来診療　outpatient care；ambulatory care

外来診療所　outpatient clinic；ambulatory clinic

外来リハビリテーション　outpatient rehabilitation；ambulatory rehabilitation

快楽原則　pleasure principle

解離性感覚障害　dissociated sensory disturbance

解離性障害　dissociative disorder：DD

解離性同一性障害　dissociative identity disorder：DID

カイロプラクティック　chiropractic

カウンセラー　counselor

カウンセリング　counseling

家屋修理詐欺　home repair scam

下顎押し出し法　jaw thrust

過角化症　hyperkeratosis

下顎呼吸　agonal respiration；gasping respiration；respiration with mandibular movement

化学繊維　chemical fiber

化学塞栓　chemoembolization

化学的インジケータ　chemical indicator

科学的根拠　scientific evidence

化学的消化　chemical digestion

化学物質食中毒　chemical food poisoning

化学療法　chemotherapy

*かかりつけ医　primary doctor；primary care physician

蝸牛神経　cochlear nerve

核黄疸　kernicterus

角化型疥癬　Norwegian scabies

角化症　keratosis

角化症病変　keratotic lesions

顎下腺　submandibular gland

*核家族　nuclear family

かくし包丁　hidden knife work

学習　learning

学習障害　learning disability；learning disorder：LD

学習性無力感　learned helplessness

学習性無力感理論　learned helplessness theory

学習能力　learning ability

学習理論　learning theory

覚せい剤依存　drug addiction

学生納付特例制度　national pension premium

exemption for students

拡大家族　extended family

拡大読書器　magnification device

喀痰　sputum

喀痰吸引　sputum suction

拡張期血圧　diastolic pressure

かくはん　stirring ; mixing

角膜移植　cornea transplant

角膜反射　corneal reflex

隔離　isolation

隔離室　isolation room

隔離病院　isolation hospital ; pest house

隔離病室　isolation room

隔離病棟　isolation unit

学力検査　academic achievement test

隔離予防策　isolation precaution

•家計　household budget ; family budget

家計調査　household budget survey

加工食品　processed food

過呼吸発作　hyperventilation attack

下肢　lower extremity

家事　housework ; homemaking

家事援助　homemaker services ; homemaking services

下肢装具　lower extremity orthosis

過食　overeating

過食症　bulimia

可処分所得　disposable income

下肢リンパ浮腫　lower extremity lymphedema

家事労働　housekeeping ; domestic labor

過伸展　hyperextension

下垂体　pituitary gland

ガス壊疽　gas gangrene

ガス交換　gas exchange

ガスコンロ　gas stove

仮性球麻痺　pseudobulbar paralysis

仮性認知症　pseudodementia

•家政婦　housekeeper

火葬　cremation

画像診断　diagnostic imaging

過疎化　depopulation

•家族　family

家族介護　family caregiving

家族介護支援事業　family caregiver support services

家族介護者　family caregiver

家族介護者の会　family caregiver support group

家族介護負担感尺度　Family Caregiver Burden Scale

家族関係　family relationship

家族形態　types of family

家族ケースワーカー　family caseworker

家族ケースワーク　family casework

家族構成　family structures

家族支援　family support

家族支援センター　family support center

家族指向ケア　family-oriented care

家族システム　family system

家族システムズアプローチ　family systems approach

家族システム理論　family system theory

家族周期　family life cycle

家族ソーシャルワーカー　family social worker

家族ソーシャルワーク　family social work

家族中心ケア　family-based care

家族手当　family allowance

家族と世帯　family and household

加速歩行　festination

家族療法　family therapy

家族類型　family patterns ; family types ; households by type

家族歴　family history

可塑性　plasticity

下腿義足　transtibial prosthesis ; below-knee prosthesis

課題遂行能力　task performance ability

下腿切断　lower extremity amputation ; below-knee amputation

課題中心アプローチ　task-centered approach

課題の明確化　clarification of the Issues

課題分析　task analysis

肩関節亜脱臼　shoulder subluxation

肩関節周囲炎　adhesive capsulitis ; frozen shoulder

肩関節脱臼　shoulder dislocation

和英

| あ | か | さ | た | な | は | ま | や | ら | わ |

片栗粉　potato starch
片手駆動式普通型車いす　single hand manual drive wheelchair ; one hand manual drive wheelchair
片手動作　one-handed activity
•片麻痺　hemiplegia
カタルシス　catharsis
カタルシス法　cathartic method
カタレプシー　catalepsy
価値　value
価値観　sense of values
価値財　merit goods
渇感　sense of thirst
脚気　beriberi ; thiamine deficiency ; vitamin B₁ deficiency
喀血　hemoptysis
学校法人　school corporation
活性酸素　active oxygen
活性炭　active charcoal
活性炭素　active carbon
葛藤　conflict
•活動（ICF）　activity
活動記録　activity progress notes
•活動制限（ICF）　activity limitations
活動的平均余命　active life expectancy
活動と参加　activity and participation
活動理論　activity theory
•合併症　complication
括約筋　sphincter
括約筋障害　sphincter disturbance
家庭　family
家庭医　family doctor
過程叙述体　narrative process recording
家庭生活の意義　significance of family
家庭相談員　family counselor
家庭内暴力　domestic violence : DV
家庭訪販　door-to-door sales
家庭用品品質表示法　Household Goods Quality Labeling Act
カテーテル関連感染　catheter-associated infection
カテーテル関連血流感染　catheter-associated bloodstream infection : CABSI

カテーテル由来感染　catheter-related infection
カテーテル由来菌血症　catheter-related bacteremia
カテーテル由来血流感染　catheter-related bloodstream infection : CRBSI
カテーテル留置法　catheterization
果糖　fructose
寡動　hypokinesia
可動性　mobility
カナタイプライター　Japanese kana-letter typewriter
カニューレ　cannula
加熱調理　heat cooking
可搬型スロープ　portable wheelchair ramp
下半身麻痺　paraplegia
過敏性腸症候群　irritable bowel syndrome
寡夫　widower
•寡婦　widow
カフェイン　caffeine
寡夫期　widowerhood
寡婦期　widowhood
寡婦給付　widow benefit
寡婦控除　tax deduction for widows ; windows tax deduction
寡婦年金　widow's pension
寡婦福祉資金貸付制度　financial loan system for widows
花粉症　hay fever
貨幣的ニード　monetary needs
芽胞　spore
過保護　overprotection
過補償　overcompensation
過密人口　overpopulation
仮面うつ病　masked depression
仮面様顔貌　mask-like face
かゆみ　pruritus ; itchiness
過用症候群　overuse syndrome
過用性筋力低下　overwork weakness
ガラクトース　galactose
空の巣症候群　empty nest syndrome
カリウム　potassium
カルシウム（欠乏症）　calcium (deficiency)
•加齢　aging ; ageing

加齢黄斑変性症　age-related macular degeneration

加齢関連認知低下　aging-associated cognitive decline : AACD

加齢性疾患　age-related disease

加齢性難聴　presbycusis

カロテノイド　carotenoid

カロテン　carotene

カロリー　calorie

カロリー制限　caloric restriction

*がん　cancer ; malignancy

眼圧　intraocular pressure ; eye pressure

眼圧計　tonometry

簡易栄養状態アセスメント　Mini Nutritional Assessment : MNA

簡易口腔衛生検査　Brief Oral Health Status Examination : BOHSE

簡易損傷スケール　Abbreviated Injury Scale : AIS

がん遺伝子　cancer gene

簡易疼痛調査票　Brief Pain Inventory : BPI

簡易疲労一覧表　Brief Fatigue Inventory : BFI

簡易浴槽　portable bathtub

肝炎　hepatitis

肝炎対策基本法　Basic Hepatitis Control Act

感音(性)難聴　sensorineural hearing loss : SNHL ; sensorineural deafness

寛解　remission

眼科医　ophthalmologist

感覚　sense

感覚過敏　hyperesthesia

感覚記憶　sensory memory

感覚機能　sensory function

感覚障害　sensory disturbance

感覚消失　anesthesia

感覚神経　sensory nerve

感覚性失語(症)　sensory aphasia

感覚代行　sensory substitution

感覚代行機器　sensory substitution devices : SSD

感覚統合　sensory integration

感覚鈍麻　hypesthesia ; hypoesthesia

感覚麻痺　sensory paralysis

肝がん　liver cancer

がん患者　cancer patient

*換気　ventilation

肝機能検査　liver function test : LFT

眼球振盪　nystagmus

*環境因子(ICF)　environmental factors

環境危険物質　environmental hazards

環境基本法　Basic Environment Act

環境権　environmental rights

環境サーベイランス　environmental surveillance

眼鏡士　optometrist

環境ホルモン　environmental hormone

環境由来疾患　disorder of environmental origin

含気量・含気率(被服の)　pore size and porosity (of clothing materials)

関係妄想　delusion of reference ; idea of reference

緩下剤　laxative

間欠性跛行　intermittent claudication

間欠導尿　intermittent urethral catheterization

*看護　nursing

*肝硬変　(liver) cirrhosis ; hepatic cirrhosis ; cirrhosis of the liver

看護覚え書き　Notes on Nursing

看護過程　nursing process

看護基礎教育　basic nursing education

看護休暇制度　family and medical leave system ; nursing care leave system

看護計画　nursing care plan

喚語困難　word finding difficulty

*看護師　nurse

看護師長　director of nursing

看護師等の人材確保の促進に関する法律　Recruitment and Retention of Nursing Personnel Act

看護師の倫理綱領　code of ethics for nurses

看護師不足　nursing shortage

喚語障害　word finding disorder

看護小規模多機能型居宅介護　small-scale multi-functional nursing care services

看護職員　nursing staff

看護助手　nurse aide ; nursing assistant	関節角度計　goniometer
看護専門職　nursing professional	*関節可動域　range of motion : ROM
看護の基準　standards of nursing practice	関節可動域訓練　range of motion exercise
監査　survey ; inspection	関節可動域テスト　range of motion testing :
監査官　surveyor ; inspector	ROM-T
観察　observation	間接言語　indirect language
観察法　observational method	関節拘縮　joint contracture ; joint stiffness
監視　surveillance	間接接触感染　indirect contact infection ;
鉗子　forceps	indirect contact transmission
乾式加熱　dry heating ; dry-heat cooking	間接接触伝播　indirect contact spread
乾式洗濯　dry cleaning	関節置換術　joint replacement
鉗子生検　forceps biopsy	関節痛　arthralgia
カンジダ・アルビカンス　candida albicans	間接焼き　indirect grilling
カンジダ食道炎　candida esophagitis	*関節リウマチ　rheumatoid arthritis : RA
肝疾患　liver disease	関節離断　disarticulation
間質性肺炎　acute interstitial pneumonia	感染　infection
患者　patient	汗腺　sweat glands
患者会　self-help group ; patient support	感染菌　bacteria
group	感染経路　routes of infection ; routes of
患者記録　patient records	transmission
患者中心医療　patient-centered medicine	感染源　source of infection
患者中心療法　patient-centered therapy	感染源隔離　source isolation
患者調査　patient survey	感染後咳そう　post-infection cough
患者の安全　patient safety	*感染症　infectious disease ; communicable
患者の権利　patients' rights	disease ; transmissible disease
患者擁護　patient advocacy	感染症サーベイランス　infection surveillance
感受性試験　sensitivity test	感染症対策　infection prevention and control
感情気分質問票　Feeling Tone Questionnaire :	感染症の予防及び感染症の患者に対する医療に
FTQ	関する法律　Infection Prevention and
感情失禁　emotional incontinence	Treatment for Patients with Infections Act :
感情転移　transference	Prevention and Treatment of Infections Act
冠状動脈（冠動脈）　coronary artery	感染症法　Prevention and Treatment of
感情鈍麻　flat affect ; blunted affect	Infections Act ; Infection Prevention and
感情の反射　reflection of feeling	Treatment for Patients with Infections Act
眼振　nystagmus	完全静脈栄養　total parenteral nutrition : TPN
がん性疼痛　carcinomatous pain	感染性胃腸炎　infectious gastroenteritis
眼精疲労　asthenopia ; eye strain	感染性医療廃棄物　infectious medical waste
関節　joint	感染制御　infection control
関節運動　joint motion	感染性心内膜炎　infective endocarditis
関節運動学的アプローチ　arthrokinematic	感染性腸炎　infectious enteritis
approach : AKA	感染性廃棄物　infectious waste
関節炎　arthritis	感染対策　infection control
間接援助技術　indirect social work practice	完全尿失禁　genuine stress incontinence

感染予防　prevention of infection ; infection prevention

肝臓　liver

乾燥症　xerosis

肝臓専門医　hepatologist

乾燥・防湿剤（被服の）　desiccant and dehumidifier (for clothing)

患側　affected side of the body

桿体　rod

がん対策基本法　Cancer Control Act

浣腸　enema ; clyster

がん治療　cancer treatment

眼底出血　hemorrhage in ocular fundus

冠動脈　coronary artery

冠動脈疾患　coronary artery disease : CAD

冠動脈性心疾患　coronary heart disease : CHD

冠動脈攣縮性狭心症　vasospastic angina pectoris

眼（内）圧　intraocular pressure

眼内レンズ　intraocular lens : IOL

陥入爪　ingrown toenail ; onychocryptosis

乾熱滅菌　dry heat sterilization

観念運動失行　ideomotor apraxia

観念失行　ideational apraxia

観念奔逸　flight of ideas

間脳　diencephalon

肝斑　liver spots

眼病　eye disease

カンピロバクター　campylobacter

カンファレンス　conference

鑑別診断　differential diagnosis

感冒　cold ; flu

甘味　sweet ; sweet taste ; sweetness

顔面神経麻痺　facial paralysis

がん抑制遺伝子　tumor suppressor gene

管理栄養士　dietitian

寒冷ストレス　cold stress

寒冷地加算　supplemental cold district allowance

寒冷療法　cold therapy

関連痛　referred pain

緩和医療　palliative medicine

緩和ケア　palliative care

緩和ケア病床　palliative care bed

緩和ケア病棟　palliative care unit

き

奇異行動　strange behavior ; unusual behavior

奇異性尿失禁　paradoxical incontinence

キーパーソン　significant other

既往歴　medical history

記憶　memory

記憶障害　memory impairment

記憶障害検査　Memory Impairment Screen : MIS

機械的消化　mechanical digestion

機械的軟食　mechanical soft diet

機会の平等　equality of opportunity ; equal opportunity

機械浴　mechanically assisted bathing

気管　trachea ; windpipe

義眼　artificial eye ; glass eye

気管カニューレ　tracheal cannula ; tracheostomy tube

気管支　bronchus ; bronchi

気管支炎　bronchitis

気管支拡張剤　bronchodilator

気管支鏡　bronchoscopy

気管支喘息　bronchial asthma

気管支ドレナージ　bronchial drainage

気管切開　tracheostomy

基幹相談支援センター　core center of consultation and support services

気管内異物　intratracheal foreign body

気管内注入　intratracheal injection

気管内麻酔　endotracheal anesthesia

危機介入　crisis intervention

危機介入アプローチ　crisis intervention approach

危機管理　risk management

利き手　handedness

企業年金　corporate pension

企業の社会的責任　corporate social responsibility : CSR

起居動作	bed mobility
起居様式	lifestyle
危険因子	risk factor
危険区域	hot zone
危険物	hazardous material
危険防止	risk prevention
危険有害物質	hazardous material
•起座位	sitting leaning-forward position ; sitting leaning-forward against a support
器材関連感染	device-related infection
起座呼吸	orthopnea ; orthopnoea
きざみ食	chopped diet
•義歯	denture ; artificial tooth
義肢	prosthesis ; artificial limb
義肢学	prosthetic
義肢訓練	prosthetic training
•義肢装具士	prosthetist and orthotist : PO
義肢装具士法	Prosthetists and Orthotists Act
気質	temperament ; personality traits ; personality characteristics
器質精神病	organic psychosis
器質性精神障害	organic mental disorder
器質性便秘	organic constipation
希死念慮	suicidal ideation
気腫	emphysema
義手	upper-limb prosthesis
気腫性腎盂腎炎	emphysematous pyelonephritis
基準介護	standardized care
基準該当介護予防サービス	standard qualified preventive care services
基準該当居宅介護支援	standard qualified care management services
基準該当居宅サービス	standard qualified home-based care services
基準該当サービス	standard qualified services
基準該当障害福祉サービス	standard qualified disability services
基準体重	ideal body weight : IBW
議事録	minutes
規制緩和	deregulation
寄生虫	parasites
寄生虫病	parasitic disease

既製服	ready-made clothing ; ready-to-wear clothing
季節労働	seasonal work
義足	lower-limb prosthesis
基礎控除	standard deduction
基礎食品	basic food group
基礎体温	basal body temperature
基礎代謝	basal metabolism
基礎代謝量	basal metabolic rate : BMR
基礎縫い	basic sewing stitches
基礎年金	basic pension
基礎年金制度	basic pension system
喫煙	smoking
ギックリ腰	strained back
拮抗	antagonism
拮抗筋	antagonist
キットウッド, T.	Tom Kitwood
気道	airway
気道確保	airway maintenance ; maintenance of airway
気道感染隔離	respiratory isolation
気道管理	airway management
気道狭窄	airway stenosis
気道虚脱	airway collapse
気道洗浄	airway cleaning
気道抵抗	airway resistance
気道内圧	airway pressure
気道熱傷	airway burn
気道閉鎖	airway closure
気道閉塞	airway obstruction
絹	silk
機能	function
機能維持	functional maintenance
機能回復	functional recovery
機能局在	functional localization
•機能訓練	functional training
機能訓練指導員	functional training instructor
機能再建	functional reconstruction
機能肢位	functional position
•機能障害	impairment
機能状態質問票	Functional Status Questionnaire : FSQ
機能性精神障害	functional mental disorder

機能性成分　functional component

機能性尿失禁　functional incontinence ; functional urinary incontinence

機能性便秘　functional constipation

機能的アプローチ　functional approach

機能的作業療法　functional occupational therapy

機能の残気量　functional residual capacity

機能の自立　functional independence

機能の自律　functional autonomy

機能的自立度評価法　functional independence measure : FIM

機能的電気刺激　functional electrical stimulation : FES

機能年齢　functional age

機能評価　functional assessment

機能分化　functional differentiation

機能予後　functional prognosis

気晴らし　relaxation ; recreation ; diversion

気晴らし的作業療法　diversional occupational therapy

寄付　donation

寄付金税控除　tax deduction for charitable contributions

ギプス　cast

気分　mood

気分循環性障害　cyclothymic disorder

気分障害　mood disorder

気分変調性症　dysthymic disorder ; dysthymia

基本肢位　fundamental position

基本指針　basic guidelines

基本相談支援　basic consultation services

基本的人権　fundamental human rights ; basic human rights

基本的欲求　basic needs ; deficiency needs

義務教育　compulsory education

記銘　encoding

記銘力障害　encoding deficit

逆隔離　reversed isolation

逆説睡眠　paradoxical sleep ; rapid eye movement sleep

•虐待　abuse

逆転移　countertransference

客観的事実　objective fact

客観的情報　objective information ; objective data

逆向健忘　retrograde amnesia

•ギャッチベッド　gatch bed

きゅう　moxibustion

吸引　suctioning

吸引器　aspirator ; suction machine

吸引細胞診　aspiration cytology

吸引生検　suction biopsy

救援関係　therapeutic relationship

休暇　leave of absence : LoA

嗅覚　sense of smell ; olfaction

嗅覚消失症　anosmia

嗅覚低下　loss of smell

救急医療　emergency medical services ; urgent care

救急外来　emergency room : ER

•救急救命士　emergency medical technician : EMT ; first aider

救急救命室　emergency room : ER

救急車　ambulance

救急処置　first aid ; emergency treatment

救急蘇生　emergency care and resuscitation

休業給付　leave benefit

休業補償　compensation for leave of absence

救護施設　almshouse ; shelter

救護法　Relief Act

きゅう師　moxibustion therapist

吸湿性繊維　hygroscopic fiber

吸湿性（被服地の）　hygroscopic properties (of clothing materials)

吸収　absorption

吸収性無気肺　absorption atelectasis

求職者　job seeker

求職者給付　job seeker's benefit

求心性視野狭窄　concentric contraction of the visual field

求心性収縮　concentric contraction

吸水性繊維　water-absorbing fiber

吸水性（被服地の）　water absorption (of clothing materials)

急性　acute

急性灰白髄炎 acute poliomyelitis	教育リハビリテーション educational rehabilitation
旧生活保護法 Repealed Public Assistance Act	共依存 co-dependency
急性冠症候群 acute coronary syndrome : ACS	•仰臥位 supine position
急性期 acute phase ; acute stage	境界域高血圧 borderline hypertension
急性期リハビリテーション acute phase rehabilitation	•共感 empathy
急性呼吸窮迫症候群 acute respiratory distress syndrome : ARDS	共感的態度 empathetic attitude
急性骨髄性白血病 acute myelogenous leukemia ; acute myeloid leukemia ; acute myelocytic leukemia : AML	•共感的理解 empathic understanding
急性出血後貧血 acute posthemorrhagic anemia	協議会 council
急性心筋梗塞 acute myocardial infarction	狂牛病 mad-cow disease
急性膵炎 acute pancreatitis	狂犬病 rabies
急性腸炎 acute enterocolitis ; acute coloenteritis	恐慌性障害 panic disorder
急性腸炎(小腸) acute enteritis	共済年金 mutual aid pension
急性腸炎(大腸) acute colitis	胸式呼吸 chest respiration
急性脳症候群 acute brain syndrome	行事食 seasonal meal
急性肺傷害 acute lung injury	狭心症 angina pectoris
急性膀胱炎 acute cystitis	狭心症発作 angina attack
急性リンパ性白血病 acute lymphocytic leukemia ; acute lymphoblastic leukemia ; acute lymphoid leukemia : ALL	強心薬 cardiotonic drug
休息 respite ; rest ; break	胸髄損傷 thoracic spinal cord injury
吸入 inhalation ; aspiration	行政改革 administrative reform
吸入薬 inhaler	共生社会 symbiosis society
9の法則 rule of nines	矯正視力 corrected visual acuity
救貧院 almshouse ; poorhouse	行政手続における特定の個人を識別するための番号の利用等に関する法律 The Use of Numbers to Identify a Specific Individual in the Administrative Procedure Act : My Number Act
給付 benefit	強制入院 involuntary hospitalization
給付基準 benefits standards	強制入所 involuntary admission
給付費審査委員会 Benefit Review Committee	競争的雇用 competitive employment
キューブラー．ロス，E. Elisabeth Kübler-Ross	きょうだい間葛藤 sibling conflict
球麻痺 bulbar palsy	きょうだい間競争 sibling rivalry
きゅう療法 moxibustion	協調 coordination
キュプラ cuprammonium rayon	強直 ankylosis
教育 education	強直間代発作 tonic-clonic seizure ; grand mal seizure
教育給付 education benefit	強直性脊椎炎 ankylosing spondylitis : AS
教育扶助 education aid	胸痛 chest pain
	協同組合 cooperative association
	共同作業所 workshop
	•共同生活援助 group home
	共同生活介護 care home
	共同負担 copayment ; copay

共同募金　community chest
共同募金活動　community chest campaign
共同保険　co-insurance
強度行動障害　severe behavioral disorder
強迫観念（かんねん）　obsession
強迫行為　compulsion ; compulsive act
強迫性障害　obsessive-compulsive disorder :
　OCD
胸部圧迫　chest compression
胸部エックス線　chest X-ray : CXR
恐怖症　phobia
胸部痛　chest pain
業務独占　exclusive license
業務マニュアル　practice manual
共鳴　resonance
共有スペース　common area
虚血　ischemia
虚血性心疾患　ischemic heart disease : IHD
虚血性大腸炎　ischemic colitis
虚血性発作（ほっさ）　ischemic stroke
虚弱　frailty ; fragile ; weakness
虚弱高齢者　fragile elderly ; frail elderly
虚弱児　fragile child ; frail child
居住環境　residential environment
居住環境整備　home modification
居住空間　living space
居住ケア　residential care
居住サポート事業　housing assistance
　services ; housing assistance program
居住、滞在及び宿泊並びに食事の提供に係る利
　用料等に関する指針　Institutional Billing
　Guidelines for Room and Board
居住地特例　domicile exception
挙上（きょじょう）　elevation
拒食症（きょしょくしょう）　anorexia
拒絶症　negativism
居宅介護（サービス）　home-based care
　(services)
居宅介護サービス計画費　care plan
　development fee
居宅介護サービス費　reimbursement for
　home-based care services
居宅介護支援　care management

居宅介護支援事業　care management services
居宅介護支援事業者　care management
　provider
居宅介護支援事業所　care management
　center
居宅介護支援費　reimbursement for care
　management
居宅介護住宅改修　home modification
居宅介護住宅改修費　reimbursement for home
　modifications ; home modification
　reimbursement
居宅介護福祉用具購入費　reimbursement for
　purchasing adaptive equipment ;
　reimbursement for purchasing technical aids
居宅サービス計画　care plan
居宅保護　outdoor relief
居宅療養管理指導　medical management
許容一日摂取量　acceptable daily intake : ADI
ギラン・バレー症候群　Guillain-Barre
　syndrome : GBS
起立訓練　standing exercise
起立性調節障害　orthostatic dizziness ;
　orthostatic vertigo
*起立性低血圧　orthostatic hypotension ;
　postural hypotension
起立・歩行動作測定法　Timed Get up and Go
　Test : TUG
*記録　progress notes ; documentation
記録（介護の）　(nursing) progress notes ;
　(nursing) documentation
筋　muscle
*筋萎縮（いしゅく）　muscular atrophy
筋萎縮性側索硬化症（そくさくこうかしょう）　amyotrophic lateral
　sclerosis : ALS
禁煙　smoking cessation ; abstinence from
　smoking
筋炎　myositis
緊急措置入院　urgent involuntary
　hospitalization
緊急通報（サービス）　emergency call (services)
緊急通報装置　emergency alarm system
緊急扶助　emergency assistance : EA
緊急連絡先　emergency contact information

筋強直性ジストロフィー　myotonic dystrophy

筋緊張　muscle tonus

筋緊張亢進　muscle hypertonia

筋緊張低下　muscle hypotonia

筋筋膜性疼痛症候群　myofascial pain syndrome：MPS

筋痙攣　muscle cramp

菌血症　bacteremia

筋交感神経活動　sympathetic muscle nerve activity

筋拘縮症　muscle contracture

菌交代症　superinfection

筋骨格疾患　musculoskeletal disease

筋骨格系　musculoskeletal system

筋再教育　muscle reeducation

近視　myopia；near-sightedness；short-sightedness

筋弛緩　muscle relaxation

筋持久力　muscle endurance

筋ジストロフィー　muscular dystrophy

禁酒　alcohol abstinence；abstinence from alcohol

筋生検　muscle biopsy

近赤外線　near-infrared

筋線維タイプ　muscle fiber type

金銭管理　money management

•金銭給付　cash benefit

近代化　modernization

近代化論　modernization theory

禁断症状　withdrawal symptom

緊張型頭痛　tension-type headache

緊張亢進　hypertonia

緊張性頸反射　tonic neck reflex

緊張低下　hypotonia

筋痛性脳脊髄炎　myalgic encephalomyelitis：ME

筋電図　electromyogram：EMG

筋電図検査　electromyography

筋肉　muscle

筋肉内　intramuscular：IM

筋肉内注射　intramuscular injection

筋肥大　muscle hypertrophy

筋疲労　muscle fatigue

筋膜炎　fasciitis

筋無力症　myasthenia gravis

金融商品の販売等に関する法律　Financial Products Sales Act

筋力　muscle strength

筋力維持　muscle maintenance

筋力強化　muscular strengthening

筋力強化訓練　muscle strengthening exercise

筋力測定　muscle strength measurement

筋力低下　muscular weakness

筋力テスト　muscular strength testing：MMT

勤労所得税額控除　earned income tax credit：EITC

く

空間失認　spatial agnosia

空間認知　spatial perception

空気感染　airborne infection

空気感染隔離　airborne infection isolation：AII

空気塞栓症　air embolism

空気調和　heating, ventilation and air-conditioning：HVAC

空気伝播　airborne transmission

空気予防策　airborne precaution

空気ろ過装置　air filter

空中細菌　airborne bacteria

空中塵埃　airborne particle

空腹感　sense of hunger

空腹時血糖　fasting blood sugar

空腹時高血糖　impaired fasting glucose：IFG

クーリング・オフ制度　cooling-off rule

クオリティ・オブ・ライフ　quality of life：QOL

苦情　complaint；grievance

•苦情解決　grievances and complaints resolution

薬　medication；drug

口すぼめ呼吸　pursed lip breathing

口対口人工呼吸　mouth-to-mouth breathing

口対鼻人工呼吸　mouth-to-nose breathing

駆虫剤　anthelmintic

屈曲　flexion

屈曲拘縮　flexion contracture

クックチル　cook chill
クッシング症候群　Cushing's syndrome
靴べら式装具　shoe horn brace：SHB
組合管掌健康保険　society-managed health insurance；association-managed Health Insurance
*くも膜下出血　subarachnoid hemorrhage：SAH
クライシス・インターベンション　crisis intervention
クラッチ　crutch
クリアランス　clearance
グリーフケア　grief care
繰入金　carry over
グリコーゲン　glycogen
繰越金　carry forward balances；balance carried forward
グリセミック・インデックス（指数）　glycemic index：GI
クリティカルパス　critical pathway：CP
クリニカルスキル　clinical skill
クリニカルパス　clinical pathway
グルーピング　grouping
グループアプローチ　group approach
グループインタビュー　group interview
グループ運動　group exercise
グループカウンセリング　group counseling
グループ診療　group practice
グループスーパービジョン　group supervision
グループダイナミックス　group dynamics
グループレクリエーション　group recreation；group activity
グループワーカー　group worker
*グループワーク　group work
グルコサミン　glucosamine
グルタルアルデヒド　glutaraldehyde
グルテン　gluten
*車いす　wheelchair
クレアチニン　creatinine
クレープ　crepe fabric
グレーブス病　Graves' disease
グレシャムの法則　Gresham's law
クレペリン, E.　Emil Kraepelin

クレンザック足継手　Klenzak ankle joint
クロイツフェルト・ヤコブ病　Creutzfeldt-Jakob disease：CJD
クローズド・クエスチョン　closed-question
グローバリゼーション　globalization
クローン病　Crohn's disease
クロタミトン製剤　crotamiton
*クロックポジション　clock position
クロルヘキシジングルコン酸塩溶液　chlorhexidine gluconate solution
くん煙　smoking
群発頭痛　cluster headache
訓練　training；exercise；practice
訓練等給付費　training benefit

け

*ケア　care
*ケアカンファレンス　care conference
ケア計画　care plan
ケアコーディネーション　care coordination
ケアサービス　care services
ケアサービスの三つの基本理念　three philosophies of care
*ケアチーム　care team
ケア付住宅　board and care home
ケアの個別化　individualized care
ケアの質　quality of care
ケアの標準化　standardized care
*ケアハウス　care home；low-cost elder home
ケアパス　care pathway
*ケアプラン　care plan
ケアホーム　care home
ケアマニュアル　long-term care policies and procedures manual
*ケアマネジメント　care management
ケアマネジメントモデル　care management model
*ケアマネジャー　care manager
ケア目標　goal of care；care goal
経過観察病棟　observation unit
計画相談支援　disability services planning and consultation

計画相談支援給付費　reimbursement for disability services planning and consultation

計画的行動理論　theory of planned behavior : TPB

計画の実施（介護過程）　implementation of care plans (care process) ; care plan implementation (care process)

計画の修正（介護過程）　revision of care plans (care process) ; care plan revision (care process)

計画の立案（介護過程）　development of care plans (care process) ; care plan development (care process)

•経管栄養法　tube feeding

経気道感染　sinopulmonary infection

経口　by mouth : PO ; oral

経口感染症　infection by oral route

経口摂取　oral intake

蛍光増白　fluorescent whitening

経口的投与法　oral administration of medications

経口補液療法　oral rehydration therapy

脛骨近位部骨折　proximal tibia fracture

脛骨高原骨折　tibial plateau fracture

経済協力開発機構　Organization for Economic Cooperation and Development : OECD

経済的虐待　financial abuse ; fiduciary abuse

経済連携協定　Economic Partnership Agreement : EPA

軽擦法　effleurage ; stroking

傾斜路　ramp

痙縮　spasticity

芸術療法　art therapy

頸髄損傷　cervical spinal cord injury ; cervical cord injury

痙性　spastic

痙性斜頸　spastic torticollis

痙性対麻痺　spastic paraparesis

形成不全　dysplasia ; malformation ; deformity

痙性麻痺　spastic paralysis

継続看護　continuum of care ; health continuum

継続サービス利用支援　continuum of disability services planning and monitoring

継続性理論　continuity theory

継続的改善活動　continuous quality improvement

継続理論　continuity theory

形態異常　abnormal deformity

形態認知　tactual form recognition

携帯用会話補助装置　voice output communication aid : VOCA ; speech-generating device

•傾聴　active listening

経腸栄養　transintestine nutrition

痙直型四肢麻痺　spastic quadriplegia

痙直型両麻痺　spastic diplegia

頸椎　cervical spine

頸椎牽引　cervical traction

頸椎後縦靭帯骨化症　ossification of the posterior longitudinal ligament of the cervical spine

頸椎根症　cervical radiculopathy

頸椎装具　cervical orthosis

頸椎捻挫　neck distortion

頸動脈　carotid artery

頸動脈狭窄　carotid artery stenosis

軽度認知（機能）障害　mild cognitive impairment : MCI

経皮　transdermal : TD

経鼻　nasal : NAS

経皮感染　percutaneous infection

経鼻経管栄養　nasal tube feeding

経皮酸素飽和度モニター　pulse oximeter

軽費老人ホーム　low-cost elder home

軽費老人ホームの設備及び運営に関する基準　equipment maintenance and facility operation standards for low-cost elder homes

警報安全システム　alert safety system

傾眠　somnolence ; drowsiness

•契約　contract

契約施設　contract-based facility

契約書　contract document

軽量化　down sizing

痙攣　convulsion ; spasm

敬老　respect for the elderly	血漿　blood plasma
敬老会　senior citizens club	結晶関節症　crystal arthropathy
敬老の日　Respect for the Aged Day	血漿グルコース　plasma glucose
ケーゲル訓練（法）　Kegel exercises	結晶性知能　crystallized intelligence
*ケースカンファレンス　case conference	結晶性能力　crystallized ability
ケース記録　case records	血小板　platelet
ケーススタディ　case study	結晶誘発性関節炎　crystal induced arthritis
ケースヒストリー　case history	欠神発作　absence seizure
ケースマネジメント　case management	血清　blood serum
ケースミックス　case mix	血清アルブミン値　serum albumin level
ケースミックス指数　Case Mix Index : CMI	血清肝炎　serum hepatitis
ケースワーカー　case worker	血清コレステロール　serum cholesterol
*ケースワーク　casework	結石　calculus
外科用マスク　surgical mask	血栓　thrombosis
劇症肝炎　fulminant hepatitis	血栓溶解療法　thrombolytic therapy
*下血　melena	欠損家庭　single-parent family ; one-parent
下剤　laxative	family
*血圧　blood pressure	血中ウイルス感染症　bloodborne virus
血圧計　blood pressure manometer	infection
血液　blood	血液尿素窒素　blood urea nitrogen : BUN
血液ガス分析　arterial blood gas analysis	結腸人工肛門　colostomy
血液検査　blood test	結腸内視鏡　colonoscope
血液中酸素濃度　blood oxygen level	結腸内視鏡検査　colonoscopy
血液透析　hemodialysis	血糖　blood sugar
血液媒介感染　bloodborne infection	*血糖値　blood sugar level
血液由来病原体　bloodborne pathogen	血尿　hematuria
*結核　tuberculosis	血便　hematochezia
結核腫　tuberculoma	結膜炎　conjunctivitis
欠格条項　disqualification criteria ; criteria for	血友病　hemophilia
disqualification	血流感染　bloodstream infection
結核対策　tuberculosis control	結露　condensation
結核対策特別促進事業　tuberculosis control	解毒剤　antidote
program	解熱剤　antipyretic medication
月額保険料　monthly premium	ケミカルスコア　chemical score
*血管性認知症　vascular dementia ; multi-	煙感知器　smoke detector
infarct dementia	ケラー, H.　Helen Adams Keller
血管造影　angiogram ; vascular imaging	*下痢　diarrhea
血管内留置カテーテル　intravascular catheter	ケリー・パッド　Kelly pad
血管内留置カテーテル関連感染症	牽引（療法）　traction (treatment)
intravascular catheter-related infection	検疫　quarantine
血球　blood cell ; hemocyte	減塩食　low salt diet ; low sodium diet
血色素　hemoglobin	限界集落　marginal village
血腫　hematoma	*幻覚　hallucination

検眼医 optometrist	言語訓練 speech and language training
衒奇症（げんきしょう） mannerism	•言語障害 speech and language disorders
幻嗅（げんきゅう） olfactory hallucination ; phantosmia ; phantom smell	言語性IQ verbal IQ : VIQ
	言語性記憶 verbal memory
研究倫理 ethics in research	言語中枢 speech center
現金給付 cash benefit	言語聴覚訓練 speech-language-hearing training
献血 blood donation	
言語 language	•言語聴覚士 speech-therapist : ST ; speech-language-hearing therapist
•健康 health	
健康維持 health maintenance	言語聴覚士法 Speech Therapists Act
健康型有料老人ホーム private active adult home	言語聴覚リハビリテーション speech-language-hearing rehabilitation
健康観察 health observation	言語聴覚療法 speech-language-hearing therapy
健康管理 health management	
健康関連QOL health-related quality of life	腱固定 tenodesis
健康危機管理 health risk management	言語的攻撃 verbal aggression
健康教育 health education	言語的コミュニケーション verbal communication
健康行動理論 health behavior theory	
健康指標 health indicator	言語能力 language capability
健康寿命 healthy life expectancy : HALE	言語療法 speech therapy
健康状態 health status ; health condition	言語療法士 speech therapist
健康状態の把握 clarification of health status	顕在性不安尺度 Manifest Anxiety Scale
健康食品 health food	顕在的ニーズ stated needs
健康診査（診断） physical examination (diagnosis) ; health examination (diagnosis)	検死 autopsy
	幻視 visual hallucination
健康診断証明書 certificate of physical examination	原刺激（げんしげき） primary stimulus
	幻肢痛 phantom limb pain
健康信念モデル health belief model	現実見当識訓練（げんとうしき） reality orientation training : ROT
健康増進 health promotion	
健康増進センター health promotion center ; center for health promotion	現実性の原理 reality principle
	原始反射 primitive reflex
健康増進の三原則 three principles of health promotion	幻肢（ファントム・リブ） phantom limb
	健常者 healthy person
健康増進法 Public Health Promotion Act ; Health Promotion Act	健常人 healthy volunteer
	幻触 tactile hallucination
健康相談 health counseling	検診 screening
健康チェック health check-up	健側 unaffected side of the body
健康手帳 health handbook	現代化 modernization
健康保菌者 healthy carrier	検体収集 specimen collection
•健康保険 health insurance	建築基準法 Building Standards Act
健康保険給付 health insurance benefit	幻聴 auditory hallucination
健康保険法 Health Insurance Act	見当識（けんとうしき） orientation
言語機能 speech function	見当識・記憶・集中テスト Orientation-

Memory-Concentration Test

* 見当識障害　disorientation

腱板損傷　rotator cuff injury

* 現物給付　in-kind benefit ; non-cash benefit

検便　stool specimen

健忘（症）　amnesia

健忘失語　anomia

腱膜瘤　bunion

幻味　gustatory hallucination

権利章典　Bill of Rights

* 権利擁護　human rights advocacy

権利擁護業務　advocate services ; advocacy services

こ

誤飲　accidental ingestion

更衣　dressing

広域連合　cross-regional federation ; inter-jurisdiction federation

後遺症　sequela ; sequelae ; late effect

行為障害　conduct disorder

抗ウイルス薬　antiviral drug

抗うつ薬　antidepressant

公営住宅　public housing

* 公益事業　public-benefit services

抗炎症薬　antiinflammatory drug

* 構音障害　articulation disorder ; dysarthria

高温やけど　thermal burn ; heat burn

口蓋垂　uvula ; palatine uvula

口蓋扁桃　palatine tonsil

高額医療合算介護サービス費　Long-Term Care Insurance reimbursement for catastrophic medical and long-term care expenses

口角炎　angular cheilitis

高額介護合算療養費　Health Insurance reimbursement for catastrophic health and long-term care expenses

高額介護サービス費　Long-Term Care Insurance reimbursement for catastrophic long-term care expenses

高額障害福祉サービス等給付費　reimbursement for catastrophic disability expenses

高額療養費　reimbursement for catastrophic health care expenses

口渇感　sense of thirst

高カリウム血症　hyperkalemia

高カロリー輸液　hyperalimentation

高カロリー輸液療法　intravenous hyperalimentation : IVH

抗がん剤　anticancer drug

交感神経　sympathetic nerve

抗乾癬薬　antipsoriatic drug

* 後期高齢者　elderly aged 75 and above

後期高齢者医療広域連合　Association of Medical Care for Senior Citizens

後期高齢者医療制度　Health Care System for the Elderly Aged 75 and Above ; Medical Care System for Senior Citizens

高機能自閉症　high-functioning autism : HFA

公共交通機関　public transportation

抗凝固剤　anticoagulant

公共職業安定所　public employment security office ; Hello Work

公共職業訓練　public vocational training

公共政策　public policy

公共の福祉　public welfare

抗菌　antibacterial

抗菌性石鹸　antibacterial soap

抗菌防臭加工　antibacterial and deodorization processing

抗菌・防臭素材　antibacterial and deodorization material

抗菌薬　antibacterial drug ; antibacterial agent

抗菌薬抵抗性　antimicrobial resistance

口腔　oral cavity

口腔衛生　oral health

口腔温　oral temperature

口腔がん　oral cancer

口腔乾燥症　xerostomia ; dry mouth

* 口腔ケア　oral health care ; oral care

* 口腔検温　oral thermometry

口腔疾患　oral disease

口腔状態　oral status

口腔清掃行動　oral hygiene

口腔相 oral propulsive phase

口腔保健アセスメント oral health assessment

•合計特殊出生率 total fertility rate：TFR

攻撃 aggression；acting out

攻撃的行動 aggressive behavior

•高血圧（症） hypertension

抗血小板薬 antiplatelet agent

抗血清 antiserum

高血糖症 hyperglycemia

後見 conservatorship；guardianship

抗原 antigen

抗原抗体反応 antigen-antibody reaction

抗原性 antigenicity

後見制度 conservatorship；guardianship

後見人 conservator；guardian

膠原病 collagen disease

咬合異常 malocclusion

抗甲状腺薬 antithyroid medication

交互型四脚歩行器 reciprocal walker

交互三点歩行 alternate three-point gait

交互式歩行器 reciprocal walker

交互歩行装具 reciprocating gait orthosis：
RGO

高コレステロール血症 hypercholesterolemia

抗細菌 antimicrobial

交差汚染 cross contamination

交差感染 cross infection

抗酸化物 antioxidant

抗酸化薬 antioxidant agent

抗酸化療法 antioxidant therapy

高脂血症 hyperlipidemia

高次脳機能 higher order brain function

高次脳機能障害 neuropsychological
disorder；higher order brain dysfunction

高次脳機能障害及びその関連障害に対する支援
普及事業 program for popularization of
assistance services for people with
neuropsychological disorder and related
disabilities

公私分離の原則 principle of separation of
public and private responsibilities

口臭 halitosis；bad breath

公衆衛生 public health

公衆衛生法 Public Health Services Act

後縦靭帯骨化症 ossification of the posterior
longitudinal ligament：OPLL

抗重力筋 antigravity muscle

抗重力姿勢 antigravity position

•拘縮 contracture

拘縮予防 contracture prevention

公助 public assistance；public aid

控除 deduction

恒常性 homeostasis

甲状腺 thyroid gland

甲状腺がん thyroid cancer

甲状腺機能亢進症 hyperthyroidism

甲状腺機能低下症 hypothyroidism

甲状腺刺激ホルモン thyroid-stimulating
hormone：TSH；thyrotropin；thyrotropic
hormone

甲状腺疾患 thyroid disease

甲状腺腫 goiter

甲状腺髄様がん medullary thyroid cancer

甲状腺乳頭がん papillary thyroid cancer

甲状腺ホルモン thyroid hormone

甲状腺未分化がん anaplastic thyroid cancer

甲状軟骨 thyroid cartilage

公証人 notary public

更新 renewal

口唇期 oral stage

抗真菌性 antifungal

抗真菌性抗生物質 antifungal antibiotic

口唇・口蓋裂 cleft lip and cleft palate

更新申請 renewal application

香辛料 spice

厚生 welfare

更生 rehabilitation

更生医療 medical rehabilitation

向性検査 extraversion-introversion test

公正原理 principle of justice

抗生剤 antibiotic

更正施設 rehabilitation facility；correctional
facility

構成失行 constructional apraxia

構成障害 constructive disability

公正証書 notarial deed

抗精神病薬　antipsychotic medication

向精神薬　psychotropic medication

合成繊維　synthetic fiber

合成洗剤　synthetic detergent

更生相談　rehabilitation counseling

更生相談所　rehabilitation counseling center for people with disabilities

厚生年金基金　Employees' Pension Fund : EPF

厚生年金保険　Employees' Pension Insurance

厚生年金保険法　Employees' Pension Insurance Act

合成ピレスロイド　synthetic pyrethroid

抗生物質　antibiotic

厚生労働省　Ministry of Health, Labour and Welfare

公設民営　privatization of public enterprise

酵素　enzyme

•拘束　restraint

抗体　antibody

叩打法　percussion

高窒素血症　azotemia

高中性脂肪血症　hypertriglyceridemia

高張性脱水症　hypertonic dehydration

硬直　ankylosis

交通バリアフリー法　Promotion of Accessibility for Elderly and Persons with Disabilities Act

肯定的差別　positive discrimination

公的介入　public intervention

公的責任　public responsibility

公的年金制度　public pension system

公的扶助　public assistance

公的扶助受給者　public assistance recipient

抗てんかん薬　antiepileptic drug : AED ; antiseizure drug

後天性障害　acquired disabilities ; acquired disorders

•後天性免疫不全症候群　acquired immune deficiency syndrome : AIDS

行動アセスメント　behavior assessment

行動援護　escort services for people with behavioral difficulties

喉頭蓋　epiglottis

行動科学　behavioral science

喉頭がん　laryngeal cancer ; laryngeal carcinoma

行動観察　behavioral observation

喉頭気管炎　laryngotracheitis

行動言語　behavioral language

行動障害　behavioral disorder ; behavioral symptom

後頭神経痛　occipital neuralgia ; C2 neuralgia ; Arnold's neuralgia

抗糖尿病薬　antidiabetic

行動パターン　behavior pattern

行動評価スケール　behavioral assessment scale

行動変容アプローチ　behavior modification approach

行動変容法　behavior modification

行動変容モデル　behavior modification model

行動目標　behavioral objective

行動リハーサル　behavior rehearsal

行動療法　behavior therapy

行動理論　behavioral theory

高度先進医療　highly advanced medical technology : HAMT

口内炎　stomatitis ; canker sore

高尿酸血症　hyperuricemia

•更年期　menopause

更年期うつ病　menopausal depression

更年期障害　menopausal disorder ; climacteric disturbance

高年齢者等の雇用の安定等に関する法律　Older Age Employment Stability Act

後発医薬品　generic drug

広汎性発達障害　pervasive developmental disorder : PDD

広範脊柱管狭窄症　extended spinal stenosis

高比重リポたんぱく質　high density lipoprotein

抗ヒスタミン剤　antihistamine

公費負担　public funding

公費負担医療　publicly funded health care

公費負担医療制度と介護保険　publicly funded health and long-term care

高頻度接触面　high-touch surface

抗不安薬　antianxiety medication

高福祉・高負担　high level of welfare, high level of taxation

幸福追求権　the right to the pursuit of happiness

幸福な老い　successful aging

後腹膜血腫　retroperitoneal hematoma

抗浮腫性　antiedemic

交付税　local allocation tax grants

高分子吸水体(吸水性ポリマー)　high molecular absorbent ; super absorbent polymer

公平　equity

公募指定　open invitation for applications for designation

硬膜外血腫　epidural hematoma

硬膜下血腫　subdural hematoma

香味　flavor

公民権(運動)　civil rights (movement)

肛門　anus

肛門括約筋　anal sphincter muscle

肛門期　anal stage

肛門鏡　anoscope ; anal speculum

肛門鏡検査　anoscopy

合理化　rationalization

公立病院　public hospital

合理的配慮　reasonable accommodation

抗利尿　antidiuresis

高齢化　population aging

高齢化委員会　Conference on Aging

高齢化社会　aging society

高齢化率　the rate of population aging

高齢期活動　later-life activity

高齢期障害　aging-associated disease

•高齢者　elderly person ; old person

高齢者医療　medical care for the elderly

高齢者医療確保法　Assurance of Medical Care for the Elderly Act

高齢者医療制度　medical care system for the elderly

高齢者円滑入居賃貸住宅　senior apartment

•高齢社会　aged society

高齢者介護　elderly care ; senior care ; aged care

高齢者介護施設　long-term care facility for the elderly

高齢社会対策基本法　Basic Aged Society Act

高齢社会対策大綱　Guiding Principles for the Aged Society

高齢者が居住する住宅の設計に係る指針　Senior Housing Design Guidelines

高齢者看護　geriatric nursing

•高齢者虐待　elder abuse

高齢者虐待の防止、高齢者の養護者に対する支援等に関する法律　Prevention of Elder Abuse and Support for Attendants of Elderly Persons Act : Elder Abuse Prevention Act

高齢者虐待防止　prevention of elder abuse ; elder abuse prevention

高齢者虐待防止ネットワーク　elder abuse prevention network

•高齢者虐待防止法　Elder Abuse Prevention Act ; Prevention of Elder Abuse and Support for Attendants of Elderly Persons Act

高齢者ケア　elderly care ; senior care

高齢者雇用　employment of older workers

高齢者雇用対策　employment promotion initiatives for older workers

高齢者サービス調整チーム　service coordination team for the elderly

高齢者住宅　senior housing

高齢者、障害者等の移動等の円滑化の促進に関する法律　Promotion of Accessibility for Elderly and Persons with Disabilities Act : Barrier-Free Act

高齢者人口　elderly population

高齢者、身体障害者等が円滑に利用できる特定建築物の建築の促進に関する法律　Promotion of Building Accessibility for Elderly and Persons with Disabilities Act : Heart Building Act

高齢者住まい法　Senior Housing Act ; Assurance of Stable Housing for Older Persons Act

高齢者生活福祉センター　welfare center for the elderly

高齢者世帯　elder household

高齢者世帯向公営住宅　senior public housing apartment

高齢者世話付住宅　assisted living

高齢者専門医　geriatrician

高齢者専用賃貸住宅　senior rental housing

高齢者総合相談センター　comprehensive consultation services for the elderly

高齢者総合的機能評価　Comprehensive Geriatric Assessment : CGA

高齢者多目的福祉センター　multipurpose senior center

高齢者単独世帯　elderly living in single-person households

高齢者ネグレクト　elder neglect

高齢者の安全な薬物療法ガイドライン Guidelines for Medication Therapy

高齢者の生きがいと健康づくり推進事業 promotional program for improving motivation and health status of the elderly

高齢者の医療の確保に関する法律　Assurance of Medical Care for the Elderly Act

高齢者能力開発情報センター　vocational training and resource center for the elderly

高齢者の居住の安定確保に関する法律 Assurance of Stable Housing for Older Persons Act : Senior Housing Act

高齢者の経済生活に関する意識調査　financial awareness survey among the elderly

高齢者の住宅と生活環境に関する意識調査 housing and living environmental awareness survey among the elderly

高齢者の尊厳　dignity of the elderly

「高齢者のための新たな医療制度等について（最終とりまとめ）」　New Health Insurance System for the Elderly (Final Summary Report)

高齢者の地域社会への参加に関する意識調査 community participation awareness survey among the elderly

高齢者評価・マネジメントプログラム　geriatric evaluation and management programs

高齢者福祉　welfare of old people ; welfare of the elderly

高齢者福祉サービス　welfare services for the elderly

「高齢者保健福祉推進十か年戦略」 Ten-Year-Strategy to Promote Health and Welfare for the Elderly : Gold Plan

高齢者向け住宅　senior housing

高齢者向け優良賃貸住宅　high-quality senior rental housing

高齢者無料職業紹介所　vocational training and resource center for the elderly

高齢者問題　issues affecting the elderly ; issues in the elderly

高齢単身無職世帯　retired single elderly household

高齢発症関節リウマチ　elderly-onset rheumatoid arthritis : EORA

高齢無職世帯　retired elderly household

口話　verbal communication

後弯　kyphosis ; roundback

声かけ　verbal encouragement : VE

誤嚥　pulmonary aspiration

誤嚥性肺炎　aspiration pneumonia

コーディネーター　coordinator

コーピング（行動）　coping (behavior)

コーホート　cohort

氷枕　ice pillow ; ice pack

ゴールドプラン　Gold Plan ; Ten-Year-Strategy to Promote Health and Welfare for the Elderly

ゴールドプラン21　Gold Plan 21 ; Next Five-Year-Plan to Promote Health and Welfare for the Elderly

コカイン型依存　cocaine addiction

股関節骨折　hip fracture

小刻み歩行　shuffling gait ; festinating gait

呼吸　breathing ; respiration

呼吸運動　external respiration ; respiratory movement

呼吸器　respiratory organ

呼吸器感染　respiratory infection

呼吸器機能障害　respiratory dysfunction ; functional respiratory disorder

呼吸器疾患　respiratory disease

呼吸訓練　respiratory exercise ; breathing exercise

呼吸困難　dyspnea ; shortness of breath ; breathlessness

呼吸障害　respiratory disorder

呼吸不全　respiratory failure

呼吸麻痺　respiratory paralysis

呼吸リハビリテーション　pulmonary rehabilitation

呼吸療法　respiratory therapy

国際衛生年　International Year of Sanitation : IYS

国際化学年　International Year of Chemistry : IYC

国際家族年　International Year of the Family : IYF

国際規格　International Standard : IS

国際規格分類　International Classification for Standards : ICS

国際厚生事業団　Japan International Corporation of Welfare Services

国際高齢者年　International Year of Older Persons : IYOP

*国際疾病分類　International Classification of Diseases : ICD

国際児童年　International Year of the Child : IYC

国際社会福祉協議会　International Council on Social Welfare : ICSW

国際障害者年　International Year of Disabled Persons : IYDP

*国際障害分類　International Classification of Impairments, Disabilities and Handicaps : ICIDH

国際人権規約　International Covenant on Human Rights

国際人権憲章　International Bill of Human Rights

国際人権擁護団体　International Human Rights Organization : IHRO

国際身体障害者スポーツ大会　Paralympic Games

*国際生活機能分類　International Classification of Functioning, Disability and Health : ICF

国際生物多様性年　International Year of Biodiversity : IYB

国際長寿センター　International Longevity Center : ILC

国際標準化機構　International Organization for Standardization : ISO

国際婦人年　International Women's Year : IWY

国際リハビリテーション協会　Rehabilitation International : RI

国際レクリエーション協会　World Leisure and Recreation Association : WLRA

国際連合　United Nations : UN

国際連盟　League of Nations : LON

国際労働機関　International Labour Organization : ILO

国際老年精神学会　International Psychogeriatric Association : IPA

国勢調査　national census

国内総生産　gross domestic product : GDP

国民医療費　national health expenditures

国民皆年金　universal pension

国民皆保険　national universal health insurance

国民健康・栄養調査　National Health and Nutrition Survey

国民健康保険組合　National Health Insurance Society

国民健康保険(制度)　National Health Insurance (system)

国民健康保険団体連合会　National Health Insurance Organization

国民健康保険法　National Health Insurance Act

国民健康保険料　National Health Insurance premium

国民健康保険料減免　National Health Insurance premium deduction

国民所得　national income : NI

国民生活基礎調査　Comprehensive Survey of Living Conditions

国民生活センター　National Consumer Affairs

Center of Japan：NCAC

国民総生産　gross national product：GNP

国民総福祉　gross national welfare：GNW

国民年金　National Pension

国民年金基金　National Pension Fund

国民年金法　National Pension Act

国民年金保険　National Pension Insurance

国民年金保険料　National Pension premiums

国民年金保険料免除　National Pension premium deduction and exemption

国民負担率　tax burden ratio to national income

国立医薬品食品衛生研究所　National Institute of Health Sciences

国立がん研究センター　National Cancer Center

国立感染症研究所　National Institute of Infectious Diseases

国立国際医療研究センター　National Center for Global Health and Medicine

国立社会保障・人口問題研究所　National Institute of Population and Social Security Research

国立循環器病研究センター　National Cerebral and Cardiovascular Center

国立成育医療研究センター　National Center for Child Health and Development

国立精神・神経医療研究センター　National Center of Neurology and Psychiatry

国立長寿医療研究センター　National Center for Geriatrics and Gerontology

国立病院　national hospital

国立保健医療科学院　National Institute of Public Health

国連・障害者の十年　United Nations Decade of Disabled Persons

誤見当　disorientation

こころのケア　mental health care；emotional care

心の理論　theory of mind：ToM

腰掛便座　sitting toilet

個室　private room

個室化　privatization of rooms

固縮　rigidity

孤食　eating alone

故人　deceased

誤診　misdiagnosis

•個人因子（ICF）　personal factors

個人衛生　personal hygiene

個人情報　personal information

個人情報の窃盗　identity theft

個人情報の保護に関する法律　Personal Information Protection Act

個人情報保護　protection of personal information

個人情報保護法　Personal Information Protection Act

個人内変動　personal change

個人年金　personal pension

個人番号　taxpayer identification numbers；identification number

個人防護用装備　personal protective equipment：PPE

子育て　parenting；child rearing

子育て支援　parenting support；child rearing support

五大栄養素　five essential nutrients

誇大妄想　delusion of grandeur

5Ｗ1Ｈ　Five W's and One H；who, what, where, when, why, and how

固着　fixation

骨萎縮　bone atrophy

骨塩量　bone mineral density

骨格　skeleton

骨格筋　skeletal muscle

国家公務員共済組合　National Government Employees' Mutual Aid Association

国家最低基準　national minimum standards

国家最低賃金　national minimum wage

骨化性筋炎　myositis ossificans

国家責任　national responsibility

骨減少性　osteopenia

骨疾患　bone disease

骨髄　bone marrow

•骨折　fracture

•骨粗鬆症　osteoporosis

骨粗鬆症検診　osteoporosis-related test

骨転移　bone metastasis

骨軟化症　osteomalacia

骨盤骨折　pelvic fracture

骨盤帯　pelvic band

骨盤底筋群　pelvic floor muscles

骨盤底筋訓練法　pelvic floor muscle exercises ; Kegel exercises

骨盤底弛緩　pelvic floor relaxation

骨密度　bone density

固定式歩行器　walker

固定ジストニア　fixed dystonia

古典的条件づけ　classical conditioning ; Pavlovian conditioning

孤独　loneliness

孤独死　lonely death ; dying alone

言葉かけ（レクリエーションでの） verbal encouragement (during activities)

言葉の明瞭性　speech clarity

子ども手当　child allowance

コノプカ, G.　Gisela Konopka

小振り歩行　swing-to gait

個別援助活動　social case work

個別援助技術　social casework techniques ; social casework skills

*個別援助計画　individualized care plan

個別化　individualization

個別介護　individualized care

*個別ケア　individualized care

個別支援計画　individualized care plan

鼓膜　tympanic membrane

*コミュニケーション　communication

*コミュニケーションエイド　communication aid

コミュニケーション手段　communications tool ; communication method

コミュニケーション障害　communication disorder

コミュニケーションの構成要素　components of communication

コミュニケーションの阻害要因　factors affecting communication

コミュニケーション評価　communication evaluation ; evaluation of communication

コミュニティ　community

コミュニティ・オーガニゼーション　community organization

コミュニティケア　community care

コミュニティ・ソーシャルワーク　community social work

コミュニティ・ベイスド・リハビリテーション community-based rehabilitation : CBR

コミュニティワーカー　community worker

コミュニティワーク　community work

コメディカルスタッフ　ancillary medical personnel ; paramedical personnel

誤薬　medication error

固有感覚　proprioception

固有受容性欠陥　proprioception deficit

誤用症候群　misuse syndrome

雇用の分野における男女の均等な機会及び待遇の確保等に関する法律　Equal Employment Opportunity Act

雇用保険（制度）　employment insurance (system)

雇用保険法　Employment Insurance Act

雇用率　employment rate

雇用率制度　employment system for people with disabilities

コラーゲン　collagen

娯楽　recreation ; amusement ; entertainment

糊料　gelling, thickening and stabilizing agents

五類感染症　category V infection ; 5th-category infection

コルサコフ症候群　Korsakoff's syndrome ; Korsakoff's amnesic syndrome

コルサコフ精神病　Korsakoff's psychosis

コルチゾール　cortisol

*コレステロール　cholesterol

コレラ　cholera

コロストミー　colostomy

婚姻証明書　marriage certificate

根拠にもとづく医療　evidence-based medicine : EBM

根拠にもとづく看護　evidence-based nursing : EBN

根拠にもとづくケア　evidence-based care : EBC

混合型認知症　mixed dementia

混合性難聴　mixed hearing loss

「今後5か年間の高齢者保健福祉施策の方向」
（ゴールドプラン21）
Next Five-Year-Plan to Promote Health and
Welfare for the Elderly : Gold Plan 21

今後の介護人材養成の在り方に関する検討会報
告書　Report on the Recruitment and
Training of Future Long-Term Care Personnel

「今後の社会福祉のあり方について」
The Future of Social Welfare

「今後の社会保障改革の方向性に関する意見
―21世紀型の社会保障の実現に向けて―」
Opinion Regarding the Future Direction of
Social Security Reform : Toward the
Establishment of Social Security for the 21st
Century

今後の障害保健福祉施策について（改革のグラン
ドデザイン案）　Future of Health and Welfare
Policies for Persons with Disabilities
(Proposed Grand Design for the Reform)

コンサルテーション　consultation

*昏睡　coma

昏睡状態　comatose

*献立作成　menu planning

コンチネンス　continence

コンビネーションシステム　combination systems

コンピュータ断層撮影　computed tomography :
CT

*昏眠　sopor

*昏迷　stupor

混乱期　stage of anger ; period of anger

さ

サーカディアンリズム　circadian rhythm

サージカルマスク　surgical mask

SARS　severe acute respiratory syndrome

サービス管理責任者　disability services
manager

サービスコード　service code

*サービス担当者会議　service providers
meeting

サービス調整　coordination of services

サービス付き高齢者向け住宅　assisted living

サービス提供圏　service area

サービス提供責任者　home-help services
manager

サービス等利用計画　disability services plan

サービスの継続性　continuum of services

サービスパッケージ　package of services

サービス利用支援　disability services planning
and coordination

サービス利用者　service recipient

サーベイランス　surveillance

サーモグラフィー　thermography

*座位　sitting position ; seating position

*再アセスメント　reassessment

サイアミン欠乏症　thiamine deficiency

在院　hospital stay ; hospitalization

災害　disaster ; accident

災害救助法　Disaster Relief Act

災害給付　disaster benefit

災害保険　disaster insurance

災害補償　accident insurance

再課題分析　reanalysis of problems

サイキアトリック・ソーシャル・ワーカー
psychiatric social worker : PSW

細気管支炎　bronchiolitis

細菌　bacterium ; bacteria

細菌性食中毒　bacterial food poisoning

細菌性肺炎　bacterial pneumonia

細菌尿　bacteriuria

座位訓練　sitting exercise

採光　daylighting

再興型インフルエンザ　re-emerging influenza

再興感染症　re-emerging infectious disease

最高血圧　systolic blood pressure

罪業妄想　delusion of guilt ; delusion of
self-accusation

サイコドラマ　psychodrama

座位姿勢　sitting posture ; upright sitting
position

最終臥床期間　bedridden period before
death : BPbd

最終滅菌　terminal sterilization

最小可聴値　absolute threshold of hearing
在職証明書　proof of employment ; employment verification
財政安定化基金　Financial Stability Funds
再生医療　regenerative medicine
再生繊維　recycled fabric
再生不良性貧血　aplastic anemia
最大筋力　maximum muscle strength
最大酸素摂取量　maximum oxygen consumption : VO2 max ; maximum oxygen uptake
最大随意収縮圧　maximum squeeze pressure : MSP
最大静止圧　maximum resting pressure : MRP
最大耐容量　maximum tolerable volume : MTV
最大歩行速度　maximal gait velocity ; maximum gait speed
在宅医　home care physician
在宅医療　home care medicine
在宅医療サービス　medical home care services
*在宅介護　home care
在宅介護支援センター　home care support center
在宅介護者リフレッシュ事業　caregivers' refresh program
在宅看護（ケア）　home health (care)
在宅ケア（サービス）　home care (services)
在宅高齢者福祉サービス　in-home elderly welfare services
在宅サービス　home care services
在宅サービス事業者　home care services provider
在宅酸素療法　home oxygen therapy : HOT
在宅人工呼吸療法　home mechanical ventilation
在宅ターミナルケア　in-home hospice care
在宅中心静脈栄養　home parenteral nutrition : HPN
在宅治療　home treatment
在宅透析療法　home dialysis
在宅福祉サービス　in-home welfare services
在宅ホスピス　in-home hospice care

在宅リハビリテーション　home rehabilitation
在宅療養支援診療所　medical clinic for supporting community living
在宅レクリエーション　home-based activity
最低血圧　diastolic pressure
最低生活水準　minimum standard of living
最低生活費　minimum cost of living
最低生活保障　guaranteed minimum standard of living
最低賃金（制度）　minimum wage (system)
再動機づけ　remotivation
細動脈　arteriole
サイドレール　side rail
採尿器（尿器）　urine collection device
再認　recognition
再認定　recertification
座位バランス　sitting balance
再分配　redistribution
採便　fecal sampling
座位補助具　seating aid
催眠　hypnosis
催眠療法　hypnotherapy
財務管理　financial management
サイロキシン　thyroxine : T4
詐欺　fraud ; scam
作業記憶　working memory
作業耐性　work tolerance
作業調整　work adjustment
作業能力　work capacity
*作業療法　occupational therapy : OT
*作業療法士　occupational therapist : OT
錯語　paraphasia
酢酸　acetic acid
酢酸塩　acetate
サクセスフル・エイジング　successful aging
錯乱　confusion ; disorientation
作話　confabulation
坐骨神経痛　sciatica
差し込み便器　bedpan
左心房　left atrium
させられ思考　made thinking
させられ体験　made experience
錯覚　illusion

殺菌　sterilization
擦式法　rubbing method
サテライト型施設　satellite facility ; branch facility
サテライト方式　satellite system
里親　foster parent
差別　discrimination
座薬　suppository
左右失認　left-right disorientation
サルコイドーシス　sarcoidosis
サルコペニア　sarcopenia
サルモネラ菌　salmonella
サルモネラ食中毒　salmonella food poisoning
酸　acid
酸塩基調節　acid-base regulation
酸塩基平衡　acid-base balance
酸化　oxidation
*参加（ICF）　participation
三角巾　sling
*参加制約（ICF）　participation restrictions
参加の原則　principles of participation ; self-determination
酸化防止剤　antioxidant
三脚づえ　tripod cane
産休　maternity leave
産業化　industrialization
酸血症　acidosis
散剤　powdered medication
三叉神経痛　trigeminal neuralgia : TN
三次元歩行分析　three-dimensional gait analysis
三肢麻痺　triplegia
36項目健康調査票　Medical Outcomes Study 36-Item Short-Form Health Survey : MOS SF-36 Health Survey
産褥感染症　puerperal infection ; postpartum infection
三色食品群　three-color classification system for food groups
産褥熱　puerperal fever ; childbed fever
三次予防　tertiary prevention
参政権　suffrage
三世代家族　three-generation family

三世代世帯　three-generation family household
産前産後休暇　maternity leave
三尖弁　tricuspid valve
酸素　oxygen
酸素（経鼻）カニューレ　nasal cannula : NC
酸素消費　oxygen consumption
酸素摂取　oxygen intake
酸素濃縮器　oxygen concentrator
酸素療法（酸素吸入）　oxygen therapy
残存感覚　remaining sense
残存感覚機能　residual sensory function
*残存能力　residual functional capacity : RFC
三大栄養素　three essential nutrients
三大死因　three leading causes of death ; top three causes of death
三団体ケアプラン策定研究会方式　Three-Organization Care Plan Development Study Group Method
三点歩行　three-point gait
酸度　acidity
三動作歩行　three-point gait
残尿　residual urine
残尿感　sensation of incomplete emptying of bladder
三人移乗法　three-person transfer
散髪　haircut
散布　spray
酸味　sour ; sour taste ; sourness
酸無水物　acid anhydride
三類感染症　category III infection ; 3rd-category infection

し

死　death
次亜塩素酸ナトリウム溶液　sodium hypochlorite solution
指圧　acupressure
指圧師　acupressurist
指圧法　acupressure
COPD　chronic obstructive pulmonary disease

C型肝炎（ウイルス）　hepatitis C (virus)

CTスキャン　computed tomography scan : CT scan

シーティング　seating

死因　cause of death : COD

死因別死亡割合　proportional mortality rate : PMR

ジェスチャー　gesture

ジェネリック医薬品　generic drug

ジェネリックソーシャルワーク　generic social work

ジェノグラム　genogram

支援機器　assistive device

支援グループ　support group

ジェンダー　gender

支援費制度　disability support payment system

塩味　salty taste ; saltiness

塩抜き　removal of excessive salt

歯科　dentistry

自我　ego

歯科医師　dentist

自我意識　ego-consciousness

歯科医師法　Dental Practitioners Act

紫外線療法　ultraviolet therapy

•歯科衛生士　dental hygienist

歯科衛生士法　Dental Hygienists Act

歯科技工士　dental technician

視覚　sense of sight ; visual perception

視覚失認　visual agnosia

•視覚障害　visual impairment ; visual disorder ; visual deficit

視覚障害者　person with visual impairments ; blind person

視覚障害者更生施設　rehabilitation facility for the blind and visually impaired

視覚障害者情報提供施設　information center for the blind and visually impaired

視覚障害者用信号機　audible pedestrian traffic signal ; audible traffic signal

視覚障害者用補助機器　adaptive equipment for the blind and visually impaired ; technical aids for the blind and visually impaired

視覚代行　vision substitution

歯科疾患　dental disease

自我障害　self-disturbance

歯科診療所　dental clinic

耳下腺　parotid gland

自家中毒　autointoxication

自我同一性　ego identity

自我の欲求　esteem needs

直火焼き　grilling

弛緩　flaccid ; flaccidity

弛緩性便秘　atonic constipation

弛緩性麻痺　flaccid paralysis

歯間歯磨き　dental floss ; flossing teeth

時間預託制　volunteering in exchange for long-term care

磁気共鳴血管撮影　magnetic resonance angiography : MRA

磁気共鳴装置　magnetic resonance imaging : MRI

磁気共鳴断層撮影　magnetic resonance imaging : MRI

色盲　color blindness

子宮がん　uterine cancer

持久訓練　endurance exercise ; endurance training

子宮頸がん　cervical cancer

子宮頸部異形成　cervical dysplasia

持久性　endurance

糸球体濾過量　glomerular filtration rate : GFR

子宮脱　uterine prolapse

視空間失認　visual spatial agnosia

刺激　stimulation

刺激性皮膚炎　irritant dermatitis

•止血　hemostasis ; haemostasis : Hb

耳血腫　aural hematoma

止血点　pressure point to stop bleeding

自己愛性介護者　narcissistic caregiver

自己愛性人格障害　narcissistic personality disorder

歯垢　dental plaque

耳垢　earwax ; cerumen

嗜好飲料　beverage

•思考障害　thought disorder

思考制止　inhibition of thought

耳垢塞栓（じこうそくせん）　cerumen impaction ; earwax blockage

思考途絶　thought blocking

自己開示　self-disclosure

自己改善　self-improvement

自己概念　self-concept

自己開発　personal development ; broadening of knowledge

*自己覚知　self-awareness

自己感染　self-infection

自己教示訓練　self-instructional training

*自己決定　self-determination

自己決定の原則　principle of self-determination

自己嫌悪　self-hatred ; self-loathing

死後硬直　rigor mortis

自己効力感　self-efficacy

自己コントロール理論　self-control theory

*自己実現　self-actualization

自己支払い　out-of-pocket

自己受容体　autoreceptor

自己消化　autolysis ; self-digestion

自己責任　self-responsibility

自己他動運動　self-assisted exercise

自己注射　self-injection

自己調節　autoregulation

自己調節鎮痛法　patient-controlled analgesia : PCA

自己同一性　self-identity

自己投資型個人年金　self-invested personal pension : SIPP

自己導尿　self-catheterization

仕事中毒　workaholic

死後のケア（処置）　postmortem care

自己破産　voluntary bankruptcy

事故抜管（ばっかん）　accidental extubation

事故評価　accident evaluation

自己評価　self-evaluation

事後評価　post evaluation ; post assessment

自己評価式抑うつ性尺度　Self-Rating Depression Scale : SDS

自己表現　self-expression

自己負担金　co-payment

自己負担割合　copayment rate

自己防衛型　armored type

事故報告書　incident report

自己放任　self-neglect

自己免疫（めんえき）　autoimmunity

自己免疫性肝炎　autoimmune hepatitis

自己溶解　autolysis

自己擁護運動　self-advocacy movement

視細胞　photoreceptor

自在輪　caster

自殺　suicide

自殺幇助（ほうじょ）　assisted suicide

自殺予防　suicide prevention

資産税　property tax

資産調査　means test

死産率　fetal mortality rate

四肢（しし）　limbs ; extremities

支持　support

脂質　lipid

*脂質異常症　dyslipidemia

資質向上の責務　responsibility for quality improvement

脂質蓄積症　lipid storage disease

支持的作業療法　supportive occupational therapy

支持棒　support bar

*四肢麻痺（ししまひ）　quadriplegia

死者　deceased

歯周炎　periodontitis

歯周疾患　periodontal disease

歯周組織　periodontium

歯周病　gum disease ; periodontal disease

自主退院　discharge against medical advice

自助　self-help

視床下部　hypothalamus

*自傷行為　self-harm : SH ; self-injury ; self-mutilation

自傷他害行為　danger to self or others

市場メカニズム　market mechanism

自助、共助、公助　self-help, mutual aid and public assistance

049

和英

あ
か
し
た
な
は
ま
や
ら
わ

*自助具 self-help device ; adaptive equipment ; assistive device
*自助グループ self-help group : SHG
指診 digital examination
視神経萎縮 optic nerve atrophy
ジスキネジア dyskinesia
JISサイズ表示（衣料の） Japanese Industrial Standards for clothing size labeling
システム理論 systems theory
ジストニア dystonia
姿勢 posture
*死生観 view of life and death
姿勢訓練 postural exercise
姿勢反射 postural reflex
姿勢反射障害 postural reflex impairment
姿勢反応 postural reaction
自責（内罰）型 self-hater
施設 facility ; institution
施設運営 facility administration
肢節運動失行 limb kinetic apraxia
施設介護 institutional care
施設介護サービス費 reimbursement for institutional care
施設介護支援 institutional care
施設基盤型サービス facility-based services
施設ケア institutional care
*施設サービス institutional care services
施設サービス計画 in-facility care plans ; institutional care plan
施設実習 institutional practical training
施設収容 institutionalization
施設内感染 nosocomial infection ; hospital-acquired infection
施設入所支援 personal care services for institutionalized disabled persons
施設の社会化 socialization of institution ; open the facility to community
慈善 charity
自然災害 natural disaster
慈善組織協会 Charity Organization Society : COS
自然毒食中毒 food poisoning by naturally occurring toxins

自然発生的退職者コミュニティ naturally occurring retirement community
事前評価 pre-evaluation ; pre-assessment
自走式階段昇降機 stair-climbing wheelchair
歯槽膿漏 pyorrhea alveolaris
自走用標準型車いす self-propelled wheelchair
持続携帯式腹膜透析 continuous ambulatory peritoneal dialysis : CAPD
持続牽引 continuous traction
持続伸張 prolonged stretching
持続性吸息 apneusis
持続他動運動 continuative passive motion : CPM
持続的気道陽圧 continuous positive air pressure : CPAP
自尊心 self-esteem
死体解剖 autopsy
死体検案書 medical certificate of cause of death
*肢体不自由 orthopedic impairment ; physical disability
自治会 self-government association ; local self-government
視知覚 visual perception
自治事務 autonomous affairs
市中感染 community-acquired infection
市町村 municipality
市町村介護保険事業計画 municipality's long-term care insurance planning
市町村社会福祉協議会 Municipal Council of Social Welfare
市町村障害者計画 municipal basic disability plan
市町村障害福祉計画 municipal welfare planning for persons with disabilities
市町村審査会 municipal committee on persons with disabilities ; municipal disability committee
市町村相互財政安定化事業 mutual stabilization of the municipal budget for long-term care insurance
市町村地域生活支援事業 municipal government-administered community living

050

assistance program

市町村特別給付　municipal government's special long-term care benefits

市町村保健センター　municipal health center ; local health center

市町村老人福祉計画　municipal welfare planning for the elderly

質改善活動　quality improvement : QI

疾患　disease ; disorder

疾患管理　disease management : DM

実技試験　practice examination

失業　unemployment

失業給付　unemployment benefit

失業手当　unemployment compensation ; unemployment benefit

失業保険　unemployment insurance

失業率　unemployment rate

• 失禁　incontinence

失禁アセスメント　urinary incontinence assessment

失禁ケア　incontinence care

シックハウス症候群　sick building syndrome : SBS ; sick house syndrome

失見当識　disorientation

• 失語　aphasia

失行　apraxia

実行機能障害　executive function disorder : EFD

失語症　aphasia

失算　acalculia ; dyscalculia

湿式加熱　boiling

湿式洗濯　wet cleaning

• 実支出　actual expenditure

実支出以外の支払　disbursements other than expenditures

実質賃金　actual wage

実質的違法性阻却論　justifiable reason for noncompliance with a law

• 実収入　actual income

実収入以外の受取　household receipts other than income

実収入以外の収入　income other than actual income

失書　agraphia ; dysgraphia

失神　fainting

湿疹　eczema

湿性温熱　moist heating

失声症　aphonia

失調　coordination impairment ; lack of coordination

失調性歩行　ataxic gait

失読　alexia

嫉妬妄想　delusional jealousy

室内気候　indoor climate

• 失認（症）　agnosia

湿熱滅菌　moist heat sterilization

実年齢　chronological age

湿布　cataplasm ; poultice

疾病　disease ; illness ; sickness

疾病影響プロフィール　Sickness Impact Profile : SIP

疾病管理予防センター　Center for Disease Control and Prevention : CDC

疾病休暇　sick leave

疾病否認　denial of illness

疾病保険　sickness insurance

実務経験証明書　certification of work experience ; verification of work experience

実務者研修　training program for non-certified care workers

質問紙（法）　questionnaire ; survey ; survey method

指定　designation ; certification

指定一般相談支援事業者　designated general consultation services provider

指定感染症　specified infection

指定管理者制度　designation system for public facility management

指定居宅介護支援事業者　designated care management provider

指定居宅サービス　designated home-based care services

指定事業者　designated provider

指定市町村事務受託法人　designated corporation for municipal affairs

指定障害福祉サービス事業者　designated disability services provider

指定情報公表センター　designated public information center

指定都市　designated city

指定都道府県事務受託法人　designated corporation for prefectural affairs

指定病院　designated hospital

児童　child ; children

児童委員　commissioned child welfare volunteer

•自動運動　active movement

自動介助運動　active assisted exercise

自動可動域　active range of motion : AROM

児童期障害　childhood disorder

児童虐待　child abuse

児童虐待の防止等に関する法律　Child Abuse Prevention Act

児童虐待防止法　Child Abuse Prevention Act

自動訓練　active exercise

児童憲章　Children's Charter

児童権利宣言　Declaration of the Rights of the Child

児童厚生施設　children's recreational center

自動思考　autonomic thought

自動症　automatism

児童自立支援　supportive services for children's independence

児童相談員　child counselor

児童相談所　children's resource and consultation center

自動体外式除細動器　automated external defibrillator : AED

児童手当　child allowance

児童手当法　Children's Allowances Act

自動排泄処理装置　automatic urine collection device

児童福祉　child welfare

児童福祉機関　child welfare agency

児童福祉計画　child welfare planning

児童福祉サービス　child welfare services

児童福祉司　child welfare officer

児童福祉施設　child welfare facility

児童福祉審議会　Advisory Council on Child Welfare

児童福祉法　Child Welfare Act

児童扶養手当　child allowance ; child dependency allowance

児童保護サービス　child protective services

児童保護施設　children's shelter

児童養護施設　children's home ; orphanage

シニア住宅　senior housing

シニアボランティア　senior volunteer

歯肉　gingiva

歯肉炎　inflamed gum

視能訓練　orthoptic exercise

視能訓練士　orthoptist : ORT

死の質　quality of death : QoD

自発活動　spontaneous activity

自発的活動支援事業　supportive program for spontaneous voluntary community activities

死斑　livor mortis ; postmortem lividity

市販薬　over-the-counter medication

耳鼻咽喉科医　otolaryngologist ; ear, nose, and throat specialist

耳鼻咽喉検査　ear, nose and throat evaluation

自費支払い　out-of-pocket

尿瓶　urinal

ジフテリア　diphtheria

•自閉症　autism

自閉症スペクトラム障害　autism spectrum disorder : ASD

死別　separated by death

脂肪　fat

死亡　death

司法解剖　forensic autopsy

脂肪酸　fatty acid

死亡診断書　death certificate ; certificate of death

脂肪組織　adipose tissue

死亡届　notification of death ; death notification

死亡率　mortality rate ; death rate

市民的及び政治的権利に関する国際規約　International Covenant on Civil and Political Rights : ICCPR

シムス位　Sims' position
閉め出し理論　crowding-out theory
諮問委員会　advisory council
視野　peripheral vision
シャイ・ドレーガー症候群　Shy-Drager syndrome：SDS
社会医学　social medicine
社会意識　social consciousness
社会医療法人　social medical corporation
社会運動（論）　social movement (theory)
社会・援護局　Social Welfare and War Victims' Relief Bureau
社会改良　social reform
社会活動　social activity
社会活動法　social action
社会教育　social education
社会恐怖　social anxiety disorder；social phobia：SAD
社会計画　social planning
社会権　social rights
社会構造　social structure
社会サービス　social services
社会参加　social participation
社会支援（サービス）　social support (services)
社会事業　social program
•社会資源　social resources
社会集団　social group
社会主義　socialism
社会情動的選択理論　socioemotional selectivity theory：SST
社会診断　social diagnosis
社会生活技能訓練　social skills training：SST
社会生活評価尺度　Life Assessment Scale for Mental Illness：LASMI
社会生活力　social functioning ability：SFA
社会政策　social policy
社会精神医学　social psychiatry
社会性の原理　principles of social welfare
社会秩序　social order
社会調査　social work research method
社会手当（制度）　social allowance (system)
社会適応訓練　social adaptability and social skill training

社会的及び文化的権利に関する国際規約　International Covenant on Economic, Social and Cultural Rights
社会的介護　social care
社会的隔離　social isolation
社会的危険　social risk
社会的支援（ネットワーク）　social support (network)
社会的受容　social inclusion
社会的障壁　social barrier
社会的相互作用　social interaction
社会的促進　social facilitation
社会的適用　social adequacy
社会的手抜き　social facilitation
社会的統合　social integration
社会的入院　social hospitalization
社会的ネットワーク　social network
•社会的不利　handicap；social disadvantage
社会的包摂　social inclusion
社会的役割の実現　Social Role Valorization：SRV
社会的役割（論）　social role (theory)
社会的欲求　belongingness and love needs
社会的リハビリテーション　social rehabilitation
社会踏査　social survey
社会ニーズ　social needs
社会認知理論　social cognitive theory
•社会福祉　social welfare；social services
社会福祉運営管理　social welfare administration
社会福祉援助活動　social work activity
社会福祉援助技術　social work practice
社会福祉基準　social welfare standards
社会福祉基礎構造改革　Basic Structural Reform of Social Welfare
社会福祉協議会　Council of Social Welfare
社会福祉計画法　social welfare planning；social planning
社会福祉現場実習　social work practicum
社会福祉サービス　social welfare services；social services
•社会福祉士　social worker：SW

社会福祉士及び介護福祉士法　Social Workers and Care Workers Act

•社会福祉事業　social welfare services

社会福祉事業に従事する者の確保を図るための措置に関する基本的な指針　Basic Guidelines on the Recruitment and Retention of Social Welfare Personnel

社会福祉事業法　Social Welfare Services Act

社会福祉士国家試験　National Certification Examination for Social Workers

社会福祉施設　social welfare facility

社会福祉実践　social work practice

社会福祉士登録　Social Work Registry

社会福祉士登録証　social worker certificate

社会福祉従事者　social welfare personnel

社会福祉主事　social welfare officer

社会福祉士養成施設　school of social work

社会福祉審議会　Social Welfare Council

社会福祉振興・試験センター　Center for Social Welfare Promotion and National Examination

社会福祉政策　social welfare policy

社会福祉制度　social welfare system

社会福祉専門職　social welfare professional

社会福祉調査法　social work research

社会福祉の給付形態　types of welfare benefits

社会福祉法　Social Welfare Act

社会福祉法人　social welfare corporation

社会福祉六法　Six Acts of Social Welfare ; six welfare laws

社会扶助　social assistance

社会復帰　social rehabilitation

社会奉仕　volunteering ; voluntary services

•社会保険　social insurance

社会保険事務所　social insurance office

社会保険審査会　Examination Committee of Social Insurance

社会保険診療報酬　social insurance reimbursement for health care

社会保険診療報酬支払基金　Social Insurance Medical Fee Payments Fund

社会保険制度　social insurance system

社会保険料　social insurance premium

社会保険料控除　tax deduction for social insurance premiums

社会保険労務士　certified social insurance and labor consultant

•社会保障　social security

社会保障関係費　social security-related cost

社会保障給付　social security benefit

社会保障給付費　social security benefits and expenses

社会保障構造改革　structural reform of Social Security

•社会保障審議会　Advisory Council on Social Security

社会保障税　social security tax

社会保障制度　social security system

社会保障制度改革推進法　Promotion of Social Security Reform Act

社会保障制度審議会　National Advisory Council on the Social Security System

社会保障制度に関する勧告　Recommendations for the Establishment of the Social Security System

社会保障費用　social security costs

社会保障費用統計　statistics on social security ; statistics on social security benefits

社会保障負担　burden of social security

社会保障法　Social Security Act

社会民主主義的福祉国家　social democratic welfare state

社会モデル　social model

社会リハビリテーション　social rehabilitation

視野狭窄　visual field restriction

弱化予防　deconditioning prevention

弱視　weak eye sight ; poor eye sight

若年性関節リウマチ　juvenile rheumatoid arthritis

若年性糖尿病　juvenile diabetes

若年性認知症　early-onset dementia : EOD ; younger-onset dementia ; working-age dementia

若年性認知症ケア　care for patients with early-onset dementia ; care for patients with younger-onset dementia ; care for patients

with working-age dementia
若年性パーキンソン病　juvenile Parkinsonism
若年性ポリープ　juvenile polyps
若年性ミオクローヌスてんかん　juvenile myoclonic epilepsy : JME ; Janz syndrome
視野障害　visual field defect
尺屈　ulnar deviation
しゃっくり　hiccups
煮沸消毒　boiling
斜面台　tilting table
斜文織　twill
シャワー　shower
シャワー用車いす　shower wheelchair
シャワー浴　shower bath
・収益事業　profit-making business ; for-profit business
就学指導　academic advising ; academic advisement
就学指導委員会　Academic Advising Committee
住環境　living environment
週間ケア計画　weekly care plan
週間サービス計画　weekly service plan
宗教　religion
従業員　employee ; staff
従業員満足度　employee satisfaction : ES
就業規則　employee rules and regulations
就業構造　employment structure
就業人口　working population
宗教法人　religious corporation
住居機能　housing performance
住居平面　floor plan ; house plan
充血　hyperemia
充血除去剤　decongestant
自由権　the right to freedom
集合住宅　apartment complex
集合ホーム　congregate home
周産期死亡率　perinatal mortality rate
収支項目分類　classification of receipts and disbursements
収集癖　hoarding
自由主義的福祉国家　liberal welfare state
収縮期圧　systolic pressure

収縮期血圧　systolic blood pressure
重症急性呼吸器症候群　severe acute respiratory syndrome : SARS
重症筋無力症　myasthenia gravis : MG
重症心身障害　severe physical and mental disabilities
重症心身障害児　severely mentally and physically disabled child ; child with severe mental and physical disabilities
重症心身障害児施設　facility for severely mentally and physically disabled children
重症心身障害児通園事業　day care services program for severely mentally and physically disabled children
重症心身障害者通園事業　day care services program for severely mentally and physically disabled people
住所地特例　exception to domiciliary rule
終身雇用（制度）　lifelong employment (system)
重心図　locus of center of gravity
終身建物賃貸借　life lease ; life occupancy lease
終身年金　lifelong pension
・従属人口　dependent population
従属人口指数　dependency ratio
住宅安全　home safety
・住宅改修　home modification
住宅改修給付　home modification benefit
住宅型有料老人ホーム　private senior home
住宅政策　housing policy
住宅性能表示制度　housing performance labeling system
住宅内事故　home accident
住宅入居等支援事業　rental housing assistance program
住宅の品質確保の促進等に関する法律　Manufactured Home Quality Assurance Act
住宅扶助　housing aid
住宅用火災警報器　home smoke alarm ; home fire alarm ; smoke detector
集団　group
集団援助活動　social group work
集団援助技術　social group work practice

和英	
あ か **し** た な は ま や ら わ	

集団隔離　cohort isolation

集団給食サービス　congregate meal program

集団住宅センター　congregate housing center

集団精神療法　group psychotherapy

集団発生　outbreak

集団力学　group dynamics

集団療法　group therapy

集団レクリエーション　group recreational activity ; groups activity

羞恥心　sense of shame

執着(性)気質　immobilithymia ; immodithymia

集中的ケアマネジメント　intensive care management

重点施策実施5か年計画　Five-Year-Plan to Implement Disability-Related Policies

柔道整復師　judo therapist ; judo orthopedist

重度障害者等包括支援　comprehensive support services for people with disabilities

重度身体障害者更生援護施設　rehabilitation and assistance center for people with severe physical disabilities

重度身体障害者授産施設　sheltered workshop for people with severe physical disabilities

重度・重複障害　severe and/or multiple disabilities

重度訪問介護　home care services for people with severe disabilities

柔軟加工剤　softening agent

柔軟体操　flexibility exercise

十二指腸潰瘍　duodenal ulcer

収尿器　urine collector

柔捻法　petrissage ; petrissage-kneading

周辺視野　peripheral vision

*周辺症状　behavioral and psychological symptoms of dementia : BPSD ; neuropsychiatric symptoms of dementia

*終末期　end-of-life ; terminal stage

*終末期の介護　end-of-life care ; terminal care

住民運動　resident movement

住民基本台帳　basic resident registration

住民基本台帳カード　basic resident registration card

住民参加　community participation ; public participation ; citizen participation

住民参加型在宅福祉サービス　community cooperative home services

住民主体の原則　principles of community work

住民税　resident tax

絨毛膜下血腫　subchorionic hematoma

重要事項説明書　important safety instructions and warnings

収容保護　indoor relief

自由連想法　free association technique

就労移行支援　vocational education and training for people with disabilities ; job training for people with disabilities

就労移行支援事業所　agency for vocational education and training

就労継続支援　continuous vocational education and training for people with disabilities

就労継続支援A型　type A continuous vocational education and training for people with disabilities

就労継続支援B型　type B continuous vocational education and training for people with disabilities

就労自立給付金　cash benefits for employment

受益者　beneficiary

受益者負担　benefit principle

主介護者　primary caregiver

主観的幸福感　subjective well-being : SWB ; subjective happiness

主観的幸福感尺度　Subjective Happiness Scale

主観的情報　subjective information ; subjective data

主観的ニーズ　subjective needs

受給者　recipient

受給要件　eligibility requirements

縮絨　fulling ; tucking

縮瞳　miosis ; myosis

宿泊型自立訓練　facility-based independence training program for people with disabilities

宿便　fecal impaction
主菜　main dish
•主治医　primary doctor ; attending physician
•主治医意見書　physician's report
樹脂加工　resin finishing treatment ; resin treatment ; anti-wrinkle finishing treatment
手指失認　finger agnosia
手指消毒　hand antisepsis
手術　surgery
手術室　operating room : OR ; operating theater
手術創感染　surgical wound infection
手術創(分類)　surgical wound (classification)
手術部位感染　surgical site infection
朱子織　satin fabric
主訴　chief complaint : CC
主題統覚検査　Thematic Apperception Test : TAT
•手段的ADL　instrumental activities of daily living : IADL
手段的日常生活動作　instrumental activities of daily living : IADL
腫脹　swelling
出血　bleeding
出血性水疱　hemorrhagic bullae
出血性卒中　hemorrhagic stroke
術後感染　postoperative infection
出産　childbearing ; delivery
出産手当　maternity allowance
出産適齢　childbearing age
出産扶助　maternity aid
出生家族　family of orientation
出生証明書　birth certificate
出生前診断　prenatal diagnosis ; prenatal screening
出生動向基本調査　National Fertility Survey
出生率　birth rate
術前不安　preoperative anxiety
受動喫煙　secondhand smoke
主動筋　prime mover
手動車いす　manual wheelchair
受動免疫　passive immunity
手動リフト式普通型車いす　manual height

adjustable wheelchair ; wheelchair with lift seat elevator
主任介護支援専門員　senior care manager
主任介護支援専門員研修　training for senior care managers
主任ケアマネジャー　senior care manager
守秘　confidentiality
•守秘義務　duty of confidentiality
手部　hand
趣味　hobby
寿命　life span
腫瘍　tumor
受容　acceptance
腫瘍医　oncologist
腫瘍遺伝子　oncogene
腫瘍壊死因子　tumor necrosis factor : TNF
受容的態度　receptive attitude
受容の原則　principle of acceptance
•手浴　hand bath
受理　acceptance
•手話　sign language
手話通訳士　registered sign language interpreter : RSLI
手話通訳者　prefecture-certified sign language interpreter
手話奉仕　sign language interpreting services
手話奉仕員　municipal-certified sign language interpreter
手話奉仕員養成研修事業　training program for municipal-certified sign language interpreter
純音聴力検査　pure tone audiometry : PTA
巡回介護　care rounding ; hourly rounding
循環型社会形成推進基本法　Fundamental Law for Establishing a Sound Material Cycle Society
循環器　cardiology ; circulatory system ; cardiovascular system
循環気質　cyclothymia ; cyclothymic temperament
循環器疾患　cardiovascular disease
准看護師　licensed practical nurse
循環的因果律　circular causality
準拠集団　reference group

準拠集団論　reference group theory

順行性洗腸　antegrade colonic enema : ACE

遵守率　compliance rate

除圧　decompression

情意鈍麻　blunted affect ; flat affect

昇華　sublimation

消化　digestion

傷害　injury

*障害　disability

障害一時金　temporary disability allowance

障害学　disability study

生涯学習　lifelong learning ; Lifelong Learning Education and Training

障害過大視　exaggeration of disability ; overstatement of the extent of disability

*障害基礎年金　Basic Disability Pension

生涯教育　lifelong education

障害厚生年金　employees' disability pension

障害高齢者の日常生活自立度判定基準　criteria for determining the independence level of elderly with disabilities

障害後性格　post-disability personality ; post-injury personality

障害児　child with disabilities ; disabled child

障害支援区分　categories of disability

障害児施設　care facility for children with disabilities

障害児等療育支援事業　support services for children with disabilities

障害児福祉手当　child disability allowance

障害者　person with disabilities ; disabled person

障害者運動　disability rights movement

障害者介護給付費等不服審査会　Appeals Board for Disability Benefits

障害者加算　supplemental disability allowance

障害者基本計画　basic disability plan

障害者基本法　Persons with Disabilities Basic Act

障害者虐待　disability abuse ; abuse of disabled people

障害者虐待の防止、障害者の養護者に対する支援等に関する法律　Persons with Disabilities Abuse Prevention Act

障害者虐待防止法　Persons with Disabilities Abuse Prevention Act

障害者ケアガイドライン　Guidelines for Care of Persons with Disabilities

障害者ケアマネジメント　care management for persons with disabilities ; disability care management

障害者計画　municipal disability plan

障害者権利条約　Convention on the Rights of Persons with Disabilities

障害者控除　tax deduction for persons with disabilities

障害者更生センター　rehabilitation center for persons with disabilities

障害者更生相談所　rehabilitation and counseling center for persons with disabilities

障害者雇用　employment of people with disabilities

障害者雇用促進　employment promotion for persons with disabilities

障害者雇用促進対策　employment promotion initiatives for persons with disabilities

障害者雇用促進法　Employment Promotion for Persons with Disabilities Act

障害者雇用納付金　grants for hiring persons with disabilities

障害者雇用率制度　mandatory employment rates of people with disabilities

障害者作業所　workshop for persons with disabilities

障害者差別解消法　Elimination of All Forms of Discrimination against Persons with Disabilities Act

障害者支援施設　facility-based support services for persons with disabilities

障害者施策推進協議会　Council on Promotion of Measures for Persons with Disabilities

障害者施策推進本部　Headquarter for Promoting Measures for Persons with Disabilities

障害者就業・生活支援センター　employment

and daily living support center for persons with disabilities

障害者情報ネットワーク　information network for persons with disabilities

障害者職業訓練　vocational education and training for people with disabilities

障害者職業訓練施設　vocational education and training facility for persons with disabilities

障害者職業センター　career center for persons with disabilities

障害者自立支援法　Comprehensive Social and Daily Living Assistance for Persons with Disabilities Act

障害者自立生活運動　independent living and disability rights movement

障害者スポーツ　disabled sports ; adaptive sports ; parasports

障害者政策委員会　Commission on Disability Policy

障がい者制度改革推進本部　Headquarter for Promoting Disability Policy Reform

「障害者制度改革の推進のための基本的な方向について」　Direction for Promoting Disability Policy Reform

障害者総合支援法　Comprehensive Social and Daily Living Assistance for Persons with Disabilities Act

「障害者総合福祉法の骨格に関する総合福祉部会の提言―新法の制定を目指して―」　Comprehensive Welfare Subcommittee's Proposals for a Framework of Comprehensive Disability Laws : Toward the Enactment of New Laws

障害者団体　disability organization ; organization for persons with disabilities

障害者駐車許可証　disabled person parking permit

障害者手当　disability allowance

障害者の権利宣言　Declaration on the Rights of Disabled Persons

障害者の権利に関する条約　Convention on the Rights of Persons with Disabilities

障害者の雇用の促進等に関する法律　Promotion of Employment for Persons with Disabilities Act

障害者の十年　decade of disabled persons

障害者の尊厳　dignity of people with disabilities ; dignity of the disabled

障害者のための国際シンボルマーク　international symbol of accessibility : ISA

障害者のための施策に関する基本的な計画　basic plan for persons with disabilities

障害者の日常生活及び社会生活を総合的に支援するための法律　Comprehensive Social and Daily Living Assistance for Persons with Disabilities Act

障害者福祉　welfare of persons with disabilities

障害者福祉年金　disability welfare pension

障害者扶助　financial aid for persons with disabilities

障害者プラン　Seven-Year Normalization Strategy for Persons with Disabilities

障害受容　adjustment to a disability ; acceptance of a disability

障害前性格　pre-disability personality ; pre-injury personality

障害手当金　disability allowance

障害程度区分　categories of disability

障害等級　degrees of disability

障害認定　disability certification ; certification of disability

障害年金　disability pension

障害の医学モデル　medical model of disability

障害の概念　concept of disability

障害の社会モデル　social models of disability

障害の受容　acceptance of disability

障害の発生予防　disability prevention ; prevention of disability

障害の三つのレベル　three levels of disability

生涯発達　life-span development

障害福祉計画　welfare planning for persons with disabilities ; disability action plan

障害福祉サービス　disability services

障害福祉年金　disability welfare pension

障害保険　disability insurance：DI

障害モデル　models of disability

紹介料　referral fee

障害老人の日常生活自立度（寝たきり度）判定
基準　criteria for determining the
independence level of the disabled elderly

障害をもつアメリカ人法　Americans with
Disabilities Act：ADA

障害を理由とする差別の解消の推進に関する法律
Elimination of All Forms of Discrimination
against Persons with Disabilities Act

消化管出血　gastrointestinal bleeding

消化管ストーマ　intestinal stoma

消化管ホルモン　gastrointestinal hormones

消化器疾患　digestive disease

消化器内科医　gastroenterologist

消化吸収　digestion and absorption

消化酵素　digestive enzyme

消化性潰瘍　peptic ulcer；peptic ulcer
disease

松果体　pineal body；pineal gland；epiphysis
cerebri

償還払い　reimbursement

使用期限　expiration date；best before date；
best if used by date

上気道咳症候群　upper airway cough
syndrome

小規模作業所　small-scale workshop

小規模身体障害者療護施設　small-scale
custodial care facility for persons with
physical disabilities

小規模生活単位型特別養護老人ホーム
small-scale unit-based welfare facility for the
elderly

•小規模多機能型居宅介護　small-scale multi-
functional home-based care services

小規模多機能型居宅介護事業　small-scale
multi-functional home-based care services
program

小規模多機能型居宅介護事業者　small-scale
multi-functional home-based care services
provider

小規模特別養護老人ホーム　small-scale
welfare facility for the elderly

蒸気滅菌　steam sterilization

状況反射　situational reflection

消去現象　extinction phenomenon

常勤換算　full-time equivalent：FTE

上下関係　vertical relationship

条件刺激　conditioned stimulus

条件づけ　conditioning

条件反射　conditioned reflex；conditioned
response

条件反応　conditioned response

症候群　syndrome

症候性てんかん　symptomatic epilepsy

症候性貧血　symptomatic anemia

猩紅熱　scarlet fever；scarlatina

錠剤　tablet

常在菌　resident bacteria；resident flora

小細胞肺がん　small cell lung cancer：SCLC

上肢　upper extremity

•少子化　depopulation

少子化社会　society with falling fertility rates

•少子・高齢化　depopulation and aging

上肢装具　upper extremity orthosis

消臭加工　deodorization processing

症状　symptom

症状精神病　symptomatic psychosis

症状てんかん　symptomatic epilepsy

常食　regular diet

上肢リンパ浮腫　upper extremity lymphedema

脂溶性ビタミン　fat-soluble vitamin

常染色体　autosome

常染色体異常　autosomal abnormality

常染色体優性　autosomal dominant

常染色体優性遺伝　autosomal dominant
inheritance

常染色体優性遺伝病　autosomal dominant
disorder

常染色体劣性　autosomal recessive

常染色体劣性遺伝　autosomal recessive
inheritance

常染色体劣性遺伝病　autosomal recessive
disorder

踵足変形　talipes calcaneus

小腸　small intestine
小腸機能障害　small intestine dysfunction
象徴的障壁　symbolic barrier
小腸ポリープ　small intestinal polyps
小腸瘤（りゅう）　enterocele
情緒障害　emotional disturbance
情動　emotion
常同行動　stereotypical behavior ; stereotyped behavior
情動失禁　emotional incontinence
常同症　stereotypy
床頭台　bedside table ; bedside cabinet
消毒　disinfection ; sterilization
消毒剤　disinfectant ; sterilization
消毒用エタノール溶液　ethanol solution for disinfection ; alcohol-based disinfectant
小児科　pediatric
小児科医　pediatrician
小児期崩壊性障害　childhood disintegrative disorder
小児在宅ケア　pediatric home care
小児在宅医療　pediatric home health care
小児自閉症　childhood autism
小児に対する二次救命心肺蘇生法　pediatric advanced life support : PALS
小児慢性特定疾患治療研究事業　treatment research program for specified forms of pediatric chronic disease ; treatment research program for specified forms of children's chronic disease
小脳　cerebellum
消費期限　expiration date ; best before date ; best if used by date
消費者　consumer
消費者安全法　Consumer Product Safety Act
消費者運動　consumer movement
消費者基本法　Consumer Protection Act
消費者行政　governmental consumer protection
消費者契約法　Consumer Contract Act
消費者権利グループ　consumer rights group
消費者主義　consumerism
消費者庁　Consumer Affairs Agency

消費者庁及び消費者委員会設置法　Establishment of the Consumer Affairs Agency and the Consumer Committee Act
消費者物価指数　consumer price index : CPI
消費者保護　consumer protection
消費税　consumption tax
消費生活協同組合　Consumers Cooperative Association
消費生活センター　Consumer Affairs Center
上皮組織　epithelial tissue
傷病休暇　medical leave ; sick leave
傷病手当　sickness and injury allowance
上部消化管　upper gastrointestinal
上部食道括約筋　upper esophageal sphincter : UES
上部食道括約筋機能障害　upper esophageal sphincter dysfunction
情報　information
情報化社会　informationalized society
情報管理　information management
情報技術　information technology : IT
情報公開　information disclosure
情報システム　information system
情報収集　information gathering
情報通信技術　information and communications technology : ICT
情報提供　dissemination of information ; distribution of information
情報ネットワーク　information network
情報の解釈（介護過程）　interpretation of information (care process)
情報の関連づけ（介護過程）　associating information with other information (care process)
情報の収集（介護過程）　information gathering (care process)
情報の統合化（介護過程）　information integration (care process)
小発作（ほっさ）　absence seizure
賞味期限　expiration date ; best before date ; best if used by date
静脈　vein
静脈栄養　parenteral nutrition

和英

あ か **し** た な は ま や ら わ

静脈炎　phlebitis
静脈血　venous blood
静脈内注射　intravenous injection
静脈瘤　varix
将来推計人口　population projection
条例　local ordinance
上腕骨近位端骨折　proximal humerus fracture ; fracture of upper end of the humerus
上腕動脈　brachial artery
•ショートステイ　short-term stay
初期発話知覚テスト　Early Speech Perception Test
初期面接　initial intake
職域保険　occupational group insurance
食育基本法　Nutrition Education Act
職員研修　staff development
食塩　salt
食塩欠乏性脱水　hyponatremic dehydration ; hypotonic dehydration
職業安定プログラム　Employment Stabilization program
職業安定法　Employment Stabilization Act
職業カウンセリング　vocational counseling ; career counseling
職業感染　occupational infection
職業教育　vocational education
職業訓練　vocational training ; job training
職業指導　vocational education ; vocational guidance
職業能力評価　vocational ability evaluation
職業曝露　occupational exposure
職業病　occupational disease
職業評価　vocational evaluation
•職業リハビリテーション　vocational rehabilitation
職業倫理　professional ethics
食(菌)作用　phagocytosis
食行動の異常　eating disorder
食事　meal
食事介助　assistance with eating ; eating assistance
食事管理　meal management

食事計画　meal planning ; menu planning
食事サービス　meal services
食事準備　meal preparation
食事制限　dietary restriction
食事宅配サービス　meal delivery service ; meals-on-wheels
食事バランスガイド　Japanese food guide spinning top
食習慣　eating habit ; dietary habit
食事用具　utensil ; eating tool ; eating device
•食事療法　medical nutrition therapy : MNT ; nutrition therapy
触診　palpation
食生活指針　Dietary Guidelines
•褥瘡　pressure ulcer ; decubitus ulcer ; pressure sore
褥瘡治癒過程スケール　Pressure Ulcer Scale for Healing : PUSH
褥瘡治療　pressure ulcer treatment
褥瘡発生予測尺度　Braden Scale for Predicting Pressure Sore Risk ; Braden Scale for Predicting Pressure Ulcer Risk
褥瘡予防　prevention of pressure ulcer ; pressure ulcer prevention
触知覚低下　loss of touch sensation
•食中毒　food poisoning ; food-borne illness
食中毒の予防　prevention of food poisoning ; food poisoning prevention
食道　esophagus
食道運動障害　esophageal motility disorder
食道がん　esophageal cancer
食道相　esophageal phase
食道内圧検査　esophageal manometry
食道裂孔ヘルニア　hiatal hernia ; hiatus hernia
触読　Braille reading ; touch reading
職場外訓練　off-the-job-training : OFF-JT
職場訓練　on-the-job-training : OJT
職場適応援助者　job coach
食品安全基本法　Basic Food Safety Act
食品衛生　food sanitation
食品衛生監視員　food inspector
食品衛生管理者　food sanitation supervisor
食品衛生法　Food Sanitation Act

食品汚染　food contamination

食品群　food groups

食品交換表　food exchange lists

食品成分表　food composition table

食品添加物　food additives

食品の凝固　coagulation in cooking

食品表示　nutrition labeling

食品表示法　Nutrition Labeling Act

•植物状態　vegetative state ; unresponsive wakefulness syndrome

植物（状態の）人間　vegetative patient

食文化　food culture

食物アレルギー　food allergy

食物関連障害　food-related disorder

食物繊維　dietary fiber

食物媒介感染　food-borne infection

•食欲　appetite

食欲中枢　appetite center

食欲低下　loss of appetite ; poor appetite

食欲不振　loss of appetite ; poor appetite

助言　advice ; suggestion

徐呼吸　bradypnea

助産師　midwife ; maternity nurse ; nurse-midwife

助産所　midwife center

書字訓練　writing exercise

書字障害　dysgraphia

除脂肪体重　lean body mass : LBM

叙述体　narrative recording

女性性　roles of women

女性の社会参加　social participation of women

食塊　bolus ; alimentary bolus

触覚　sense of touch

ショック　shock

ショック期　stage of shock ; phase of shock

所得税　income tax

所得テスト　income test

所得保障　income security

ジョハリの窓　Johari window

ジョブコーチ　job coach

処方集　formulary

処方箋　prescription

徐脈　bradycardia

初老期うつ病　involutional depression

•初老期認知症　presenile dementia

白子眼　ocular albinism

自律　autonomy

•自立　independence

私立学校教職員共済　Mutual Aid Pension for Private School Personnel

自立訓練　independent living training

自立訓練（機能訓練）　functional independent training

自立訓練（生活訓練）　independent living skills training

自律訓練法　autogenic training

•自立支援　independent living support

自立支援医療　supportive health services for independent living

自立支援給付　reimbursement for supportive independent living services

自立支援協議会　Council on Independent Living

自立支援プログラム　independent living support program

自律神経　autonomic nerve

自律神経過反射　autonomic hyperreflexia ; autonomic dysreflexia

自律神経機能障害　autonomic dysfunction

自律神経系　autonomic nervous system

自律神経失調　dysautonomia

自律神経障害　autonomic nerve disorder

自律神経症状　autonomic symptom

自立生活　independent living : IL

自立生活運動　independent living movement : ILM

自立生活スキル　independent living skill

自立生活センター　Center for Independent Living : CIL

自立生活プログラム　independent living program

自律尊重原則（医療倫理）　autonomy (health care ethics)

自立的ニーズ　needs for independence

自立度　level of independent living

視力　vision ; visual acuity

視力障害　visual impairment ; visual disturbance

資力調査　means test

シルバーカー　four-wheel walker with seat and shopping basket ; walker with seat and shopping basket

シルバーサービス　senior services

シルバーサービス振興会　Elderly Service Providers Association

シルバー人材センター　Silver Human Resources Center

シルバーハウジング・プロジェクト　elderly housing project

シルバー110番　Comprehensive Counseling Center for the Elderly

シルバーマーク制度　symbol system for qualified elderly services

事例研究　case research

•事例検討　case study

ジレンマ　dilemma

腎移植　kidney transplant ; kidney transplantation ; renal transplant

心因　psychogenesis

心因性精神障害　psychogenic psychosis

心因性頻尿　psychogenic pollakiuria

心因反応　psychogenic reaction

腎盂炎　pyelitis

腎盂腎炎　pyelonephritis

腎盂造影　pyelography

心エコー　echocardiography ; cardiac ECHO

心エコー図　echocardiogram

腎炎　nephritis

新エンゼルプラン　New Angel Plan

人格　personality

人格検査　personality test

人格障害　personality disorder

人格的欲求　psychological needs

人格変化　personality change

新型インフルエンザ　new flu virus strains ; novel influenza

新型インフルエンザ等感染症　infections with the new strains of influenza

新型特養　unit-based welfare facility for the elderly

腎がん　kidney cancer

新感染症　novel infectious disease ; new infectious disease

•心気症　illness anxiety disorder : IAD ; hypochondria ; hypochondriasis

腎機能　kidney function ; renal function

腎機能障害　kidney failure ; renal failure ; renal insufficiency

新規発症持続性連日性頭痛　new daily persistent headache : NDPH

心気妄想　hypochondriacal delusion

鍼灸　acupuncture and moxibustion

新救貧法　New Poor Law

心胸郭比　cardiothoracic ratio

真菌感染　fungal infection

心筋虚血　myocardial ischemia

真菌血症　fungemia ; fungaemia

心筋梗塞　myocardial infarction

真菌症　mycosis

真菌性眼内炎　fungal endophthalmitis

寝具乾燥サービス　drying of beddings service ; drying of futon service

神経因性膀胱　neurogenic bladder

神経学的検査　neurological examination

神経学的状態　neurological status

神経筋疾患　neuromuscular disease

神経筋接合部　neuromuscular junction

神経筋促通法　neuromuscular facilitation technique

神経原性筋萎縮　neurogenic muscle atrophy

神経原性ショック　neurogenic shock

神経原性疼痛　neuropathic pain

神経原性肺水腫　neurogenic pulmonary edema

神経腫瘍医　neuro-oncologist

神経循環無力症　neurocirculatory asthenia

神経症　neurosis

神経障害　neuropathy

神経症候　neurological symptom

神経症性障害　neurotic disorder

神経心理学的検査　neuropsychological test

神経心理学的評価　neuropsychological evaluation

神経性食欲不振症　anorexia nervosa : AN

神経性大食症　bulimia nervosa

神経性無食欲症　anorexia nervosa : AN

神経生理学的アプローチ　neurophysiological approach

神経組織　nervous tissue

神経痛　neuralgia

神経ブロック　nerve block

神経変性疾患　neurodegenerative disease

心血管疾患　cardiovascular disease

腎結石　kidney stone

親権　parental authority

人権　human rights

心原性ショック　cardiac shock

心原性脳塞栓　cardiogenic cerebral embolism

心原性肺水腫　cardiogenic pulmonary edema

人口移動　population movement

新興感染症　emerging infectious disease

人工甘味料　artificial sweetener

人工喉頭　artificial larynx ; voice generator

人工肛門　stoma ; artificial anus

人工股関節全置換術　total hip replacement : THR

•人工呼吸　rescue breathing ; artificial respiration

人工呼吸器　artificial ventilator ; artificial respirator ; mechanical ventilator

新興・再興感染症　emerging and re-emerging infectious diseases

人口推計　population estimates

進行性球麻痺　progressive bulbar palsy

進行性筋ジストロフィー　progressive muscular dystrophy : PMD

人口静態　static population

進行性ミオクローヌスてんかん　progressive myoclonus epilepsy : PME

人口置換水準　replacement level fertility

人口転換論　demographic transition theory

人口統計　demographic statistics

人工透析　hemodialysis ; dialysis

人口動態　population dynamics

人工妊娠中絶　elective abortion

人口爆発　population explosion

人工膀胱　artificial bladder

「新・高齢者保健福祉推進十か年戦略」 New Ten-Year-Strategy to Promote Health and Welfare for the Elderly ; New Gold Plan

人工レンズ　artificial lens

新ゴールドプラン　New Gold Plan ; New Ten-Year-Strategy to Promote Health and Welfare for the Elderly

新国民生活指標　People's Life Indicators

人材確保指針　Guidelines on the Recruitment and Retention of Social Welfare Personnel

審査請求　appeal

•心疾患　heart disease

腎疾患　kidney disease ; renal disease

心室期外収縮　premature ventricular contraction : PVC

心室細動　ventricular fibrillation

心室中隔欠損　ventricular septal defect : VSD

寝室の住環境整備　optimization of bedroom environment

心シャント　cardiac shunt

人獣共通感染症　zoonosis ; zoonotic disease

人種差別　race discrimination

人種差別主義　racism

滲出性中耳炎　serous otitis media : SOM ; otitis media with effusion

腎症　nephropathy

新障害者プラン　Five-Year-Plan to Implement Disability-Related Policies

•身上監護　personal guardianship

寝床気候　bedding microclimate

寝食分離　separation of spaces for eating and sleeping

•心身機能（ICF）　body functions

心神耗弱　diminished capacity

•心身症　psychosomatic disorder : PSD ; psychophysiologic disorder

心身障害者　person with physical and mental disabilities

心身障害者世帯向公営住宅　public housing for persons with disabilities

065

和英	

心身障害者ホームヘルプ　home help services for persons with physical and mental disabilities

心神喪失　insanity

診診連携　collaboration between outpatient clinics

新生児　neonate ; newborn infant

新生児行動評価　Neonatal Behavior Assessment Scale : NBAS

新生児死亡率　neonatal mortality rate

申請者　applicant

真性腹圧性尿失禁　genuine stress incontinence

真正妄想　primary delusion ; true delusion

振戦　tremor

振戦せん妄　delirium tremens : DTs

心尖拍動　apex beat ; apical impulse

振戦法　oscillation massage ; vibration massage

心臓　heart

腎臓　kidney

腎臓移植　kidney transplant ; kidney transplantation

心臓カテーテル法　heart catheterization

心臓機能障害　functional cardiac disorder ; disorders of cardiac function

心臓超音波検査　ultrasound cardiography

腎臓内科医　nephrologist

心臓病　heart disease

心臓不整脈　cardiac arrhythmia ; cardiac dysrhythmia

心臓弁膜症　valvular heart disease

心臓マッサージ　cardiac massage

心臓リハビリテーション　cardiac rehabilitation

親族　relative

身体依存　physical addiction

身体介護　physical care

身体活動レベル　physical activity level : PAL

身体機能　physical function

身体機能検査　physical performance test : PPT

身体構造（ICF）　body structures

身体拘束　physical restraint ; body restraint

身体拘束ゼロ　Guidelines for No Use of Physical Restraints

身体障害者　person with physical disabilities

身体障害者更生施設　rehabilitation facility for persons with physical disabilities

身体障害者更生相談所　rehabilitation and counseling center for persons with physical disabilities

身体障害者社会参加支援施設　support center for social participation of people with physical disabilities

身体障害者障害程度等級表　list of disability physical grading

身体障害者相談員　physical disability counselor

身体障害者短期入所　short-term stay for people with physical disabilities

身体障害者デイサービス　day care services for people with physical disabilities

身体障害者手帳　physical disability certification handbook

身体障害者の利便の増進に資する通信・放送身体障害者利用円滑化事業の推進に関する法律　Telecommunications and Broadcasting Access Enhancement for Persons with Physical Disabilities Act

身体障害者のレクリエーション　recreational activity for persons with physical disabilities

身体障害者福祉　welfare of persons with physical disabilities

身体障害者福祉司　welfare officer for persons with physical disabilities

身体障害者福祉審議会　Advisory Council on the Welfare of Physically Disabled Persons

身体障害者福祉センター　welfare center for persons with physical disabilities

身体障害者福祉法　Welfare of Physically Disabled Persons Act

身体障害者補助犬法　Service Dogs for Persons with Physical Disabilities Act

身体障害者療護施設　custodial care facility for persons with physical disabilities

身体症状障害　somatic symptom disorder

身体像　body image
身体的虐待　physical abuse
身体的攻撃　physical aggression
身体的欲求　biological and physiological needs
新体力テスト　New Physical Fitness Test
診断　diagnosis
診断群分類　diagnosis procedure combination : DPC
診断群別所定報酬額支払方式
　diagnostic related groups-prospective payment system : DRG-PPS
伸張運動　stretching exercise
新陳代謝　metabolism
心的外傷　psychic trauma
心的外傷後ストレス障害　posttraumatic stress disorder : PTSD
人的資源　human resources ; manpower
腎摘除　nephrectomy
心電図検査　electrocardiogram : EKG
親等　degree of kinship
振動　oscillation ; vibration
人頭払い制　capitated payment
心肺機能　cardiopulmonary function
心肺蘇生法　cardiopulmonary resuscitation : CPR
心肺脳蘇生法　cardiopulmonary cerebral resuscitation : CPCR
心拍　heartbeat
心拍出量　cardiac output
心拍数　heart rate
審判的態度　judgmental attitude
深部感覚　deep sensation
深部静脈血栓症　deep vein thrombosis
心不全　heart failure
腎不全　kidney failure ; renal failure ; renal insufficiency
心房　atrium
心房細動　atrial fibrillation
心房中隔欠損症　atrial septal defect : ASD
信用失墜行為の禁止　prohibition of acts bringing discredit
•信頼関係　rapport

心理学的援助技術　psychological intervention techniques
心理過程　psychological process
心理劇　psychodrama
心理劇療法　psychodrama therapy
心理検査　psychological test
心理社会評価　psychosocial assessment
心理・性的段階　psychosexual stages
心理・性的発達理論　psychosexual development
心理的虐待　psychological abuse ; emotional abuse
心理的ケア　psychological care ; emotional care
心理的準備　psychological preparation ; mental preparation
心理的欲求　psychological needs
心理テスト　psychological test
心理判定　mental health assessment ; psychological assessment
心理判定員　mental health assessor
心理評価　psychological assessment
診療所　clinic ; doctor's office
診療の補助　nursing
診療放射線技師　radiologic technologist
診療報酬　reimbursement for health care services ; health care reimbursement
診療報酬支払相対評価スケール方式
　Resource-Based Relative Value Scale : RBRVS
診療報酬制度　health care reimbursement system
診療予約　doctor's appointment
心理力動論　psychodynamics
心理療法　psychotherapy
進路指導　academic and career counseling
進路指導教官　academic and career counselor ; school counselor

す

素揚げ　frying without breading or batter
随意運動　voluntary movement

随意収縮　voluntary contraction
膵液（すいえき）　pancreatic juice
膵炎（すいえん）　pancreatitis
水銀中毒　mercury poisoning
水系感染　waterborne infection
遂行機能障害　executive function disorder：EFD；disorder of executive function
遂行機能障害症候群　dysexecutive syndrome
水剤（内服用の）　oral liquid medication
水晶体　crystal lens
水腎症　hydronephrosis
膵臓（すいぞう）　pancreas
膵臓がん　pancreatic cancer
錐体（すいたい）　cone
錐体外路症状（がいろしょうじょう）　extrapyramidal symptoms；extrapyramidal side effects：EPS
錐体路　pyramidal tract
垂直感染　vertical disease transmission
推定一日摂取量　estimated daily intake
推定エネルギー必要量　Estimated Energy Requirement：EER
水痘（すいとう）　varicella；chicken pox
水痘感染　varicella infection
水道水　tap water
水痘帯状疱疹ウイルス（すいとうたいじょうほうしん）　varicella zoster virus：VZV
随伴性　contingency
水分　fluid；moisture
水分欠乏性脱水　hypertonic dehydration
水分摂取　fluid intake
水分バランス　fluid balance
*水分補給　rehydration；fluid intake
水疱（すいほう）　blister
髄膜炎　meningitis
髄膜白血病　meningeal leukemia
睡眠関連呼吸障害　sleep-related breathing disorder
睡眠剤　hypnotic
睡眠時無呼吸　sleep apnea
睡眠時無呼吸症候群　sleep apnea syndrome：SAS
*睡眠障害　sleep disorder；somnipathy
睡眠薬　hypnotic drug；sleeping pill

水溶性ビタミン　water-soluble vitamin
水溶性汚れ　water-based stain
スイングアーム介助バー　swing away bed rail；swing away grab bar
数値評価スケール　Numeric Rating Scale：NRS
スーパー・エゴ　superego
*スーパーバイザー　supervisor
*スーパーバイジー　supervisee
*スーパービジョン　supervision
スクールカウンセラー　school counselor
スクールソーシャルワーカー　school social worker
すくみ足歩行　freezing of gait：FOG
鈴木 - ビネー式知能検査　Suzuki-Binet Intelligence Scale
*頭痛　headache；cephalalgia
スティグマ　stigma
ステープル・ファイバー　staple fiber
ステッキ型つえ　walking stick
ステューデント・スーパービジョン　student supervision
ステレオタイプ　stereotype
ステロイド　steroid
ストーマ（ケア）　stoma (care)
ストーマ用装具（ようそうぐ）　stoma bags and stoma care accessories
ストライド　stride
ストライド長　stride length
*ストレス　stress
ストレス反応　stress reaction
ストレスマネジメント　stress management
ストレス免疫訓練（めんえき）　stress inoculation training
ストレスモデル　stress model
ストレッサー　stressor
ストレッチ体操　stretching exercise
*ストレッチャー　stretcher
*ストレングス視点　strengths perspective
ストレングスモデル　strength model；strength-based model
スパンデックス　spandex
スピリチュアルケア　spiritual care
スピリチュアルペイン　spiritual pain

滑り止めマット　non-slip mat ; non-slip rug

スポーツ　sports

スポーツ基本法　Basic Sports Act

スポーツドリンク　isotonic drink ; isotonic sports drink

スポーツ・文化施設　sports and cultural center

スポンジブラシ　foam brush

スライディングシート　sliding sheet ; transfer sheet

スライディングボード　sliding board ; transfer boards

スライディングマット　sliding mat

擦り傷　abrasion

スリング　sling

スロープ　slope

せ

性格　personality ; character

性格検査　personality test

性格の特性論　trait theory of personality ; personality trait theory

性格の類型論　type theory of personality ; personality type theory

生活　life ; living ; livelihood

*生活援助　home help services ; home care

生活介護　day care services for persons with disabilities

生活課題　concerns in daily living ; needs and concerns

生活環境　living environment

生活関連活動　activities parallel to daily living : APDL

生活機能（ICF）　functioning

生活技能訓練　life skills training

生活協同組合　consumers cooperative association

生活期リハビリテーション　home-based rehabilitation ; maintenance phase of rehabilitation

生活空間　life space

生活経営　family resource management

生活圏域　living space

生活構造　life structure

生活困窮者　needy ; needy person

生活困窮者自立支援法　Independent Support Services for the Low-Income and Needy Act

生活支援　disability support services

生活支援員　disability support services personnel

生活支援サービス　disability support services

生活支援ハウス　welfare center for the elderly

生活時間　time use ; time allocation

生活施設　live-in facility

生活指導員　public assistance personnel

生活習慣　lifestyle

*生活習慣病　lifestyle disease ; lifestyle-related disease

生活周期　life cycle

生活水準　standard of living

生活相談員　social services designee

生活年齢　chronological age

*生活の質　quality of life : QOL

生活のしづらさなどに関する調査　National Survey of Children and Adults with Disabilities

生活場面ソーシャルワーク　life space social work

生活場面面接　life space interview

生活不活発病　disuse syndrome

生活福祉資金貸付制度　welfare fund loan system

生活扶助　living aid ; general relief aid

*生活保護　public assistance ; livelihood protection

生活保護基準　standards of public assistance

生活保護受給者　public assistance recipient

生活保護制度　public assistance system ; public assistance program

生活保護の原理・原則　principles and rules of public assistance

生活保護の種類　types of public assistance programs

生活保護への移行防止措置　prevention of long-term care insurance recipients from becoming public assistance recipients

和英	

生活保護法　Public Assistance Act
生活満足度　life satisfaction
生活モデル　life model
生活療法　living learning
*生活歴　personal life history ; life history
性器期　genital stage
正規曲線　normal curve
正義原則（医療倫理）　justice (health care ethics)
性機能障害　sexual dysfunction
正球性貧血　normocytic anemia
請求対象期間　billing period
生業扶助　occupational aid
税金　tax
税金還付　tax rebate
静菌作用　bacteriostatic action
整形靴　corrective shoes ; orthopedic shoes
整形外科　orthopedics
生計費調整　cost-of-living adjustment : COLA
生計費用　cost of living
生検　biopsy
生検鉗子　biopsy forceps
制限食　restricted diet
性行為感染症　sexually transmitted disease : STD
税控除　tax deduction
性差　gender difference
正座位　kneel sitting
政策　policy
政策立案者　policymaker
静座不能　akathisia
性差別　sex discrimination ; gender discrimination
生産年齢人口　working-age population ; productive age population
制止　inhibition
*清拭　sponge bath
誠実義務　duty of good faith
正常圧水頭症　normal pressure hydrocephalus
正常血圧　normal blood pressure
正常細菌叢　normal flora
正常値　normal value

正常歩行　normal gait
生殖家族　family of procreation
生殖性　generatively
精神安定剤　anxiolytic ; tranquilizer
精神医学　psychiatry
精神医学的リハビリテーション　psychiatric rehabilitation
精神依存　psychological addiction
精神医療審査会　Committee on Mental Health
精神衛生　mental hygiene ; mental health
精神衛生法　Mental Hygiene Act
精神および行動の障害　mental and behavioral disorder
精神科医　psychiatrist
精神科作業療法　psychiatric occupational therapy
*精神科ソーシャルワーカー　psychiatric social worker : PSW
精神科ソーシャルワーク　psychiatric social work
精神科デイ・ケア（センター）　psychiatric day care (center)
精神科デイ・ナイト・ケア　psychiatric day and night care
精神科ナイト・ケア　psychiatric night care
精神科病院　psychiatric hospital ; mental hospital
精神科リハビリテーション　psychiatric rehabilitation
精神鑑定　court-ordered psychological evaluation ; forensic psychological and neuropsychological evaluation
成人教育　adult education
成人呼吸窮迫症候群　adult respiratory distress syndrome
*精神障害　mental illness ; mental disorder ; psychiatric disorder
精神障害作業療法　psychiatric occupational therapy
*精神障害者　person with mental illness
精神障害者ケアガイドライン　Guidelines for Mental Health Care of Persons with Mental Illness

精神障害者社会適応訓練事業　social rehabilitation program for persons with mental illness

精神障害者社会復帰促進センター　social rehabilitation center for persons with mental illness

精神障害者地域移行・地域定着支援事業　community living support program for transition of persons with mental illness from hospitals into the community

精神障害者通所授産施設　sheltered workshop for persons with mental illness

精神障害者福祉　welfare of persons with mental illness

精神障害者保健福祉手帳　psychological disability certification handbook

精神障害の原因　cause of mental illness ; cause of mental disorders ; cause of psychiatric disorders

精神障害の診断と統計の手引き　Diagnostic and Statistical Manual of Mental Disorders : DSM

精神障害の分類　classification of mental disorders ; psychiatric nosology ; psychiatric taxonomy

成人潜在性自己免疫性糖尿病　latent autoimmune diabetes in adults : LADA

精神通院医療　outpatient psychiatry services

精神的虐待　psychological abuse ; mental abuse ; emotional abuse

精神的老化　psychological aspects of aging

精神年齢　mental age : MA

精神薄弱者福祉法　Mentally Frail Persons Act

成人発症　adult-onset

成人発症関節リウマチ　adult-onset rheumatoid arthritis : AORA

精神（発達）遅滞　mental retardation : MR

精神病　psychosis ; mental illness

成人病（生活習慣病）　lifestyle disease

精神病院　psychiatric hospital

精神病質　psychopathy ; psychopathic personality

精神分析　psychoanalysis

精神分析的心理療法　psychoanalytical psychotherapy

精神分析療法　psychoanalytic therapy

精神保健　mental health

精神保健及び精神障害者福祉に関する法律　Mental Health and Welfare of Persons with Mental Disabilities Act : Mental Health Act

精神保健福祉士　psychiatric social worker : PSW

精神保健福祉士法　Psychiatric Social Workers Act

精神保健福祉センター　mental health and welfare center

精神保健福祉相談員　mental health welfare advisor

精神保健福祉法　Mental Health and Welfare of Persons with Mental Disabilities Act

精神保健法　Mental Health Act ; Mental Health and Welfare of Persons with Mental Disabilities Act

成人保護サービス　adult protective services : APS

成人用顕現性不安尺度　Adult Manifest Anxiety Scale

精神療法　psychotherapy ; psychological therapy

静水圧作用　hydrostatic pressure

税制優遇措置　favorable tax treatment

性腺　gonad ; sex gland ; reproductive gland

性染色体　sex chromosome

生前信託　living trust

精巣　testicle ; testis

製造物責任法　Product Liability Act : PL Act

生存権　the right to an adequate standard of living ; the right to a decent standard of living

生存権保障　guarantee of the right to an adequate standard of living

生体肝移植　living donor liver transplantation

生体腎移植　living donor kidney transplantation

生体リズム　biological rhythm

成長障害　failure to thrive : FTT

成長ホルモン　growth hormone

和英

あ か せ た な は ま や ら わ

性的虐待　sexual abuse

性的暴力　sexual violence

性同一性障害　gender dysphoria ; gender identity disorder

●成年後見制度　adult guardianship system ; conservatorship

成年後見制度法人後見支援事業　assistance program for providing proper adult guardianship services ; assistance program for providing proper conservatorship services

成年後見制度利用支援事業　assistance program for promoting the use of the adult guardianship system ; assistance program for promoting the use of conservatorship

成年後見人　adult guardian ; conservator

正の強化　positive reinforcement

正の罰　positive punishment

政府関係法人労働組合連合　Labor Federation of Government-Related Organizations

政府管掌健康保険　government-managed health insurance

生物学的治療法　biological therapy

生物年齢　biological age

性別　gender ; sex

性別役割分業　sexual division of labor : SDL

性暴力被害者支援看護職　sexual assault nurse examiner : SANE

性ホルモン　sex hormone

整脈　eurhythmia

生命維持管理装置　life-sustaining equipment ; life-support equipment

生命・医療倫理　biomedical ethics

生命サポートサービス　advanced life support : ALS

生命徴候　vital signs

生命表　life table ; mortality table ; actuarial table

生命保険　life insurance

生命保険料　life insurance premium

生命倫理　bioethics

性役割　gender role

●整容　personal hygiene

整容支援　assistance with personal hygiene

生理的欲求　biological and physiological needs

生理的老化　physiological aging ; primary aging

政令指定都市　ordinance-designated city

セーフティネット　safety net

セーフティネット支援対策等事業　safety-net enhancement program

世界人権宣言　Universal Declaration of Human Rights : UDHR

世界大恐慌　Great Depression

世界的老化　global aging

●世界保健機関　World Health Organization : WHO

世界保健機関憲章　Constitution of the World Health Organization

世界レジャー・レクリエーション協会　World Leisure and Recreation Association : WLRA

セカンドオピニオン　second opinion

咳（せき）　cough

赤外線療法　infrared light therapy

赤十字　Red Cross

脊髄（せきずい）　spinal cord

脊髄症　myelopathy

脊髄小脳変性症　spinocerebellar degeneration ; spinocerebellar ataxia

脊髄神経　spinal nerve

●脊髄損傷（せきずいそんしょう）　spinal cord injury : SCI

脊髄反射　spinal reflex

咳喘息（せきぜんそく）　cough variant asthma : CVA

脊柱　spine ; vertebral column

脊柱管狭窄症（せきちゅうかんきょうさくしょう）　spinal stenosis

脊柱起立筋　erector spinae

脊椎圧迫骨折（せきついあっぱく）　spinal compression fracture ; vertebral compression fracture ; compression fracture of the spine

脊椎X線　spinal X-ray

脊椎穿刺（せきついせんし）　spinal tap

脊椎分離症　spondylolysis

責任　responsibility

咳反射　cough reflex : CR

赤痢（せきり）　dysentery

セクシュアリティ sexuality

セクシュアルハラスメント sexual harassment

•世帯 household

世代 generation

世代間ケア intergenerational care

世代間扶養 intergenerational support

世代間紛争 intergenerational conflict

世帯類型 classification of type of household

舌咽呼吸 glossopharyngeal breathing : GPS

舌下腺 sublingual gland

赤血球 red blood cell : RBC

舌根沈下 glossoptosis

摂食 food intake

絶食 nulla per os : NPO ; nothing by mouth

接触感染 contact infection

•摂食障害 eating disorder

摂食中枢 feeding and satiety centers

接触反射 contact reflection

舌苔 white tongue ; coated tongue

切断 amputation

切迫性 urgency

切迫性尿失禁 urge incontinence

説明責任 accountability

説明体 abstraction form

セツルメント social settlement ; settlement
house ; community center

セネストパチー cenesthopathy

セミパブリックスペース semi-public space

セミファーラー位 semi-Fowler's position

セミプライベートスペース semi-private space

背もたれ backrest

ゼラチン化 gelatinization

セラピー therapy

セラピスト therapist

セラピューティックレクリエーションサービス
therapeutic recreation services

セラピューティックレクリエーションスペシャリスト
therapeutic recreation specialist

•セルフケア self-care

セルフヘルプ self-help

セルロース cellulose

世論調査 public opinion poll

•繊維 fiber

前意識 preconscious

繊維製品取扱い表示 care labeling

繊維製品品質表示規程 care labeling rule

繊維の軟化点 softening point of textile
materials

船員保険 Seamen's Insurance

船員保険法 Seamen's Insurance Act

遷延性排尿 delayed urination

•全介助 total assistance

腺がん adenocarcinoma

前がん状態 precancerous condition ;
premalignant condition

前期高齢者 young-old ; elderly aged between
65 and 74

全血球計算 complete blood count : CBC

潜血試験 occult blood test

善行原則(医療倫理) beneficence (health care
ethics)

前向(性)健忘 anterograde amnesia

全国健康保険協会 Japan Health Insurance
Association

全国在宅障害児・者等実態調査 National
Survey of Children and Adults with
Disabilities

全国社会福祉協議会 Japan National Council
of Social Welfare

全国訪問看護事業協会 National Association
for Home-Visit Nursing Care

全国有料老人ホーム協会 Japanese
Association of Retirement Housing

全国老人クラブ連合会 Japan Federation of
Senior Citizens' Club

全国老人福祉施設協議会 Japan Council of
Senior Citizens Welfare Services

全国老人保健施設協会 Japan Association of
Geriatric Health Services Facilities

仙骨 sacrum

•洗剤 detergent

洗剤アレルギー detergent allergy

潜在意識 subconscious mind

潜在的ニーズ unstated needs

センサス census

全色盲 total color blindness

全失語　total aphasia ; global aphasia
腺腫　adenoma
占床率　occupancy rate
染色体　chromosome
*染色体異常　chromosomal abnormality
全身清拭　full-body sponge bath
全身性進行性硬化症　progressive systemic sclerosis : PSS
全人的医療　holistic medicine
全身浴　full-body bath
全数調査　population census
前脊髄動脈症候群　anterior spinal artery syndrome
*尖足　foot drop
喘息　asthma
喘息発作　asthmatic attack
全体的機能評価　Global Assessment of Functioning : GAF
全体的評価尺度　Global Assessment Scale : GAS
選択的サービス　selective services
選択的最適化論　selective optimization with compensation : SOC
選択的情報提供　selective dissemination of information : SDI
洗濯表示　care labeling
洗濯用合成洗剤　synthetic laundry detergent
洗濯用石けん　laundry soap
洗腸法　colostomy irrigation
先天異常　congenital anomaly
先天奇形　congenital malformation
先天性筋ジストロフィー　congenital muscular dystrophy : CMD
先天性股関節脱臼　congenital hip dislocation : CHD
先天性疾患　congenital disease
先天性障害　congenital disorder
先天性代謝異常　inborn errors of metabolism ; inherited metabolic disorder
先天性代謝異常検査　Newborn Screening Test
先天性ネフローゼ症候群　congenital nephrotic syndrome
蠕動運動　peristalsis

前頭側頭型認知症　frontotemporal dementia : FTD ; Pick's disease
前頭側頭葉変性症　frontotemporal lobar degeneration : FTLD
前頭葉　frontal lobe
前頭葉障害　frontal lobe dysfunction
前頭葉症状　frontal lobe syndrome
専売医薬　proprietary medicine
洗髪　shampooing ; hair washing
先発薬品　brand name medication
全般性認知症　generalized dementia
全般性不安障害　generalized anxiety disorder : GAD
潜伏感染　latent infection
潜伏期　latency period ; incubation period
潜伏期保菌者　incubatory carrier
喘鳴　wheezing
全面依存　total dependence
*せん妄　delirium
全盲　total blindness
せん妄評価尺度　Delirium Rating Scale
前立腺　prostate
前立腺炎　prostatitis
前立腺がん　prostate cancer
前立腺疾患　prostate disease
前立腺特異抗原　prostate specific antigen : PSA
前立腺肥大症　benign prostatic hyperplasia : BPH ; benign enlargement of the prostate : BEP ; (benign) prostatic hypertrophy
前輪歩行器　front wheel walker
前弯　lordosis

そ

総入れ歯　full denture
*躁うつ病　bipolar disorder ; manic-depressive illness ; manic depression
爪炎　onychia
爪下血腫　subungual hematoma
創感染　wound infection
想起　memory retrieval ; memory recall
臓器移植　organ transplant ; organ

transplantation

早期介入　early intervention

早期がん　early-stage cancer

臓器提供　organ donation

早期発見　early detection

双極Ⅰ型障害　bipolar I disorder

双極性感情障害　bipolar affective disorder ; manic-depressive illness

双極性障害　bipolar disorder

双極Ⅱ型障害　bipolar II disorder

早期離床　early ambulation

早期療育　early childhood care and education

•装具　orthosis ; brace

送迎（サービス）　transportation (service)

装甲型　armored type

爪甲鉤弯症　onychogryphosis ; ram's horn nails

総合相談　comprehensive consultation

総合相談支援業務　comprehensive consultation services

総合的品質管理活動　total quality management : TQM

総合病院　general hospital

総合リハビリテーションセンター　comprehensive rehabilitation center

相互扶助　mutual aid

総コレステロール　total cholesterol

葬祭扶助　funeral aid

挿耳型補聴器　in-the-ear hearing aid

•喪失体験　experiences of loss ; loss

巣状　focal

創傷（ケア）　wound (care)

巣症状　focal neurologic deficit ; focal neurologic sign

創傷被覆材　wound dressing

増殖　proliferation ; growth

爪真菌症　onychomycosis

創設家族　family of procreation

相続　inheritance ; succession

相続税　inheritance tax

相談　consultation

相談援助　consultation and assistance

相談援助実施機関　consultation and

assistance center

相談援助面接　consultation interview

相談支援　consultation and support

相談支援専門員　consultation and support specialist

早朝覚醒　early morning awakening

増粘剤　thickener ; thickening agent

早発性アルツハイマー病　early-onset Alzheimer's disease

躁病　mania

創分類　wound classification

相貌失認　prosopagnosia

掻痒感　itching

早老症　progeria

ソーシャルアクション　social action

ソーシャルアドミニストレーション　social administration

ソーシャルインクルージョン　social inclusion

ソーシャルウェルフェア・アドミニストレーション　social welfare administration

ソーシャルキャピタル　social capital

ソーシャルグループワーク　social group work

ソーシャルケースワーク　social case work

ソーシャルサービス　social services

ソーシャルサポート　social support

ソーシャルサポート・ネットワーク　social support network

ソーシャル・スキルズ・トレーニング　social skills training : SST

ソーシャルプランニング　social planning

•ソーシャルワーカー　social worker : SW

ソーシャルワーク　social work

ソーシャルワーク・プラクティス　social work practice

ソーシャルワークリサーチ　social work research

SOLER　squarely, open, lean, eye contact and relax

阻害因子　inhibitor

•側臥位　lateral recumbent position

塞栓　embolism

足背動脈　dorsalis pedis artery

足病　podiatric medicine

足病医　podiatrist

和英

あ か さ た な は ま や ら わ

*足浴　foot bath
側弯　scoliosis
鼠咬症　rat-bite disease
ソシオメトリー　sociometry
組織　organization
組織社会化　organizational socialization
粗死亡率　crude death rate ; crude mortality rate
*咀嚼　mastication ; chewing
咀嚼筋炎　masticatory myositis
咀嚼障害　masticatory disorder ; masticatory disturbance
咀嚼問題　chewing problem
咀嚼力　masticatory ability
粗出生率　crude birth rate : CBR
蘇生処置拒否　Do Not Resuscitate : DNR ; Do Not Attempt Resuscitation : DNAR ; Do Not Attempt Cardiopulmonary Resuscitation : DNACPR
組成表示　labelling of fiber composition of textile products ; textile labelling
措置　governmental order
措置基準　standards for allocation of elderly persons to welfare facilities
措置施設　patient allocation facility
*措置制度　patient allocation system
措置入院　involuntary hospitalization ; involuntary commitment
外開き戸　out swing door
その人らしさ　sense of self
ソフト食　soft diet
尊厳　dignity
尊厳死　death with dignity
尊厳死宣言書　living will
尊厳死法　Death with Dignity Act
損傷　injury ; trauma

た

ターナー症候群　Turner syndrome
*ターミナルケア　terminal care
タール便　tarry stool ; bloody stool
体位　position

体位設定　positioning
第1号研修（喀痰吸引等研修）　1st category training program for suctioning of phlegm and tubal feeding
第1号被保険者　1st category insured person
第1号保険料　insurance premiums of 1st category insured persons
第一次貧困　primary poverty
第一次予防　primary prevention
第一種社会福祉事業　type 1 social welfare services
体位ドレナージ　postural drainage
*体位変換　position change ; change of position
体位変換器　positioning device
退院　discharge
退院計画　discharge planning
大うつ病　major depression
体液　body fluid
*体温　body temperature
体温計　thermometer
体温調節　thermoregulation
体温調節機能障害　thermoregulatory disorder
体温調節機能（被服の）　temperature regulation (of clothing materials)
体温調節障害　thermoregulatory impairment
胎芽期　embryonic stage
*体格指数　body mass index : BMI
胎芽病　embryopathy
体幹　trunk ; torso
体幹機能障害　orthopedic impairment
体感症　cenesthopathy
体幹装具　spinal orthosis
待機児童　waitlisted children
大球性貧血　macrocytic anemia
体型　body type
*退行　regression
*退行期うつ病　involutional depression ; involutional melancholia
退行行動　regressive behavior
第3号研修（喀痰吸引等研修）　3rd category training program for suctioning of phlegm and tubal feeding

第三次教育 tertiary education

第三者委員 third-party panel

第三者評価（制度） third-party evaluation (system)

第三次予防 tertiary prevention

第三セクター方式 joint public and private co-operation ; joint public and private sector participation

胎児期 fetal stage

胎児期障害 fetal disorder

代謝 metabolism

代謝疾患 metabolic disorder

代謝当量 metabolic equivalent of task : MET

退所 discharge

代償 compensation

代償運動 compensatory movement

帯状疱疹 herpes zoster ; shingles

帯状疱疹後神経痛 postherpetic neuralgia : PHN

対症療法 symptomatic therapy

退職 retirement

退職者医療制度 retiree health care system

退職所得調査 retirement earnings test

退職手当 retirement allowance ; severance package ; severance pay

対処行動 coping behavior

退所時情報 discharge information

退所指導 discharge advice

対処戦略 coping strategy

対人援助技術 interpersonal social work skills

対人関係 interpersonal relationship

対人関係スキル interpersonal skills

対人恐怖 anthrophobia ; anthropophobia

対人ケアサービス personal care services

対人社会サービス personal social services

耐性 resistance ; tolerance

体性感覚 somatic sensation

体性神経 somatic nervous system

体操 exercise

代替医療 alternative medicine

代替機能 substitute function

大腿骨頸部骨折 femoral neck fracture

大腿四頭筋 quadriceps femoris

代替性 substitutability

大腸がん colorectal cancer ; colon cancer

大腸がん検診 colorectal cancer screening

大腸菌 Escherichia coli : E. coli

大腸ポリープ colorectal polyps ; colon polyps

大臀筋 gluteus maximus muscle

大転子部 greater trochanter

帯電防止加工 antistatic finish

耐糖能異常 impaired glucose tolerance : IGT

大動脈弁 aortic valve

大動脈弁狭窄症 aortic valve stenosis

代読 reading assistance

台所道具 kitchenware ; kitchen tools and utensils

台所の住環境整備 optimization of kitchen environment

胎内感染 prenatal infection

体内時計 biological clocks

第2号研修（喀痰吸引等研修） 2nd category training program for suctioning of phlegm and tubal feeding

第2号被保険者 2nd category insured person

第2号保険料 insurance premiums of 2nd category insured persons

第二次貧困 secondary poverty

第二種社会福祉事業 type 2 social welfare services

第二次予防 secondary prevention

大脳 cerebrum

大脳皮質 cerebral cortex

代筆 writing assistance

代弁者 advocate

代弁的機能 advocacy

大麻 marijuana ; hemp ; cannabis

対面法 face-to-face interview

耐容一日摂取量 tolerable daily intake

耐容性 tolerance

代理 substitution

代理決定 surrogate decision

対立装具 opponens splint

代理電話 telecommunications relay service : TRS

代理判断 substituted judgment

体力　physical strength ; physical energy

*ダウン症候群　Down's syndrome

唾液（だえき）　saliva

唾液機能　salivary function

唾液分泌　salivary secretion

唾液分泌過多　hypersalivation ; ptyalism ;
　sialorrhea

他害行為　danger to others : DTO

多価不飽和脂肪酸（ふほうわしぼうさん）　polyunsaturated fatty
　acid : PUFA

多関節性痛風　polyarticular gout

宅老所　old folks home

多系統萎縮症（いしゅく）　multiple system atrophy : MSA

多血症　polycythemia

多剤処方（たざい）　polypharmacy

多剤耐性（たざいたいせい）　multidrug resistance : MDR

多剤耐性結核　multidrug resistant
　tuberculosis : MDR-TB

多剤併用　polypharmacy

多次元的機能評価　Multidimensional
　Functional Assessment

多次元貧困指数　Multidimensional Poverty
　Index : MPI

多重人格障害　dissociative identity disorder :
　DID ; multiple personality disorder

多職種チーム　interdisciplinary team : IDT

多職種連携　interprofessional collaboration

多職種連携教育　interprofessional education

多臓器不全　multiple organ failure

多臓器不全症候群　multiple organ dysfunction
　syndrome : MODS

多段階免除制度　multi-level premium
　deduction system

立ち上がり運動　sit-to-stand exercise

立ちくらみ　light-headedness ; dizziness

立ち直り反応　righting reaction

*脱臼（だっきゅう）　luxation ; joint dislocation

脱健着患（だっけんちゃっかん）　undress the unaffected and dress
　the affected

脱施設（化）　deinstitutionalization

脱神経　denervation

*脱水症　dehydration

達成動機　achievement motivation

脱抑制　disinhibition

多点つえ　multi-point cane

多動　hyperactivity ; repetitive behavior

*他動運動　passive exercise

他動可動域　passive range of motion

多動性障害　hyperkinetic disorder

多糖類　polysaccharides

田中 - ビネー式知能検査　Tanaka-Binet
　Intelligence Test

ダニ　mite

ダニアレルゲン　dust mite allergy

多尿　polyuria ; excessive urine output

楽しみ志向　joy-oriented ; pleasure-oriented

多発梗塞性認知症（たはっこうそくせいにんちしょう）　multi-infarct dementia

多発性筋炎　polymyositis

多発性硬化症　multiple sclerosis : MS

多発性脳梗塞（のうこうそく）　multiple cerebral infarction

打撲　contusion

多面的療法　multimodal therapy : MMT

多問題家族　family with multiple problems

多様性　diversity

誰もが支え合う地域の構築に向けた福祉サービス
　の実現〜新たな時代に対応した福祉の提供ビ
　ジョン〜　Realization of Social Services for
　the Development of Supportive
　Communities: New Vision for a New Era of
　Social Services Delivery

単回使用器材　single-use device : SUD

団塊の世代　baby boom generation

*短下肢装具（たんかしそうぐ）　ankle-foot orthosis : AFO ; short
　leg brace

担架ネット　bath stretcher ; shower stretcher

*短期記憶　short-term memory

短期ケア施設　short-term care facility

短期入所　short-term stay

短期入所生活介護　short-term stay for
　personal care

短期入所療養介護　short-term-stay for health
　care

短期目標　short-term goal

単極性うつ病　major depression

単極性感情障害　depression

短期療法　brief therapy

男根期　phallic stage
段差　threshold
•端座位　sitting posture at the edge of the seat ; sitting position
段差解消機　lifting platform
胆汁うっ滞性肝炎　cholestatic hepatitis
断酒会　alcoholic self-help organization
単純骨折　simple fracture ; closed fracture
男女共同参画社会　gender-equal society
男女雇用機会均等法　Equal Employment Opportunity Act
単親家庭　single-parent family ; one-parent family
炭水化物　carbohydrate
ダンスセラピー　dance/movement therapy : DMT
男性性　roles of men
胆石　gallstone
短繊維　staple fiber
胆道がん　biliary tract cancer
胆道疾患　biliary tract disease
単糖無水物　monosaccharide anhydride
単糖類　monosaccharide
単独開業医　solo practitioner
単独恐怖症　autophobia ; monophobia ; isolophobia
単独事業　original program
タンニン　tannin
たんぱく質　protein
たんぱく質エネルギー　protein energy
たんぱく質エネルギー低栄養状態　protein-energy malnutrition : PEM
単麻痺　monoplegia
弾力性　elasticity

ち

•チアノーゼ　cyanosis
地域　community
地域移行支援　community transition services
地域医療　community health care
地域医療計画　community health plan ; regional health plan
地域医療支援病院　community medicine support hospital
地域援助活動　community work
地域援助技術　community work practice
地域開発　community development
地域格差　regional disparities
地域加算　regional reimbursement
地域活動支援センター　community support center
地域活動支援センター機能強化事業　enhancement program for community support centers
地域看護　community nursing
地域ケア　community care
地域ケア会議　community care conference
地域ケアネットワーク　community care network
地域計画　community planning
地域支援事業　community support program
地域社会　community
地域診断　community diagnosis
地域生活支援事業　community living assistance services
地域精神医学　community psychiatry
地域精神保健福祉活動　community mental health and welfare services ; community mental health and social services
地域相談支援　community consultation services
地域相談支援給付費　reimbursement for community consultation services for persons with disabilities
地域組織化活動　community organizing
地域定着支援　community living support
地域における医療及び介護を総合的に確保するための基本的な方針　Basic Policy on Ensuring Collaboration between Medical and Long-Term Care Services
地域のレクリエーション　community-based recreational activities
地域病院　community hospital
地域福祉　community welfare
地域福祉活動計画　community welfare action plan

地域福祉基金　community welfare fund

地域福祉計画　community planning；
community welfare planning

地域福祉コーディネーター　community social
services coordinator

地域福祉サービス　community social services；
community welfare services

地域福祉事業　community social services
program；community welfare program

地域福祉センター　community social services
center；community welfare center

地域包括ケア　comprehensive community
care

地域包括ケアシステム　community-based
integrated care system

*地域包括支援センター　comprehensive
community support center

地域包括支援センター運営協議会
management council of comprehensive
community support center

地域保健　community health

地域保健法　Community Health Act

地域密着型介護サービス　community-based
long-term care services

地域密着型介護サービス費　reimbursement for
community-based long-term care services

地域密着型介護予防サービス　community-
based preventive care services

地域密着型介護予防サービス費
reimbursement for community-based
preventive care services

地域密着型介護老人福祉施設入所者生活介護
community-based residential care

地域密着型サービス　community-based
service

地域密着型通所介護　community-based day
care services

地域密着型特定施設　community-based
specified facility

地域密着型特定施設入居者生活介護
community-based specified facility care

地域密着型訪問介護　community-based home
care

地域リハビリテーション　community-based
rehabilitation

地域連携パス　liaison critical pathway

*チームアプローチ　team-based approach

チーム医療　team-based health care

チームカンファレンス　team conference

*チームケア　team-based care

チームワーク　teamwork

*チェーンストークス呼吸　Cheyne-Stokes
respiration

知覚　sensation；perception

知覚障害　sensory impairment

知覚麻痺　sensory paralysis

逐語反射　word-for-word reflection

蓄積効果　cumulative effect

蓄尿障害　urinary storage disorder

地誌的失認　topographical agnosia

知性化　intellectualization

チック　tic

チック障害　tic disorder

*窒息　suffocation；asphyxiation

*知的障害　intellectual disability；mental
retardation

知的障害児施設　facility for children with
intellectual disabilities

知的障害者　persons with intellectual
disabilities

知的障害者グループホーム　group home for
persons with intellectual disabilities

知的障害者ケアガイドライン　Guidelines for
Care of Persons with Intellectual Disabilities

知的障害者更生施設　rehabilitation facility for
persons with intellectual disabilities

知的障害者更生相談所　rehabilitation and
counseling center for persons with
intellectual disabilities

知的障害者作業所　workshop for persons with
intellectual disabilities

知的障害者授産施設　sheltered workshop for
persons with intellectual disabilities

知的障害者相談員　counselor for persons with
intellectual disabilities

知的障害者短期入所　short-term stay for

persons with intellectual disabilities

知的障害者短期入所事業　short-term stay program for persons with intellectual disabilities

知的障害者デイサービス　day care services for persons with intellectual disabilities

知的障害者デイサービス事業　day care services program for persons with intellectual disabilities

知的障害者デイサービスセンター　day care services center for persons with intellectual disabilities

知的障害者の権利宣言　Declaration on the Rights of Mentally Retarded Persons

知的障害者のレクリエーション　recreational activities for persons with intellectual disabilities

知的障害者福祉　welfare of persons with intellectual disabilities

知的障害者福祉司　welfare officer for persons with intellectual disabilities

知的障害者福祉法　Welfare of Persons with Intellectual Disabilities Act

知的障害者福祉ホーム　welfare home for persons with intellectual disabilities

知的障害者ホームヘルプサービス　home help services for persons with intellectual disabilities

知的障害（精神遅滞）　intellectual disability (mental retardation)

知的水準　intellectual level

知的欲求　cognitive needs

*知能　intelligence

知能検査　intelligence test

*知能指数　intelligence quotient : IQ

知能障害　intellectual disability

知能年齢　intellectual age

知能偏差値　intelligence standard score : ISS

遅発性アルツハイマー病　late-onset Alzheimer's disease

地方行政　local administration

地方行政府　local government authority

地方公共団体　local public organization

地方交付税　local allocation tax

地方公務員共済組合　Local Government Employees' Mutual Aid Association

地方裁判所　district court

地方自治　local autonomy

地方自治体　local government

地方自治体連合　local authority association

地方自治法　Local Autonomy Act

地方障害者施策推進協議会　Local Council on Promotion of Measures for Persons with Disabilities

痴呆（認知症）　dementia

地方分権　decentralization

致命率　case-fatality rate

着衣失行　dressing dyspraxia

着衣スキル　dressing skill

着床前診断　preimplantation genetic diagnosis

着色料　food coloring ; color additive

着香料　food flavoring

注意獲得　attention-seeking

注意欠陥・多動性障害　attention deficit hyperactivity disorder : ADHD

注意障害　attention-deficit disorder

中央供給　central supply

中央社会福祉審議会　Central Social Welfare Council

中央障害者施策推進協議会　Central Council on Promotion of Measures for Persons with Disabilities

仲介的機能　brokerage

中核市　core city

中核症状　core features of dementia

中間施設　intermediate facility ; transitional facility

中耳炎　otitis media

注射　injection ; shot

中心暗点　central scotoma

中心カテーテル　central catheter

中心静脈圧　central venous pressure : CVP

中心静脈栄養法　central parenteral nutrition

中枢神経　central nerve

中枢神経系　central nervous system : CNS

中枢神経性障害　central nervous system disorder ; central nervous system disease

中枢性聴覚処理障害　central auditory processing disorder : CAPD

中性脂肪　triglyceride ; neutral fat

中性洗剤　neutral detergent

中途覚醒　nocturnal awakening ; middle-of-the-night insomnia

中毒性精神病　toxic psychosis

中途視覚障害　acquired visual impairment

中途視覚障害者　newly blind

中途失明　acquired blindness

中途障害　acquired disability

中途聴覚障害　acquired hearing impairment

中脳　mesencephalon ; midbrain

チューブ栄養　tube feeding

注文服　made-to-order clothing ; custom-made clothing

中立位（ちゅうりつい）　neutral position

腸　intestine

腸液　intestinal juice

腸炎ビブリオ　Vibrio parahaemolyticus

超音波　ultrasound

超音波検査　ultrasonography : US

超音波療法　ultrasound therapy

聴覚　sense of hearing ; auditory perception

聴覚音声セラピスト　auditory-verbal therapist

聴覚音声療法　auditory-verbal therapy : AVT

聴覚過敏　hyperacusis

聴覚失認　auditory agnosia

*聴覚障害　hearing impairment ; hearing loss ; auditory impairment

聴覚中枢　auditory center

聴覚的評価　audiology assessment ; hearing assessment

聴覚・平衡機能障害　hearing and balance disorder

長下肢装具（ちょうかしそうぐ）　knee-ankle-foot orthosis : KAFO ; long leg brace

腸管出血性大腸菌　enterohemorrhagic Escherichia coli : EHEC

*長期記憶　long-term memory

聴器毒性物質　ototoxic substance

腸機能　bowel function

長期目標　long-term goal

超高齢社会　super-aged society

長座位　high-Fowler's position

調剤サービス　pharmaceutical services

超自我　superego

長寿　longevity

長寿社会　longevity society

長寿社会対応住宅設計指針　Residential Design Guidelines Corresponding to the Longevity Society

長寿社会福祉基金　Social Welfare Funds for Longevity Society

超少子高齢社会　hyper-aged and depopulating society

聴神経　auditory nerve

*調整交付金　adjustment grant ; adjustment subsidy

長繊維　filament

聴導犬　hearing dog

町内会　neighborhood association

聴能訓練士　hearing therapist

*重複障害　multiple disabilities

*腸閉塞（ちょうへいそく）　ileus

腸閉塞症　intestinal obstruction ; bowel obstruction

調味料　seasonings and ingredients

調理済み食品　ready-to-serve dish ; ready-to-eat product

調理方法　recipe

調理用自助具　assistive kitchen device

聴力　hearing ; hearing ability

聴力検査　hearing test ; audiometry evaluation

聴力損失値　degree of hearing loss

聴力レベル　hearing level

腸ろう経管栄養　intestinal tube feeding

*直接援助技術　direct social work practice ; direct social work

直接言語　direct language

直接接触感染　direct contact infection ; direct contact transmission

直腸がん　rectal cancer ; cancer of the rectum

直腸機能障害　bowel dysfunction

直腸診　rectal examination
直腸脱　rectal prolapse
直腸瘤　rectocele
直角法　corner-to-corner interview ; corner position
直系家族　stem family
著変　significant change
苧麻　Boehmeria nivea ; ramie
縮緬　chirimen crepe fabric ; crepe fabric
治療食　therapeutic diet
治療的レクリエーションサービス　therapeutic recreation services
治療歴　medical history
沈下性肺炎　hypostatic pneumonia
賃金　wage
賃金格差　wage gap ; wage disparity
陳述記憶　explicit memory ; declarative memory
陳情　petition ; appeal

つ

椎間板ヘルニア　intervertebral disc herniation ; herniated disc
椎骨動脈　vertebral artery
•対麻痺　paraplegia
通院医療　outpatient care ; ambulatory health care
通院患者　outpatient
通院者率　rate of outpatient services ; outpatient utilization rates
通院等乗降介助　medical escort and travel companion services
通過菌　transient bacteria ; transient flora
痛覚　algesia
通過症候群　transitional syndrome
通気　air permeability
通気性（被服の）　air permeability (of clothing materials)
•通所介護　adult day care
通所介護施設　adult day care center
通所施設　outpatient facility
•通所リハビリテーション　outpatient

rehabilitation ; ambulatory rehabilitation
通信教育　online education
通信販売　mail order business
痛風　gout
痛風性関節炎　gouty arthritis
•つえ　cane
つえ歩行　cane-assisted gait
付添手当　attendance allowance
付添人　attendant
次々販売　reloading scam
継手　joint
ツベルクリン反応　tuberculin skin test reaction ; tuberculin reaction ; TB skin test reaction
爪　nail
爪白癬　tinea unguium ; onychomycosis
ツング自己評価式抑うつ性尺度　Zung Self-Rating Depression Scale : SDS

て

手当　allowance
•手洗い　hand washing
定位家族　family of orientation
低栄養　undernutrition
DSM　Diagnostic and Statistical Manual of Mental Disorders
低温殺菌　pasteurization
低温滅菌　low-temperature sterilization
低温やけど　moderate-temperature burn
D型肝炎（ウイルス）　hepatitis D (virus)
低カリウム血症　hypokalemia
定期巡回・随時対応型訪問介護看護　routine-visit and on-call home health care
定期的健康診断　periodic health evaluation : PHE ; regular check-up
低緊張性膀胱　bladder hypotonia
底屈　plantar flexion
デイケア　day care
•低血圧　hypotension
•低血糖症状　hypoglycemia
抵抗　resistance
デイサービス　adult day care services
低酸素血症　hypoxemia

和英

低酸素症　anoxia

DCM　Dementia Care Mapping

T字づえ　T-cane

低脂肪食　low-fat diet

低所得　low income

低所得者対策　low income assistance program

低所得世帯　low income household

低所得層　low income class

•ディスアビリティ　disability

ディスクロージャー　disclosure

低体温症　hypothermia

低たんぱく症　hypoproteinemia

低張性脱水　hypotonic dehydration；hyponatremic dehydration

低賃金労働　low-wage labor

ティッピングレバー　tipping lever

TDL　techniques of daily living

低ナトリウム血症　hyponatremia

定年　retirement

定年制　mandatory retirement system

定年退職　mandatory retirement

TPO　time, place, and occasion

デイ・ホスピタル　day hospital

呈味成分　components of taste

剃毛　shaving

テイラー顕現性不安尺度　Taylor's Manifest Anxiety Scale：TMAS

ティルト・リクライニング型車いす　tilt and reclining wheelchair

テープ止めタイプ　diapers with tape tabs

手押し型車いす　attendant-propelled wheelchair

適応　adjustment；adaptation

適応期　stage of adjustment and acceptance

適応機制　defense mechanism

適応障害　adjustment disorder

適応状況　status of adjustment

適正検査　aptitude test

出来高払い　fee-for-service：FFS

•摘便　digital removal of feces：DRF；digital removal of stools；digital evacuation

テクスチャー　texture

テクノエイド協会　Association for Technical Aids

デシベル　decibel：dB

テストステロン　testosterone

•手すり　handrail

手すりの設置　handrail installation

鉄欠乏性貧血　iron deficiency anemia

手続き記憶　procedural memory

鉄分（欠乏症）　iron (deficiency)

•手引歩行　assisted ambulation

テフロン加工　Teflon-coating

デュシェンヌ型筋ジストロフィー　Duchenne muscular dystrophy：DMD

転移　metastasis；transference

転移神経症　transference neurosis

転院　hospital transfer

伝音器官　organ of hearing

•伝音性難聴　conductive hearing loss

てんかん　epilepsy

点眼液　eye drops

転換性障害　conversion disorder：CD；functional neurological symptom disorder

てんかん発作　epileptic seizure

電気けいれん療法　electroconvulsive therapy：ECT

電気刺激　electrostimulation

電気ショック療法　electroconvulsive therapy：ECT；electroshock therapy

電気診断法　electrodiagnosis：EDX

転居ストレス　relocation stress

電気療法　electrotherapy

電撃療法　electroconvulsive therapy：ECT

点検商法　inspection fraud

•点字　Braille

電子カルテ　electronic health records：HER

転子間骨折　intertrochanteric fracture

点字器　Braille slate

電子記録　electric records

電子健康記録　electronic health records：HER

電子処方　e-prescription

点字タイプライター　Braille typewriter；Brailler

電磁調理器　electromagnetic cooker

電子内視鏡検査　electronic endoscopy

電子ビームＣＴ　electron-beam computed tomography : EBCT

転子部骨折　trochanteric fracture

点字ブロック　tactile floor tiles ; Braille blocks

点字用具　Braille writing equipment

伝染性疾病　communicable disease ; transmissible disease

伝染病　communicable disease ; transmissible disease

伝染病予防法　Communicable Diseases Prevention and Control Act

点滴　intravenous : IV

点滴静脈内注射　intravenous drip

点滴治療　intravenous therapy ; IV therapy

転倒　fall

転倒危険度　fall risk

電動吸引器　electric aspirator

•電動車いす　electric wheelchair ; powerchair ; electric-powered wheelchair

転倒後症候群　post-fall syndrome

転倒事故　fall incident

伝導失語　conduction aphasia

伝導性難聴　conductive hearing loss

転倒・転落　slips and falls from height

電動歯ブラシ　electric toothbrush

電動普通型車いす　electric wheelchair

•電動ベッド　electric bed

転倒予防　fall prevention

天然繊維　natural fiber

でんぷん　amylum ; starch

点訳　Braille translation

電話勧誘販売　telemarketing scams ; phone scams

電話補助機器　telephone assistive device

と

トイレの住環境整備　optimization of bathroom space and toilet units

トインビー・ホール　Toynbee Hall

同一化　identification

同一視　identification

同一性危機　identity crisis

動因　motivation ; motive

投影　projection

投影検査　projective test

投影（投射）　projection

投影法　projective techniques

•動悸　palpitation

動機づけ　motivation ; motive

道具的条件づけ　instrumental conditioning

凍結肩　frozen shoulder

凍結貯蔵　frozen storage

統合医療供給システム　integrated delivery system : IDS

同行援護　escort services

統合化　integration

統合教育　integrated education

統合失調感情障害　schizoaffective disorder

•統合失調症　schizophrenia

瞳孔対光反射　pupillary light reflex

橈骨遠位端骨折　distal radius fracture

橈骨動脈　radial artery

橈骨動脈瘤　radial artery aneurysm

動作性ＩＱ　performance IQ : PIQ

洞察　insight ; discernment

洞察療法　insight therapy

動作分析　motion analysis

動作法　psycho-rehabilitation method

動作歩行　point gait

糖質　saccharide

透湿性　breathability ; water vapor permeability

透湿性防水加工　waterproof breathability

投射　projection

凍傷　frostbite

同情　sympathy

同性愛　homosexuality

統制された情緒的関与　controlled emotional involvement

•透析　dialysis

透析療法　dialysis therapy

動線　workflow

当選商法　sweepstakes and lottery scams

痘そう　smallpox

085

糖蔵　food preservation by high sugar concentrations

糖代謝異常　abnormal glucose metabolism

糖値　glucose level

•疼痛（とうつう）　pain

疼痛回避性歩行　antalgic gait

疼痛管理　pain management ; pain control

疼痛性障害　pain disorder

疼痛薬　pain medication ; pain relief medication

導尿　urethral catheterization

•糖尿病　diabetes mellitus : DM

糖尿病交換表　diabetic exchange list ; diabetic food exchange list

糖尿病性神経障害　diabetic neuropathy

糖尿病性腎症　diabetic nephropathy

糖尿病性網膜症　diabetic retinopathy

逃避　avoidance ; escape

頭部外傷　traumatic brain injury : TBI ; head injury

頭部後傾法　head tilt/chin lift maneuver

動物介在活動　animal assisted activity : AAA

動物介在療法　animal assisted therapy : AAT

動物性脂肪　animal fat

動物性食品　animal source foods : ASF ; animal product

動物性たんぱく質　animal protein

動物療法　animal assisted therapy : AAT

糖分　sugar content

動脈　artery

動脈圧　arterial blood pressure : ABP ; arterial pressure

動脈血　arterial blood

•動脈硬化（症）　arteriosclerosis

動脈硬化性心疾患　arteriosclerotic heart disease : ASHD

動脈疾患　arterial disease

動脈造影　arteriography

動脈塞栓（そくせん）　arterial embolism

動脈拍動　arterial pulse

動脈閉塞症（へいそくしょう）　arterial occlusive disease : AOD

動脈瘤（りゅう）　aneurysm

投薬　medication administration

投薬過誤　medication error

投与　administration

動揺関節　flail joint

動揺性高血圧症　labile hypertension

動揺性歩行　waddling gait ; duck-like walk

投与制限　medication restriction

投与量の調整　dose modification

登録看護師　registered nurse

登録ヘルパー　registered home helper

ドーパミン　dopamine

特異的発達障害　specific developmental disorder : SDD

•特殊寝台　hospital bed ; specialty bed

特殊尿器　automatic urine collection device

特殊法人　semigovernmental corporation

特殊浴槽　medical bathtub ; specialty bathtub

読書用眼鏡　reading glasses

読唇（術）　lipreading ; speechreading

特定機能病院　advanced treatment hospital

特定健康診査　annual physical exam

特定施設　specified facility

特定施設入居者生活介護　residential care for residents of long-term care facilities

特定疾病　specified disease ; intractable disease

特定商取引に関する法律　Specified Commercial Transactions Act

特定相談支援事業　specified consultation services

特定入所者介護サービス費　reimbursement for residential care of low-income residents

特定非営利活動促進法　Promotion of Activities by Specified Nonprofit Organizations Act : NPO Act

特定非営利活動法人　specified nonprofit corporation

特定福祉用具　specified adaptive equipment ; specified technical aids

特定福祉用具販売　sale of specified adaptive equipment ; sale of specified technical aids

特定保健指導　specified health guidance

特定保健用食品　foods for special medical purposes

特定目的公営住宅　purpose-specific public housing

特定有料老人ホーム　specified private care home

特別栽培農産物　specially cultivated products

特別支援学級　special education class for children with disabilities

特別支援学校　special education school for children with disabilities

特別支援教育　special education ; special needs education

特別児童扶養手当　disability allowance for disabled children ; disabled child allowance

特別障害給付金　disability benefits for disabled adult children ; disabled adult child benefit

特別障害者控除　special tax deduction for persons with disabilities

特別障害者手当　disability allowance for disabled adult children ; disabled adult child allowance

特別税額控除　special tax deduction

特別地域加算　special regional reimbursement

特別徴収　special levy

特別治療食　special therapeutic diet

•特別養護老人ホーム　welfare facility for the elderly

特別養護老人ホームの設備及び運営に関する基準　equipment maintenance and facility operation standards for welfare facilities for the elderly

特別養護老人ホームの入所措置の基準　admission standards for welfare facilities for the elderly

特別用途食品　foods for special purposes

独立行政法人　independent administrative corporation

独立行政法人国立重度知的障害者総合施設のぞみの園　Independent Administrative Institution National Center for Persons with Severe Intellectual Disabilities, Nozominosono

特例介護予防サービス費　exceptional reimbursement for preventive care services

特例居宅介護サービス費　exceptional reimbursement for home-based care services

特例施設介護サービス費　exceptional reimbursement for residential care services

特例地域密着型介護サービス費　exceptional reimbursement for community-based care services

•読話　speechreading

•吐血　hematemesis ; haematemesis

床ずれ　pressure ulcer ; pressure sore ; decubitus ulcer

都市化　urbanization

都市ガス　town gas

都市型軽費老人ホーム　urban low-cost elder home

閉じこめ症候群　locked-in syndrome : LIS

閉じこもり　housebound

閉じこもり症候群　housebound syndrome

閉じこもり老人　housebound elderly

•徒手筋力テスト　Manual Muscle Testing : MMT

徒手療法　manual therapy

•閉じられた質問　closed-ended question

独居　living alone

独居老人　elderly living alone

突進現象　festinating gait

突然死　sudden death

突発性難聴　sudden hearing loss ; sudden sensorineural hearing loss ; sudden deafness

都道府県介護保険事業支援計画　prefectural planning of long-term care services

都道府県障害者計画　basic disability plan

都道府県障害福祉計画　prefectural welfare planning for persons with disabilities

都道府県相談支援体制整備事業　prefectural project of the establishment of the consultation and support system

都道府県地域生活支援事業　prefectural government-administered community living assistance program

都道府県老人福祉計画　prefectural welfare planning for the elderly

ドナー　donor

ドメスティック・バイオレンス　domestic violence : DV

ドライシャンプー　dry shampoo

ドライマウス　dry mouth ; xerostomia

トラウマ　trauma

トランスファー　transfer

トランスファーボード　transfer board

トリガー　trigger

取引　transaction

トリヨードサイロニン　triiodothyronine : T3

ドレーン　drain

トレッドミル　treadmill

トレンデレンブルグ体位　Trendelenburg position

トレンデレンブルグ徴候　Trendelenburg sign

とろみ剤　thickener ; thickener powder

とろみ食　thickened diet

とろみ調整食品　altered consistency diet ; modified consistency diet

な

ナーシングホーム　nursing home

ナースセンター　nurses center

内因　endogenous ; intrinsic

内因型喘息　intrinsic asthma

内因性括約筋不全　intrinsic sphincter deficiency : ISD

内因性感染　endogenous infection

内因性精神障害　endogenous mental disorder

内因性精神病　endogenous psychosis

内科　internal medicine

内向性　introversion

内呼吸　internal respiration

内耳炎　labyrinthitis

内視鏡　endoscope

内視鏡検査　endoscopy

内出血　internal bleeding

内旋　internal rotation

内臓脂肪　visceral fat ; abdominal fat

ナイチンゲール, F.　Florence Nightingale

ナイチンゲール誓詞　Nightingale Pledge

内的適応　adjustment

内転　adduction

ナイトホスピタル　night hospital

内発的動機づけ　intrinsic motivation

内反　varus

内反尖足　equinovarus foot ; clubfoot

•内部（機能）障害　visceral impairment

内服薬　oral medication

内部障害者更生施設　rehabilitation facility for people with visceral impairments

内分泌　endocrine

内分泌医　endocrinologist

内分泌器官　endocrine organs

内分泌疾患　endocrine disorder

ナイロン　nylon

中食　ready-made meal

仲間関係　peer relationship

ナショナル・ミニマム　national minimum

ナトリウム　sodium

ナラティブ・アプローチ　narrative approach

ナラティブ・セラピー　narrative therapy

軟化剤　emollient

軟化症　malacia

喃語　babbling

軟膏　ointment

軟口蓋　soft palate

軟菜食　soft diet

難治性疾患　incurable disease

•難聴　hearing loss : HL ; hard of hearing

難聴幼児通園施設　audiologic rehabilitation center for children with hearing impairments

難燃剤　fire-retardant material

難燃・防炎加工　nonflammable and flame-retardant treatment

•難病　intractable disease ; hard-to-treat disease

難病対策　intractable disease policy

難病対策要綱　outlines of the policy for intractable disease

難病の患者に対する医療等に関する法律　Medical Care of Patients with Intractable Diseases Act

難民　refugee

に

*ニーズ　needs

ニーズアセスメント　needs assessment

ニーズの階層　hierarchy of needs

ニート　Not in Education, Employment or Training：NEET

ニィリエ，ベンクト　Bengt Nirje

2型糖尿病　type 2 diabetes mellitus；type 2 diabetes

苦味　bitter；bitter taste；bitterness

二酸化炭素　carbon dioxide

二酸化窒素　nitrogen dioxide

二次医療　secondary health care

二次医療圏　secondary medical service area

二次過程　secondary process

二次感染　secondary infection

二次救命処置　advanced life support：ALS

二次障害　secondary impairment

二次心肺蘇生法　advanced cardiovascular life support：ACLS

二次性高血圧　secondary hypertension

二次的動機　secondary motive

二次的欲求　growth needs

二次的老化　secondary aging

二次判定　secondary assessment

二次被害　loss due to reloading scams

二次妄想　secondary delusion

21トリソミー　trisomy 21

21世紀における国民健康づくり運動　National Health Promotion Movement in the 21st Century：Healthy Japan 21

21世紀における第2次国民健康づくり運動　The Second Term of National Health Promotion Movement in the 21st Century

「21世紀福祉ビジョン」　Welfare Vision for the 21st Century

24時間ケア　twenty-four-hour care

24時間見守り　twenty-four-hour protective oversight

24時間連絡体制　24-hour on call

二次予防　secondary prevention

「2015年の高齢者介護～高齢者の尊厳を支えるケアの確立に向けて～」　Elderly Care for the Year 2015: Toward the Establishment of an Elderly Care System that Preserves Dignity

2025年に向けた介護人材の確保～量と質の好循環の確立に向けて～　Improvement of Shortage of Long-Term Care Workers for the Year 2025: Initiatives for Development of the Virtuous Circle of Quantity and Quality Assurance

*日常生活活動（動作）　activities of daily living：ADL

日常生活自立支援事業　independent living support services program

日常生活用具　adaptive equipment；technical aid；assistive device

日常生活用具給付等事業　adaptive equipment loan program；technical aids loan program

日常生活用具の給付等　loan of adaptive equipment；loan of technical aids

日常的金銭管理　daily money management：DMM

日常のレクリエーション　regular recreational activities

*日内変動　circadian variation

日射病　heat stroke；sun stroke

日中過睡眠　excessive daytime sleepiness：EDS

ニット　knitting；knit

ニッポン一億総活躍プラン　Japan's Plan for Dynamic Engagement of All Citizens

二動作歩行　two-point gait

ニトログリセリン　nitroglycerin：NG

二分脊椎　spina bifida

日本アイバンク協会　Japan Eye Bank Association

日本医師会　Japan Medical Association

日本介護福祉士会　Japan Association of Certified Care Workers

日本介護福祉士会方式　Japan Association of Certified Care Workers Methods

日本介護福祉士会倫理綱領　Japan Association of Certified Care Workers' Code of Ethics

日本介護福祉士養成施設協会　Japan Association of Training Institutions for Certified Care Workers

日本看護協会　Japanese Nursing Association

日本救急救命士協会　Japanese Paramedics Association

日本口腔外科学会　Japanese Society of Oral and Maxillofacial Surgeons : JSOMS

日本高齢者虐待防止センター　Japanese Center for the Prevention of Elder Abuse

日本国憲法　Constitution of Japan

日本国憲法第13条　Article 13 of the Constitution of Japan

日本国憲法第25条　Article 25 of the Constitution of Japan

日本歯科医師会　Japan Dental Association

日本式昏睡尺度　Japan Coma Scale : JCS

日本社会福祉学会　Japanese Society for the Study of Social Welfare : JSSW

日本社会福祉士会　Japanese Association of Certified Social Workers : JACSW

日本社会福祉士会方式　Japanese Association of Certified Social Workers' Assessment Forms

日本集中治療医学会　Japanese Society of Intensive Care Medicine

日本食品標準成分表　Standard Tables of Food Composition in Japan

日本私立学校振興・共済事業団　Promotion and Mutual Aid Corporation for Private Schools of Japan : PMAC

日本人の栄養所要量　recommended dietary allowance for Japanese

日本人の食事摂取基準　Dietary Reference Intakes for Japanese : DRIs

日本精神保健福祉士協会　Japanese Association of Psychiatric Social Workers

日本赤十字社　Japanese Red Cross Society

日本ソーシャルワーカー協会　Japanese Association of Social Workers : JASW

日本ソーシャルワーク教育学校連盟　Japanese Association for Social Work Education : JASWE

日本尊厳死協会　Japan Society for Dying with Dignity

日本WHO協会　WHO Association of Japan

日本年金機構　Japan Pension Service

日本脳炎　Japanese encephalitis : JE

日本微量栄養素学会　Japan Trace Nutrients Research Society

日本放射線技師会　Japan Association of Radiological Technologists : JART

日本訪問看護財団　Japan Visiting Nursing Foundation

日本訪問看護振興財団方式　Japan Visiting Nursing Foundation's Assessment and Care Planning Tool

日本薬剤師会　Japan Pharmaceutical Association

日本臨床衛生検査技師会　Japanese Association of Medical Technologists : JAMT

日本臨床工学技士会　Japan Association for Clinical Engineers

日本レクリエーション協会　National Recreation Association of Japan : NRAL

入院　hospitalization ; admission

入院医療　inpatient care

入院型緩和ケア　inpatient hospice

入院措置　involuntary hospital admission

入院保険　hospital insurance : HI

乳がん　breast cancer

入居者　resident

乳児　infant

乳児死亡率　infant mortality rate

入所　admission

入所期間　length of stay : LOS

入所施設　residential facility

入所者　resident

入所者の権利　residents' rights

入眠　falling asleep

入眠障害　sleep-onset insomnia

入浴　bathing

入浴介助　assistance with bathing

入浴サービス　bathing services

入浴台 bath board

入浴補助用具 assistive bathing aids ; bathroom aids

入浴用いす bath chair ; shower chair

入浴用車いす bathroom wheelchair ; shower wheelchair

ニューロパチー neuropathy

尿 urine

尿意 uresiesthesia

尿管皮膚瘻 ureterocutaneous fistula

尿器 urinary bottle

尿検査 urinalysis : UA

尿酸 uric acid

尿失禁 urinary incontinence

尿処理用装具 equipment for colostomy care

尿素窒素 urea nitrogen

尿糖 glycosuria ; glucosuria

尿道 urethra

尿道カテーテル urethral catheter

尿道瘤 urethrocele

尿毒症 uremia

尿取りパッド urinary incontinence pad

尿閉 urinary retention

尿路 urinary tract

尿路感染症 urinary tract infection : UTI

尿路結石 urolithiasis

尿路疾患 uropathy

尿路ストーマ urostomy

尿路由来敗血症 urosepsis

二類感染症 category II infection ; 2nd-category infection

ニルジェ，ベンクト Bengt Nirje

任意後見制度 voluntary guardianship system ; voluntary guardianship

任意事業 voluntary program

任意入院 voluntary hospitalization

人間の基本的欲求 basic human needs

人間貧困指数 human poverty index : HPI

認知 cognition

認知機能改善療法 cognitive remediation therapy : CRT ; cognitive enhancement therapy

認知行動療法 cognitive behavioral therapy : CBT

認知症 dementia

認知障害 cognitive impairment ; cognitive disorder

認知症介護研究・研修センター Center for Dementia Care Research and Practices : CDCR

認知症介護実践研修 dementia care training for long-term care personnel

認知症介護実践者等養成事業 dementia care training program for long-term care personnel

認知症カフェ dementia cafe ; memory cafe

認知症ケア専門病棟 dementia special care unit ; special care unit

認知症ケアパス dementia care pathway

認知症ケアマッピング dementia care mapping : DCM

認知症高齢者 elderly with dementia

認知症高齢者グループホーム group home for older people with dementia

認知症高齢者の日常生活自立度判定基準 criteria for determining the independence level of elderly with dementia

認知症コールセンター dementia call center ; dementia helpline

認知症サポーター dementia supporters

認知症施策推進5か年計画 Five-Year-Plan to Promote Initiatives for Elderly with Dementia

認知症施策推進総合戦略（新オレンジプラン）～認知症高齢者等にやさしい地域づくりに向けて～ Comprehensive Promotion for Dementia-Related Initiatives (New Orange Plan) : Towards the Establishment of Dementia Friendly Communities

認知症施策等総合支援事業 comprehensive support programs for dementia

認知症疾患医療センター medical center for dementia

認知症初期集中支援チーム initial-phase intensive support team

認知症専門病棟 dementia special care unit ; special care unit

認知状態　cognitive status

*認知症対応型共同生活介護　group home for people with dementia

*認知症対応型通所介護　day care services for people with dementia

認知症地域医療支援事業　dementia care education programs for physicians

認知症地域支援推進員　dementia care coordinator

認知症治療病棟　dementia special care unit ; special care unit

認知症度　degrees of dementia ; stages of dementia

認知症に伴う行動障害と精神症状　behavioral and psychological symptoms of dementia : BPSD

認知症の人のためのケアマネジメントセンター方式　Center Method to Support Persons with Dementia Commentary and Sheet Pack for Care Management

認知症評価尺度　Dementia Rating Scale

認知症ライフサポートモデル　dementia care model

認知症老人徘徊感知機器　dementia wandering alarm

認知的・経験的自己理論　cognitive-experiential self-theory : CEST

認知発達段階　stages of cognitive development

認知リハビリテーション　cognitive rehabilitation

認知療法　cognitive therapy

認定　certification

認定NPO法人　certified nonprofit corporation

認定看護師　certified nurse : CN

認定看護助産師　certified nurse midwife : CNM

認定健康教育士　certified health education specialist : CHES

認定調査　certification assessment ; accreditation survey

認定調査員　certification assessor ; accreditation surveyor

認定調査票　long-term care insurance eligibility assessment forms

認定特定行為業務従事者　authorized personnel for specific medical procedures

ぬ

縫い糸　sewing thread

縫い針　sewing needle

ね

寝返り　rolling over ; turning over

ネクター状液体食　nectar liquid diet

*ネグレクト　neglect

*寝たきり高齢者　bedridden elderly person

寝たきり症候群　disuse syndrome

寝たきり度　levels of being bedridden

寝たきり予防　prevention of becoming bedridden

寝たきり老人ゼロ作戦　bedridden eradication campaign

*熱傷　burn

熱処理　thermal processing ; heat treatment

熱水消毒　hot water disinfection

熱中症　heat stroke

ネットワーキング　networking

熱疲労　heat exhaustion

ネブライザー　nebulizer

ネフローゼ　nephrosis

ネフローゼ症候群　nephritic syndrome

年金　pension

年金基金　pension fund ; superannuation fund

年金給付　pension benefit

年金給付基準法　Pension Benefits Standards Act

年金支給開始年齢　pensionable age

年金事務所　pension office

年金受給資格　eligibility of employee pension

年金受給者　pensioner

年金審議会　National Pension Council

年金制度　pension system

年金積立基金　pension reserve fund

年金手帳　pension handbook

年金保険　pension insurance

年金保険者（介護保険）　pension insurer (long-term care insurance)

•年金保険制度　pension insurance system

年金保険料　pension insurance premium

捻挫　sprain

年少人口　youth population ; young population

粘着気質　athletic type of temperament

年齢差別　agism ; ageism

年齢調整死亡率　age-adjusted death rate : AADR

の

ノイローゼ　neurosis

脳炎　encephalitis

脳外傷　traumatic brain injury : TBI ; head injury

膿痂疹　impetigo

脳下垂体　pituitary gland ; master gland

脳幹　brain stem

脳器質（性）疾患　organic brain disease ; organic brain disorder : OBD

脳血管疾患　cerebrovascular disease : CVD

•脳血管障害　cerebrovascular disease : CVD

•脳血管性認知症　cerebrovascular dementia

•脳血栓（症）　cerebral thrombosis

脳研式知能検査　Noken Intelligence Scale

濃厚飲料　thickened liquid

•脳梗塞　cerebral infarction

濃厚はちみつ状液体食　honey-thickened liquid diet

脳挫傷　cerebral contusion

•脳死　brain death

脳死判定基準　clinical criteria of brain death

脳腫瘍　brain tumor

脳神経　cranial nerve

脳神経疾患　cranial nerve disorder

•脳性麻痺　cerebral palsy : CP

膿栓　tonsil stone ; tonsillolith

•脳塞栓（症）　cerebral embolism

脳卒中　stroke ; cerebrovascular accident

脳卒中機能障害評価法　Stroke Impairment Assessment Set : SIAS

脳卒中情報システム　stroke registry system

能動義手　body-powered prosthesis

脳動脈硬化症　cerebral arteriosclerosis

能動免疫　active immunity

•脳（内）出血　brain hemorrhage cerebral hemorrhage ; intracerebral hemorrhage

膿尿　pyuria

脳波　brain waves

脳波検査　electroencephalography : EEG

脳貧血　cerebral anemia

脳浮腫　cerebral edema

膿瘍　abscess

•能力障害　disability

•ノーマライゼーション　normalization

ノーマライゼーション 7 か年戦略　Seven-Year Normalization Strategy for Persons with Disabilities

伸び上がり歩行　vaulting gait

ノルアドレナリン　noradrenaline : NA

•ノロウイルス　norovirus

•ノンレム睡眠　non-rapid eye movement sleep : NREM sleep ; Non-REM sleep

は

歯　tooth ; teeth

パーキンソン症候群　Parkinson's syndrome

•パーキンソン病　Parkinson's disease ; Parkinson disease : PD

バーセル指数　Barthel Index : BI

パーソナリティ　personality

パーソナリティ障害　personality disorder

パーソナル・スペース　personal space

パーソナル・ソーシャル・サービス　personal social services

パーソンセンタードケア　person-centered care

ハートビル法　Heart Building Act ; Promotion of Building Accessibility for Elderly and Persons with Disabilities Act

ハーネス　harness

パールマン，H.　Helen Harris Perlman

バーンアウト・シンドローム　burnout syndrome	配膳　passing and removing meal trays ; meal
肺移植　lung transplantation	tray services
•肺炎　pneumonia	肺塞栓　pulmonary embolism : PE
肺炎球菌性髄膜炎　pneumococcal meningitis	•バイタルサイン　vital signs
肺炎球菌性肺炎　pneumococcal pneumonia	肺動脈　pulmonary artery
肺炎球菌ワクチン　pneumococcal vaccination	肺動脈閉鎖症　pulmonary atresia
肺炎レンサ球菌　Streptococcus pneumoniae	梅毒　syphilis
バイオハザードマーク　biohazard sign	排尿　urination
•俳徊　wandering	排尿管理　urinary management
背臥位　supine position	排尿訓練　bladder training
俳徊感知器　wandering alarm ; wander alarm	•排尿障害　urinary disorder ; dysuria ;
肺活量　lung capacity ; vital capacity	micturition disorder
胚芽米　brown rice	排尿中枢　micturition center
•肺がん　lung cancer	背部叩打法　back blows
•肺気腫　pulmonary emphysema	排便　defecation ; bowel movement
肺機能検査　pulmonary function tests : PFTs	排便管理　bowel management
肺機能低下　lung function decline	排便訓練　bowel training
廃棄物処理　waste disposal	•排便障害　defecation disorder ; dyschezia
配偶者　spouse	排便補助具　assistive devices for defecation
配偶者虐待　spousal abuse	肺胞　alveolus ; alveoli
配偶者控除　spousal tax deduction	肺胞ガス交換　alveolar gas exchange
背屈　dorsiflexion	肺胞換気　alveolar ventilation
•背景因子（ICF）　contextual factors	肺胞気　alveolar air
敗血　sepsis	肺胞腔　alveolar space
•肺結核　pulmonary tuberculosis	肺胞死腔　alveolar dead space
敗血症　sepsis ; septicemia	肺胞上皮細胞　alveolar epithelial cells
敗血症性ショック　septic shock	肺胞水腫　alveolar edema
背光効果　halo effect	肺胞低換気　alveolar hypoventilation
配合成分（洗剤の）　ingredients (of detergent) ;	肺胞内圧　alveolar pressure
detergent ingredients	肺胞表面張力　alveolar surface tension
肺疾患　lung disease ; pulmonary disease	肺胞浮腫　alveolar edema
配食サービス　meal delivery service ; meals-	肺胞膜　alveolar membrane
on-wheels	肺胞マクロファージ　alveolar macrophage
肺水腫　pulmonary edema	肺胞・毛細血管障壁　alveolar-capillary barrier
バイステック，F. P.　Felix Paul Biestek	•ハイムリッヒ法　Heimlich maneuver
•バイステックの七つの原則　Biestek's seven	•廃症症候群　disuse syndrome
principles of the social work relationship	•廃用性萎縮　disuse atrophy
•排泄　excretion ; toileting	廃用性機能低下　disuse-induced functional
排泄介助　assistance with toileting	decline ; functional decline due to disuse
排泄ケア　assistance with toileting ; toileting	廃用性筋萎縮　disuse muscle atrophy ; disuse
assistance ; bowel and bladder care	atrophy of muscle
排泄スケジュール　toileting schedule	廃用性拘縮　disuse-induced skeletal muscle
排泄物　body wastes	

contracture

廃用性骨粗鬆症（はいようせいこつそしょうしょう）　disuse osteoporosis

肺理学療法　chest physical therapy : CPT

ハヴィガースト, R.　Robert James Havighurst

パウチ　ostomy pouch

吐き気（はくじょう）　nausea

•白杖（はくじょう）　white cane

白癬（はくせん）　tinea ; ringworm

•白内障　cataract

跛行（はこう）　claudication

箱型補聴器　external hearing aid-box type

HACCP　Hazard Analysis Critical Control Point system

橋本甲状腺炎　Hashimoto's thyroiditis

橋本病　Hashimoto's disease

破傷風　tetanus

パス　Program Analysis of Service Systems : PASS

バスボード　bath board

•長谷川式認知症スケール（改訂版）　Hasegawa's Dementia Scale-Revised : HDS-R

パターナリズム　paternalism

肌着　underwear

8020（ハチマル・ニイマル）運動　8020 campaign

波長合わせ　tuning in

発がん　carcinogenesis

発がん遺伝子　oncogene

発汗障害　sweating disorder

発がん物質　carcinogen

罰金　fine ; monetary penalty

白血球　white blood cells : WBC ; leukocytes

白血病　leukemia

発酵　fermentation

発語失行　verbal apraxia ; apraxia of speech

撥水性（はっすいせい）　water repellency

発生（率）　incidence (rate)

発達　development

発達課題　developmental task

発達検査　developmental test

発達指数　developmental quotient : DQ

•発達障害　developmental disability ;

developmental disorder

発達障害者支援センター　Support Center for Persons with Developmental Disorders

発達障害者支援法　Developmental Disabilities Assistance Act

発達性協調運動障害　developmental coordination disorder : DCD

発達段階　stages of development

発達段階説　development theory

発達遅延　developmental delay

発達年齢　developmental age

発達保障　the right to development

発達理論　developmental theory

発熱　fever ; pyrexia

バトラー, R. N.　Robert Neil Butler

パトライト　visual-audible signal device

鼻カニューレ　nasal cannula : NC

バニオン　bunion

パニック障害　panic disorder

ハビリテーション　habilitation

パブリックスペース　public space

パブロフ　Pavlov

ハミルトンうつ病評価尺度　Hamilton Rating Scale for Depression ; Hamilton Depression Rating Scale

パラノイア　paranoia

パラメディカルスタッフ　paramedical staff

パラリンピック　Paralympics

バランス　balance

はり　acupuncture

•バリアフリー　barrier free

バリアフリー住宅　barrier-free home ; barrier-free house

バリアフリーデザイン　barrier-free design

バリアフリー法　Barrier-Free Act ; Promotion of Accessibility for Elderly and Persons with Disabilities Act

バリアフリーマップ　barrier-free map

バリアフリーリフォーム融資　barrier-free home modification loan

はり師　acupuncturist

はり師・きゅう師　acupuncture and moxibustion therapists

095

針生検　needle biopsy

針穿刺　needle puncture

バリデーション　validation

バリデーション療法　validation therapy

・バルーンカテーテル　balloon catheter

パルスオキシメーター　pulse oximeter

バルテス, P. B.　Paul B. Baltes

ハル・ハウス　Hull House

ハロー効果　halo effect

ハローワーク　Hello Work ; public employment security office

ハンカチーフサイン　skin pinch test

半跏趺坐　half lotus sitting position

反響言語　echolalia ; echophrasia ; echologia

反響症　echopathy

反響症状　echophenomenon

反響書字　echographia

反響動作　echomatism ; echopraxia ; echokinesis

反響表情　echomimia

バンク-ミケルセン, N. E.　Niels Erik Bank-Mikkelsen

半合成繊維　semisynthetic fiber

バンコマイシン耐性腸球菌　vancomycin-resistant enterococci : VRE

晩婚　late marriage

瘢痕拘縮　cicatricial contracture ; scar contracture

半座位　half-sitting position ; Fowler's position

反射運動　reflex movement

反射性交感神経性ジストロフィー　reflex sympathetic dystrophy : RSD

反射性尿失禁　reflex incontinence

半身浴　half-body bathing ; lower body bathing

伴性遺伝病　sex-linked disease ; X-linked recessive disorder

ハンセン病　Hansen's disease ; leprosy

ハンセン病対策　Hansen's disease control policy ; leprosy control policy

半側空間無視　unilateral spatial neglect : USN

半側無視　unilateral neglect

半調理　semi-prepared dish ; ready-to-cook food

ハンチントン（舞踏）病　Huntington's disease : HD ; Huntington's chorea

・ハンディキャップ　handicap

反動形成　reaction formation

ハンドライティング　handwriting

ハンドリム　handrim

反応時間　reaction time

反応性精神病　reactive psychosis

販売目的隠匿　concealment fraud

反復唾液嚥下テスト　repetitive saliva swallowing test : RSST

半盲　hemianopia

ひ

ピア・カウンセリング　peer counseling

ピアグループ　peer group

ピアグループスーパービジョン　peer group supervision

ピアサポート　peer support

ピアジェ, J　Jean Piaget

ピアスーパービジョン　peer supervision

BS 法　brainstorming technique

PFC バランス　balance of protein, fat and carbohydrate

BMI　body mass index

PL 法　PL Act ; Products Liability Act

B 型肝炎（ウイルス）　hepatitis B (virus)

ヒートショック　heat-shock response

・BPSD　behavioral and psychological symptoms of dementia

非営利組織　nonprofit organization

鼻炎　rhinitis

皮下　subcutaneous : Sub-Q

非開胸心臓マッサージ　closed-chest cardiac massage ; chest compressions

非開放性損傷　closed wound

・被害妄想　persecutory delusion

日帰り介護　adult day care services

日帰りリハビリテーション　outpatient rehabilitation

皮革製品　leather product

皮下出血　subcutaneous bleeding ; bruising
非課税世帯　tax-exempt household
非課税団体　tax-exempt organization
非価値財　demerit goods
皮下注射　hypodermic injection
非加熱調理　no-heat cooking
非貨幣的ニード　non-monetary need
光環境　lighting environments
光老化　photoaging
引きこもり　social withdrawal
引き戸　sliding door
被虐待高齢者　victim of elder abuse
被虐待児童　victim of child abuse
日暮れ時兆候　sundowning
非経口栄養　parenteral feeding
非結核性抗酸菌症　nontuberculous mycobacterial infection
*非言語的コミュニケーション　nonverbal communication
非行少年　juvenile delinquent
非合理的信念　irrational belief
腓骨神経麻痺　peroneal nerve paralysis
微細脳機能障害　minimal brain dysfunction : MBD
膝折れ　knee giving way ; giving way of the knee
皮脂　sebum
肘置き　armrest
肘台付つえ　platform crutch
皮質下血管性認知症　subcortical vascular dementia
肘這い　creeping
鼻出血　epistaxis ; nasal bleeding ; nosebleeds
肘浴　elbow bathing
非処方薬　non-prescription drug
非審判的態度　nonjudgmental attitude ; non-judgmental attitude
ヒステリー　hysteria
非政府組織　non-governmental organization : NGO
ヒゼンダニ　Acarus scabiei ; Sarcoptes scabiei ; itch mite

非専門的マンパワー　nonprofessional manpower
脾臓　spleen
肥大型心筋症　hypertrophic cardiomyopathy : HCM
肥大性骨関節症　hypertrophic osteoarthropathy : HOA
肥大性肺性骨関節症　hypertrophic pulmonary osteoarthropathy : HPOA
非代替性　nonsubstitutability
*ビタミン　vitamin
ビタミン欠乏症　vitamin deficiency
ビタミンB群　vitamin B complex
左側臥位　left lateral recumbent position : LLR
悲嘆　grief
悲嘆反応　grief reaction
非陳述記憶　implicit memory ; nondeclarative memory
筆記通訳者　blind interpreter
ピック病　Pick's disease
必須アミノ酸　essential amino acid
筆談　written communication
必要前提基準　prerequisite criteria
必要即応の原則　principles of emergency response
非定型精神病　atypical psychosis
ヒト免疫不全ウイルス（感染）　human immunodeficiency virus (infection) : HIV (infection)
ひとり親家庭　single-parent family
ひとり暮らし高齢者　single-living elderly
皮内注射　intradermal injection
避難場所　evacuation site
泌尿器科医　urologist
否認　denial
ビネー式知能検査　Binet Intelligence Test ; Binet Test
微熱　slight fever
皮膚　skin
皮膚炎　dermatitis ; eczema
皮膚科医　dermatologist
皮膚がん　skin cancer
皮膚筋炎　dermatomyositis

被服　clothe ; clothing

被服圧　clothing pressure

被服気候　clothing climate

被服材料　clothing material

皮膚疾患　skin disease

皮膚障害　skin disorder

皮膚消毒　skin antiseptic

皮膚掻痒症　skin pruritus

皮膚損傷　skin tear

被扶養者　dependent

飛蚊症　myodesopsia ; myiodesopsia ; myiodeopsia

ヒポクラテスの誓い　Hippocratic Oath

•被保険者　insured person ; insuree

飛沫感染　droplet infection

飛沫伝播　droplet transmission

飛沫予防策　droplet precaution

•肥満　obesity

肥満指数　obesity index

•秘密保持　confidentiality

秘密保持義務　obligation of confidentiality

秘密保持の原則　principle of confidentiality

ひもときシート　Himotoki Sheets ; unscramble worksheets

日雇健康保険　Day Laborers' Health Insurance

日雇労働者　day laborer

ひやりはっと　Hiyari Hatto reporting ; near-miss reporting

ピューレ状　pureed solid

病院　hospital

病院環境　hospital environment

病院感染　hospital-acquired infection : HAI

病院感染肺炎　hospital-acquired pneumonia

病院機能評価　hospital accreditation

病院基盤型サービス　hospital-based services

病院情報システム　hospital information system

病院ボランティア　hospital volunteer

評価　assessment ; evaluation

評価項目　assessment item

病原体　pathogenic organism ; pathogen

病原大腸菌　pathogenic Escherichia coli

表在感覚　superficial sensation

病識　disease awareness ; awareness of disease ; insight into disease

表示基準　labeling standards

被用者健康保険　employees' health insurance

被用者年金　employees' pension

被用者保険　employees' insurance

標準化　standardization

標準化死亡比　standardized mortality ratio : SMR

標準控除　standard deduction

標準失語症検査　Standard Language Test of Aphasia : SLTA

標準予防策　standard precautions

病床規制　hospital bed control

病診連携　collaboration between outpatient clinics and hospitals

病巣　nidus

病巣感染　focal infection

病態失認　anosognosia

氷枕　ice pillow

病的老化　pathological aging ; secondary aging

病棟　unit ; ward

平等権　equal rights

•氷のう　ice bag

漂白　bleaching

漂白剤　bleaching agent

標本調査　sample survey

費用抑制　cost containment

病理検査　pathology test

鼻翼呼吸　nasal flaring

•日和見感染症　opportunistic infection

平織　plain weave

•開かれた質問　open-ended question

開き戸　hinged door

びらん　erosion

ピリング　pilling

疲労　fatigue

広場恐怖　agoraphobia

•貧血　anemia

頻呼吸　tachypnea

貧困　poverty

貧困家庭　poor family

貧困指数　poverty index

貧困者　poor
貧困水準　poverty level
貧困調査　poverty study
品質管理活動　quality control : QC
頻尿　pollakiuria
頻便　frequent bowel movements
頻脈　tachycardia

ふ

ファーストステップ研修　first steps training
*ファーラー位　Fowler's position
ファイバースコープ　fiberscope
FAST　Functional Assessment Staging Test
ファミリー・アイデンティティ　family identity
ファミリー・ケースワーク　family casework
ファミリー・サポート　family support
ファミリー・サポート・センター　family support
　center
ファミリー・ソーシャルワーク　family social work
ファミリー・ライフサイクル　family life cycle
不安症　anxiety
*不安障害　anxiety disorder
不安神経症　anxiety neurosis
フィブリン　fibrin
フィラメント　filament
フィランソロピー　philanthropy
風疹　rubella
フードガード　food guard
フードガイドピラミッド　food guide pyramid
夫婦家族　conjugal family
夫婦関係　marital relationship
夫婦財産契約　marital property agreement
夫婦療法　marital therapy
風味　flavor
*フェイス・シート　face sheet
フェニールケトン尿症　phenylketonuria : PKU
*フォーマル・ケア　formal care
フォーマルサービス　formal service
*フォロー・アップ　follow-up
不快指数　discomfort index
不感蒸泄　insensible perspiration
腹圧性尿失禁　stress incontinence

幅員　width
*腹臥位　prone position
腹腔鏡検査　laparoscopy ; diagnostic
　laparoscopy
複合家族　joint family ; extended family
複合型サービス福祉事業　combined senior
　care services program
副交感神経　parasympathetic nerve
複雑骨折　compound fracture
*副作用　side effect
副子　splint
*福祉　welfare ; social services
福祉改革　welfare reform
福祉型障害児入所施設　welfare facility for
　children with disabilities
福祉関係八法の改正　Reform of the Eight Acts
　related to Social Welfare
*福祉機器　adaptive equipment
*腹式呼吸　abdominal breathing ;
　diaphragmatic breathing ; belly breathing
福祉教育　welfare education program
福祉行政　welfare administration
福祉圏域　welfare service area
福祉公社　public social welfare corporation
福祉国家　welfare state
福祉コミュニティ　community welfare
　organization
福祉サービス　welfare services ; social
　services
福祉(サービス)供給システム　social services
　supply system
福祉サービス第三者評価制度　third party
　quality certification system for social welfare
　services
福祉サービス利用援助事業　assistance
　program for utilization of social welfare
　services
福祉三法　Three Acts of Social Welfare ; three
　welfare laws
*福祉事務所　welfare office ; public welfare
　office
福祉社会　welfare society
福祉車両　disability vehicle

福祉住環境コーディネーター　housing and environment coordinator

福祉人材確保指針　Guidelines for the Recruitment and Retention of Social Welfare Personnel

福祉政策　welfare policy

福祉制度　welfare system

福祉専門職　social welfare professional

福祉手当　welfare allowance

福祉電話　telephone assistive device ; assistive listening and technology device

福祉ニーズ　welfare needs

福祉のまちづくり　community development

福祉避難所　special needs shelter

福祉ホーム　welfare home

福祉マンパワー　social welfare-related manpower

福祉ミックス　welfare mix

副主治医　secondary physician

*福祉用具　adaptive equipment ; technical aid ; assistive device ; assistive technology : AT

福祉用具・介護ロボット実用化支援事業　assistance program for promoting the development of the practical adaptive equipment and elder care robots

福祉用具産業　adaptive equipment industry ; technical aids industry

福祉用具JISマーク　Japanese Industrial Standards sign for adaptive equipment

福祉用具専門相談員　adaptive equipment advisor ; technical aids advisor

*福祉用具貸与　adaptive equipment rental services ; technical aids rental services

福祉用具の研究開発及び普及の促進に関する法律　Promotion of Research, Development and Dissemination of Adaptive Equipment Act

福祉用具分類コード　Classification Code of Technical Aids : CCTA

福祉用具法　Adaptive Equipment Act ; Assistive Technology Act

福祉倫理　welfare ethics

福祉レクリエーション　welfare and recreation

福祉六法　Six Acts of Social Welfare

副腎髄質　adrenal medulla

副腎皮質　adrenal cortex

腹水　ascites

フグ中毒　puffer fish poisoning ; tetrodotoxin poisoning ; fugu poisoning

腹痛　abdominalgia ; abdominal pain

腹部超音波検査　abdominal ultrasound

腹膜透析　peritoneal dialysis : PD

含み声　muffled voice

含め煮　simmering

服薬管理　medication management

服薬遵守　medication compliance

不潔区域　contaminated area

不潔行為　urination and defecation-related inappropriate behaviors

不潔創　dirty wound

不潔物収納室　dirty utility room

不顕性感染　silent infection ; inapparent infection

不顕性誤嚥　silent aspiration ; inapparent aspiration

撫擦法　stroking

父子家庭　single-father family ; motherless family

父子世帯　single-father household ; motherless household

*浮腫　edema

不織布　nonwoven fabric

婦人科医　gynecologist

不随意運動　involuntary movement

不正行為　malpractice

不正咬合　malocclusion

不正受給　public assistance fraud ; benefit fraud

不正請求　billing fraud

不整脈　arrhythmia

不全片麻痺　hemiparesis

不全四肢麻痺　incomplete quadriplegia

不全対麻痺　paraparesis

不全麻痺　paresis

二人部屋　semi-private room

負担　burden

負担率　burden rate

普通型車いす　standard wheelchair
普通出生率　crude birth rate : CBR
普通食　regular diet
普通徴収　regular levy
物価　cost-of-living
物質的虐待　material abuse
物質文化　material culture
物質誘発性精神病　substance-induced
　psychosis
物質乱用　substance abuse
物理医学　physical medicine
物理的障壁　physical barrier
物理療法　physiotherapy
不適応　maladjustment
不適応行動　maladjusted behavior
ブドウ球菌　Staphylococcus
不登校　school absenteeism
ブドウ糖　glucose
舞踏病様運動　chorea
不当労働行為　unfair labor practice : ULP
布団カバー　duvet cover
負の価値財　demerit goods
負の強化　negative reinforcement
負の罰　negative punishment
不平等　inequality
不服申立て（制度）　appeal (system)
部分介助　limited assistance
部分清拭　partial sponge bath ; partial bed
　bath
部分浴　partial bath
普遍主義　universalism
不飽和脂肪酸　unsaturated fatty acid
不眠（症）　insomnia ; sleeplessness
不明熱　fever of unknown origin : FUO
扶養義務　responsibility to support
　dependents
扶養義務者　person responsible for
　dependent family members
扶養控除　tax deductions for dependents
扶養手当　dependency allowance
•プライバシー　privacy
プライバシー空間　space of privacy
プライバシー保護　privacy protection

プライベートスペース　private space
•プライマリ・ケア　primary care
プライマリ・ケア医　primary care physician :
　PCP
プライマリ・ヘルス・ケア　primary health care :
　PHC
フラストレーション　frustration
フラストレーション耐性　frustration tolerance
プラセボ効果　placebo effect
フラッシュバック　flashback
フラッシュベル　flashing light ; flashing call
　indicator lights
プラットホームクラッチ　platform crutch
ブランチング　blanching
プラン・ドゥ・シー　plan-do-see cycle : PDS
　cycle
ブリーフセラピー　brief therapy
振り塩法　salt sprinkling
プリ・テスト　pretest
不良肢位　malposition
不良姿勢　malposture
浮力作用　buoyant effect
不慮の事故（家庭内における）　unexpected
　accident (at home)
ブルンストローム・ステージ　Brunnstrom stage
プレイセラピー　play therapy
ブレーンストーミング法　brainstorming
　technique
フロイト, S.　Sigmund Freud
ブロイラー, E.　Eugen Bleuler
ブローカ失語　Broca's aphasia
ブローカ野　Broca's area
フローとストック　stock and flow
プログラム説　programmed theory
プロゲステロン療法　progesterone therapy
プロセス　process
プロセス・ゴール　process-goal
プロセス・レコード　process recording
プロダクティブ　productive
プロダクティブ・エイジング　productive aging
プロパンガス　propane gas
憤慨型　angry men
文化的障壁　cultural barrier

和英

あ か さ た な へ ま や ら わ

文化的同化　cultural assimilation
文化変容　acculturation
文章完成テスト　Sentence Completion Test：
　SCT
分析　analysis
糞便検査　fecal examination；stool
　examination
分回し歩行　circumduction gait
分離　isolation；separation
分離不安（障害）　separation anxiety (disorder)

へ

平均在院日数　average length of stay：ALOS
*平均寿命　average life span
平均世帯人員　average household size
平均薬価　average price of drugs
*平均余命　life expectancy
閉経　menopause
平衡　equilibrium；balance
平衡（機能）障害　balance disorder
平行棒　parallel bar
米国知的・発達障害学会　American
　Association of Intellectual and
　Developmental Disabilities：AAIDD
閉鎖骨折　closed fracture
閉鎖施設　locked facility
閉鎖病棟　locked unit
閉塞性睡眠時無呼吸症候群　obstructive sleep
　apnea syndrome：OSAS
閉塞性動脈硬化症　arteriosclerosis obliterans
平熱　normal temperature
平面計画　zoning；land-use planning
ベヴァリッジ報告　Beveridge Report
ペースト食　pureed diet
*ペースメーカー　pacemaker
ベーチェット病　Behcet's disease；Behcet's
　syndrome
へき地医療体制　rural and remote healthcare
　system
ペクチン　pectin
ベック抑うつ評価尺度　Beck Depression
　Inventory：BDI

ペット　PET；positron emission tomography
ベッド柵　bedside rail
ベッド上肢位　bed positioning
ベッドリフト　bed lift
ベビーブーマー　baby boomer
ベビーブーム　baby boom
ベビーブーム世代　baby boom generation
ヘマトクリット　hematocrit
ヘモグロビン　hemoglobin：Hb
ヘリコバクター・ピロリ　Helicobacter pylori：H.
　pylori
ヘルシンキ宣言　Declaration of Helsinki
ヘルスプロモーション　health promotion
便　feces；stool；excrement
便意　bowel movement
返還請求　claims for refund
*便器　toilet bowl；bedpan
便器洗浄機　bedpan washer
変形　deformity
変形性関節症　osteoarthritis：OA
変形性頚椎症　cervical spondylosis
変形性股関節症　coxarthrosis
変形性膝関節症　knee osteoarthritis；
　gonarthrosis；(unilateral) knee osteoarthritis
変形性脊椎症　spondylosis deformans
偏見　prejudice
ベンザルコニウム塩化物溶液　benzalkonium
　chloride solution
*便失禁　fecal incontinence：FI；bowel
　incontinence
変質（食品の）　food spoilage
変質（精神医学における）　psychopathic
　degeneration
偏執病　paranoia
変色　discoloration
便処理用装具　stoma bags and accessories
片頭痛　migraine headache
変性疾患　degenerative disease
便潜血検査　fecal occult blood test：FOBT
便通　bowel movement
扁桃腺　tonsil
*便秘　constipation
返品特約　return policy

102

扁平上皮がん　squamous cell carcinoma

扁平足　pes planus ; flat foot ; fallen arches

弁別刺激　discriminative stimulus

弁膜異常　valvular abnormality

弁膜症　valvular disease

ほ

保育　nursery care

保育園　nursery school ; child day care center

保育士　certified child care worker : CCCW

保育所　nursery school ; child day care center

保育所等訪問支援事業　Onsite Assistance Program for children with disabilities

防衛機制　defense mechanism

防炎素材　flame-resistant material

防汚素材　soil-resistant material

放課後子どもプラン推進事業　promotional program for afterschool child care

放課後等デイサービス　after-school and weekend program

蜂窩織炎　cellulitis

防火対策　fire prevention ; fire prevention policy

包括医療　comprehensive health care

包括型地域生活支援　assertive community treatment : ACT

包括性　inclusion

包括的医療　comprehensive medical care ; comprehensive health care

包括的・継続的ケアマネジメント支援業務　comprehensive and continuous care management

包括的支援事業　comprehensive assistance program

包括的地域ケアシステム　comprehensive community care system

放棄　neglect

膀胱　bladder

膀胱炎　cystitis ; urocystitis

膀胱鏡検査　cystoscopy

膀胱訓練　bladder training

膀胱脱　cystocele

膀胱・直腸機能障害　bladder and bowel dysfunction

膀胱内圧測定　cystometry ; cystometrography

膀胱瘤　cystocele

膀胱瘻　bladder fistula

防護環境　protective environment : PE

防災　disaster prevention and preparedness

放射線　radiation

放射線治療　radiation therapy

法人　corporation

法人税　corporate tax ; corporation tax

法人番号　corporate identification number : CIN

防水シーツ　waterproof sheet

紡績　yarn spinning

蜂巣織炎　cellulitis

包帯　bandage

防虫剤　mothball

法定後見　legal guardian

法定後見制度　legal guardianship

法定雇用率　mandatory employment rates of people with disabilities

法定受託事務　delegated statutory duties

法定相続分　inheritance rights

法定代理受領　long-term care insurance reimbursement

法定代理人　legal representative

法定伝染病　legally designated infectious disease ; reportable infectious disease

法的義務　legal obligation

乏尿　oliguria ; hypouresis

放任　neglect

防犯対策　crime prevention policy

防腐剤　antiseptic

方面委員制度　district committee system

*訪問介護　home care

訪問介護員　home helper ; home care aide

訪問介護計画　home care plan of care ; home-care care plans

訪問介護事業　home care program

*訪問看護　home health

訪問看護計画　home health plan of care

訪問看護師　home health nurse

103

和
英

あ
か
さ
た
な
ほ
ま
や
ら
わ

訪問看護ステーション　home visiting nursing station

訪問看護療養費　reimbursement for home health and home care services

訪問教育　onsite educational program

訪問口腔衛生　mobile oral health services

訪問歯科衛生　mobile dental hygiene services

訪問歯科衛生指導　mobile oral health and dental services

訪問指導　educational home visiting program

訪問調査　onsite assessment ; onsite evaluation ; onsite inspection

訪問調査員　site assessor ; site evaluator ; site inspector

訪問入浴介護　in-home bathing services

訪問販売　door-to-door sales

訪問面接　on-site interview

訪問薬剤管理指導　home- based medication management and education

訪問リハビリテーション　home-based rehabilitation

訪問理美容サービス　mobile beauty services

法律支援　legal assistance

暴力　violence

法令違反　law violation

ポータブルトイレ　commode ; bedside commode

ポータブル浴槽　portable bathtub

ホームヘルスサービス　home health services

ホームヘルパー　home helper ; home care aide

ホームレス　homeless person

ホームレス自立支援法　Homeless Self-Reliance Support Act ; Special Initiatives to Assist Homeless to Achieve the Maximum Degrees of Self-Reliance Act

ホームレスの自立の支援等に関する特別措置法　Special Initiatives to Assist Homeless to Achieve the Maximum Degrees of Self-Reliance Act : Homeless Self-Reliance Support Act

保温性（衣服の）　thermal insulation (of clothing)

保温性加工　thermal-insulation finish

歩隔　stride width ; step width

補完医療　complementary medicine

補完代替医療　complementary and alternative medicine : CAM

保菌者　carrier

保険　insurance

保険医　insurance doctor

保険医療機関　designated insurance hospital

保健医療従事者　health care personnel

保健・医療・福祉の連携　collaboration between health and welfare sectors

保健機能食品　food with health claims

保険給付　insurance benefit

保健行動　health behavior

保健師　public health nurse : PHN

保健師助産師看護師法　Public Health Nurses, Midwives and Nurses Act

保健指導　health guidance

保険者　insurer

保健所　public health center

保険証　insurance card

保健センター　local health center

保険料　insurance premium

保険料の免除（国民年金）　premium exemption (National Pension)

保険料率　insurance premium rates

歩行　gait ; ambulation ; walk

補高　elevation

歩行介助　assistance with ambulation

歩行器　walker

歩行器型つえ　pyramid cane ; hemi walker

歩行機能評価　gait assessment

歩行訓練　ambulation training ; gait training

歩行困難　gait difficulty

歩行失行　gait apraxia

歩行車　four-wheel walker

歩行周期　gait cycle ; walking cycle

歩行障害　gait disability ; gait disorder

歩行速度　gait velocity ; gait speed

歩行動作　gait activity

歩行能力　gait ability ; ambulation ability ; walking ability

歩行パターン　gait pattern

歩行補助具　walking aid

歩行補助つえ　walking cane

歩行練習　gait training

保護施設　custodial facility

保護司法　Volunteer Probation Officers Act

保護者　guardian

保護の実施機関　public assistance provider

保佐　conservatorship

保佐人　conservator

保持　storage ; maintenance

母子及び寡婦福祉法　Welfare of Single-Mother Families and Widows Act

母子及び父子並びに寡婦福祉法　Welfare of Single-Parent Families and Widows Act

母子家庭　single-mother family ; fatherless family

母子感染　mother-to-child transmission

母子健康手帳　maternal and children health handbook

母子指導員　single-parent counselor

ポジショニング　positioning

母子世帯　single-mother household ; fatherless household

母子相談員　single-parent adviser

ポジトロン・エミッション・トモグラフィー　positron emission tomography : PET

母子福祉　welfare of fatherless families

母子福祉資金貸付制度　financial loan system for single- mothers

母子父子寡婦福祉資金　financial loan system for single-parent families and widows

母子保健　maternal and child health

母子保健法　Maternal and Child Health Act

補助技術　assistive technology : AT

補助金　subsidy

補助金の一般財源化　intergovernmental transfers of revenue from central to local government

補助具　technical aid

補助犬　service dog

補助呼吸筋　accessory respiratory muscle

ホスピス　hospice

ホスピスケア　hospice care

ホスピタリズム　hospitalism

母性　maternal ; motherhood

保清介助　assistance with personal hygiene

補装具　adaptive equipment ; assistive appliance

補装具費　disability benefits for adaptive equipment ; adaptive equipment benefit

補足給付　supplementary benefit

保存料　preservative

•補聴器　hearing aid

発作　seizure

発疹　skin rash

•発赤　erythema ; skin redness

ホットパック　hot pack

ボツリヌス菌　Clostridium botulinum

補綴　prosthetic

•ボディメカニクス　body mechanics

歩幅　step length

ホメオスタシス　homeostasis

歩容　gait

•ボランティア　volunteer

ボランティア活動　volunteering

ボランティアコーディネーター　volunteer coordinator

ボランティアセンター　volunteer center

ボランティアリズム　voluntarism

ポリープ　polyp

ポリウレタン　polyurethane

ポリエステル　polyester

ポリエステルアレルギー　polyester allergy

ポリオ　poliomyelitis : polio

ポリオ後症候群　post-polio syndrome : PPS

ホルターモニタ　Holter monitor

ホルネル症候群　Horner syndrome

ホルムアルデヒド　formaldehyde

•ホルモン　hormones

ホルモン補充療法　hormone replacement therapy : HRT

本態性高血圧　essential hypertension

ま

マーク　symbol ; sign

マイナンバー法　My Number Act : The Use of Numbers to Identify a Specific Individual in the Administrative Procedure Act

前払い型グループ診療　prepaid group practice : PGP

マクギル疼痛質問表　McGill Pain Questionnaire : MPQ

マグネシウム　magnesium

摩擦　friction

麻疹　measles ; rubeola ; morbilli

麻酔　anesthesia

麻酔剤　anesthetic

マスク　surgical mask

マズロー，A. H.　Abraham Harold Maslow

マズローの欲求段階　Maslow's hierarchy of needs

マダニ　tick

まだら認知症　lacunar dementia

末期腎不全　end-stage renal disease : ESRD

末期の水　water of the last moment

マッサージ　massage

マッサージ師　massage therapist

マッサージ療法　massage therapy

末梢血管疾患　peripheral vascular disease

末梢静脈栄養法　peripheral parenteral nutrition : PPN

末梢神経　peripheral nerve

末梢神経障害　peripheral neuropathy : PN

末梢神経性障害　peripheral nerve disorder

末梢神経麻痺　peripheral nerve palsy

末梢動脈疾患　peripheral arterial disease : PAD

末梢動脈閉塞性疾患　peripheral arterial occlusive disease : PAOD

末梢浮腫　peripheral edema

*松葉づえ　crutch ; axillary crutch ; underarm crutch

松葉づえ歩行　crutch gait

間取り　floor plan ; house plan

マネジドケア　managed care

マネジドヘルスケア　managed health care

*麻痺　paralysis ; paresis

麻痺性構音障害　ataxic dysarthria

摩耗抵抗　abrasion resistance

麻薬　narcotic ; narcotic drug

麻薬中毒　narcotic addiction

慢性胃炎　chronic gastritis

慢性肝炎　chronic hepatitis

慢性期　chronic stage ; chronic phase

慢性硬膜下血腫　chronic subdural hematoma

慢性呼吸不全　chronic respiratory failure

慢性骨髄性白血病　chronic myelogenous leukemia ; chronic myeloid leukemia : CML

慢性疾患　chronic disease

慢性疾患療法機能評価　Functional Assessment of Chronic Illness Therapy : FACIT

慢性腎臓病　chronic kidney disease : CKD

慢性腎不全　chronic renal failure : CRF

慢性疼痛　chronic pain

慢性疲労症候群　chronic fatigue syndrome : CFS

慢性閉塞性肺疾患　chronic obstructive pulmonary disease : COPD

慢性リンパ性白血病　chronic lymphocytic leukemia ; chronic lymphoid leukemia : CLL

満足度調査　satisfaction survey

マンパワー　manpower

満腹中枢　satiety center

マンモグラフィ　mammography

マンモグラム　mammogram

み

ミーンズ・テスト　means test

味覚　gustation ; sense of taste

右片麻痺　right-side hemiplegia ; paralysis on the right side of the body

*ミキサー食　blenderized diet ; blended diet : BD

右側臥位　right lateral recumbent position : RLR

未熟児　premature infant ; preemie

水飲みテスト（改訂版）　Modified Water Swallowing Test

未成年　minor

未成年後見人　guardian of minor

ミトコンドリア病　mitochondrial disease

看取り　end-of-life care

看取り介護　end-of-life care

ミニ脳卒中　mini stroke

ミニマムデータセット　Minimum Data Set : MDS

*ミニメンタルステート検査　Mini-Mental State
　Examination : MMSE

*ミネラル　mineral

ミネラル欠乏症　mineral deficiency

ミネラル補給　mineral supplementation

身分証明書　identification

耳垢　cerumen ; earwax

耳鳴り　tinnitus

*脈拍　pulse

三宅式記銘力検査　Miyake Paired Verbal
　Association Learning Test

味蕾　taste buds

民間医療保険　private health insurance

民間介護保険　private long-term care
　insurance

民間事業者による老後の保健及び福祉のための
　総合的施設の整備の促進に関する法律
　Well-Aging Community Act : WAC Act

民間年金　private pension

民間非営利組織　private nonprofit organization

民間病院　private hospital

民間保険　private insurance

民生委員　commissioned welfare volunteer

民生委員協議会　council of commissioned
　welfare volunteers

民生委員法　Commissioned Welfare
　Volunteers Act

ミンチ食　minced diet

民法　civil law

む

無為　avolition ; inaction

無意識　unconsciousness

無医地区　medically underserved area

無塩　no added salt : NAS

無塩食　no added salt diet : NAS diet

無危害原則（医療倫理）　non-maleficence
　(health care ethics)

無機質　inorganic solid

無気肺　pulmonary atelectasis

無気力　lethargy

無呼吸　apnea

無呼吸低呼吸指数　Apnea-Hypopnea Index :
　AHI

無言　mutism ; speechless ; silent

無作為抽出法　random sampling

無差別平等　equality and non-discrimination

無差別平等の原理　principles of equality and
　non-discrimination

無酸素訓練　anaerobic exercise

無酸素血症　anoxemia

無酸素症　anoxia

無酸素性作業閾値　anaerobic threshold : AT

無歯症　edentulism

無条件刺激　unconditioned stimulus

無条件反応　unconditioned response

無症候性キャリア　asymptomatic carrier

無床診療所　bedless hospital ; outpatient
　hospital ; hospital without beds

無償労働　unpaid labor

無職　unemployment ; jobless

むずむず脚症候群　restless legs syndrome

むち打ち症　whiplash

六つの基礎食品　six basic food groups

無動　akinesia

無尿　anuria

胸やけ　heartburn

無保険者　uninsured

無料　free of charge

無料商法　free trial scam

め

明暗順応　light and dark adaptation

名称　name ; title

名称独占　protected title

名称の使用制限　restriction on the use of an
　occupational title

迷信　superstition

酩酊 drunkenness ; intoxication

*メタボリックシンドローム metabolic syndrome

*メチシリン耐性黄色ブドウ球菌 methicillin-resistant Staphylococcus aureus : MRSA

*滅菌 sterilization

滅裂思考 disorganized thinking

メディカル・ソーシャルワーカー medical social worker : MSW

メニエール病 Meniere's disease ; Meniere disease

メノポーズ menopause

めまい dizziness ; vertigo

メラニン細胞 melanocyte

メラノサイト melanocyte

メラミン樹脂 melamine resin

メリット財 merit goods

メリヤス weft knitting ; course

メレンゲ meringue

綿 cotton

*免疫 immunity

免疫グロブリン immunoglobulin : Ig

免疫システム immune system

免疫不全 immunodeficiency

免疫抑制剤 immunosuppressant drug

免疫療法 immunotherapy

免許 license

面接 interview

面接技法 interviewing techniques

面接調査 interview survey

面接法（社会福祉調査） interview method (social work research)

メンタルヘルス（ケア） mental health (care)

メンタルヘルス指針 Mental Health Guidelines ; Guidelines for Promoting Mental Health Care of Workers

メンテナンス（建物の維持管理） maintenance (maintenance and management of buildings)

綿棒 cotton swab

も

喪 mourning

盲 blindness

盲学校 school for the blind and visually impaired

盲児施設 facility for blind and visually impaired children

盲人ホーム home for the blind and visually impaired

盲人用読書器 optical-to-tactile converter

*妄想 delusion ; paranoia

妄想性障害 delusional disorder

妄想反応 paranoid reaction

妄想様観念 secondary delusion ; delusion-like idea

盲導犬 guide dog ; seeing-eye dog

毛嚢炎 folliculitis

網膜 retina

網膜黄斑部変性症 macular degeneration

網膜芽細胞腫 retinoblastoma

網膜出血 retinal hemorrhage

網膜症 retinopathy

網膜中心動脈閉塞症 central retinal artery occlusion

網膜剥離 retinal detachment

盲ろう deaf-blindness

もうろう状態 twilight state

盲老人ホーム home for the elderly blind

*燃えつき症候群 burnout syndrome

目標（設定） goal (setting)

もく浴剤 bath powder

モジュール module

モジュラー型車いす modular wheelchair

モジュラー型義肢 modular prosthetic limb

求められる介護福祉士像 required roles and responsibilities of care workers

*モニタリング monitoring

物盗られ妄想 paranoid about being stolen from ; delusion of being stolen from

物忘れ forgetfulness

モラール morale

モルヒネ morphine

モルヒネ型依存 morphine addiction

問題解決アプローチ problem solving approach

問題解決過程 problem solving process

*問題行動　problem behavior
問題志向記録　problem-oriented record : POR

や

野外レクリエーション　outdoor recreational activity
夜間介護　night care ; night time care
*夜間せん妄　nighttime delirium
夜間対応型訪問介護　night time home care
夜間病院　night hospital ; night time hospital
夜間副子　night splint
夜勤　night shift
薬剤　medication ; drug
薬剤管理　medication management
*薬剤師　pharmacist
薬剤性肝炎　drug-induced hepatitis
薬剤性肝疾患　drug-induced liver disease
薬剤性急性膵炎　drug-induced acute pancreatitis
薬剤性骨粗鬆症　drug-induced osteoporosis
薬剤性膵炎　drug-induced pancreatitis
薬剤性精神病　drug-induced psychosis
薬剤性統合失調症　drug-induced Schizophrenia
薬剤性パーキンソニズム　drug-induced Parkinsonism
薬剤性慢性膵炎　drug-induced chronic pancreatitis
薬剤副作用　adverse drug reaction : ADR
薬剤誘発性ループス　drug-induced lupus
薬事監視　pharmaceutical inspection
薬事監視員　pharmaceutical inspector
薬事法　Pharmaceutical Affairs Act ; Safety Assurance and Quality Improvement of Pharmaceutical Products and Medical Devices Act
薬疹　drug rash
薬物アレルギー　drug allergy
薬物依存　drug addiction
薬物更生施設　drug rehab center
薬物拘束　chemical restraint
薬物相互作用　medication interaction

薬物中毒　drug intoxication
薬物乱用　drug abuse ; substance abuse
*薬物療法　pharmacotherapy ; drug therapy
役割　role
役割演技　role play ; role playing
役割葛藤　role conflict
役割行動　role behavior
役割認知　role perception
役割理論　role theory
火傷　burn
ヤコブ病　Creutzfeldt-Jakob disease : CJD
矢田部 - ギルフォード性格検査　Yatabe-Guilford Personality Test
薬局　pharmacy
夜尿症　nocturia ; nycturia
夜盲症　night blindness ; nyctalopia

ゆ

遺言者　testator
遺言書　will ; testament
友愛組合　friendly society
友愛訪問　friendly visiting ; friendly visiting program
友愛訪問員　friendly visitor
誘因　incentive ; motive
USBフラッシュメモリ　USB flash drive
有機食品表示　organic food labeling
有機農産物・特別栽培農産物　organic agricultural products and specially grown products
有給休暇　paid time off : PTO
有機溶剤依存　organic solvent abuse
遊戯療法　play therapy
夕暮れ症候群　sundown syndrome ; sundowning
有効視野　useful field of view : UFOV
有床診療所　outpatient clinic with inpatient beds
有償ボランティア　paid volunteer
優性遺伝　dominant inheritance
優生学　eugenics
優性保護　eugenic protection

109

優先座席　priority seat

有訴者率　rates of subjective symptoms

有痛性脂肪症　adiposis dolorosa ; Dercum disease

有痛性歩行　antalgic gait

誘電加熱　dielectric heating

誘導加熱　induction heating

有病　prevalence

有病率　prevalence rate

遊離脂肪酸　non-esterified fatty acid : NEFA

遊離ホルムアルデヒド　free formaldehyde

有料老人ホーム　private elderly care home ; retirement home

有料老人ホーム協会　Japanese Association of Retirement Housing

有料老人ホーム設置運営標準指導指針　Standards and Guidelines for the Establishment and Administration of Private Elderly Care Homes

浴衣　bathrobe

輸血　blood transfusion

輸血後肝炎　post-transfusion hepatitis

油脂　fats and oils

ユニセフ　United Nations Children's Fund : UNICEF

ユニット　unit

ユニット型特別養護老人ホーム　unit-based welfare facility for the elderly

ユニットケア　unit-based care

ユニバーサルデザイン　universal design

ユニバーサルデザイン政策大綱　General Principles of Universal Design Policy

ユニバーサルファッション　universal fashion ; universal style

ユネスコ　United Nations Educational, Scientific and Cultural Organization : UNESCO

指文字　fingerspelling ; dactylology

ゆりかごから墓場まで　from the cradle to the grave

よ

要介護高齢者のレクリエーション　recreational activity for long-term care recipients

養介護施設　elderly care facility

要介護者　care-required ; certified as needing care

要介護状態　in need of care

要介護状態区分　classification of level of care-required

要介護度　classification of level of care-required

要介護認定　certification of long-term care insurance care-required benefits

要介護認定等基準時間　standard hours of care per day for long-term care insurance benefits

要介護認定の審査判定基準　certification standards for long-term care insurance care-required benefits

要介護認定有効期間　validity period of certification of long-term care insurance care-required benefits

要介護被保険者　care-required category insured person

養護　foster care ; custodial care

養護委託　adult foster care

養護学校　school for children with disabilities ; school for disabled children

擁護活動　advocacy

養護施設　children's residential care home ; children's home

養護者　caregiver

養護受託者　foster caregiver

養護老人ホーム　adult foster care facility

養護老人ホームの設備及び運営に関する基準　equipment maintenance and facility operation standards for adult foster care facilities

養護老人ホームの入所措置の基準　admission standards for adult foster care facilities

葉酸　folic acid

養子　adopted child

養子縁組　adoption
•要支援者　assistance-required ; certified as needing assistance
要支援状態　in need of assistance
要支援状態区分　classification of level of assistance-required
•要支援認定　certification of long-term care insurance assistance-required benefits
要支援認定の審査判定基準　certification standards for long-term care insurance assistance-required benefits
要支援認定有効期間　validity period of certification of long-term care insurance assistance-required benefits
腰髄損傷　lumbar spinal cord injury
陽性症状　positive symptom
陽性所見　positive finding
陽性モデル　positive mold
ヨウ素　iodine
腰椎　lumbar vertebrae
腰椎圧迫骨折　lumbar compression fracture
腰椎椎間板ヘルニア　lumbar herniated disc
•腰痛　low back pain ; lumbago
•腰痛予防　prevention of low back pain
陽電子放射断層撮影法　positron emission tomography : PET
羊毛　wool
要約記録　summary recording
要約体　summary style
要約筆記者　blind interpreter
養老院　almshouse
余暇　leisure
余暇時間　leisure time ; spare time ; free time
余暇生活　leisurely living
余暇(生活)設計　leisure planning
余暇(生活)相談　leisure consulting
余暇政策　leisure policy
余暇の善用　good use of leisure time
余暇プログラム　leisure program
余暇問題　issues in recreation and leisure
抑圧　repression
抑うつ　depression
抑うつ自己評価尺度　Center for Epidemiological Studies Depression Scale : CES-D
抑うつ状態　depressive state
抑うつ神経症　depressive neurosis
浴室改修　bathroom modification
浴室の住環境整備　optimization of bathroom environment
浴比　detergent-to-load ratio ; laundry detergent ratio
予後　prognosis
横出しサービス　supplemental service
予後予測　prognosis and prediction
予算　budget
予算編成　budgeting
四次予防　quaternary prevention
欲求　needs
欲求階層説　hierarchy of needs theory
欲求の五段階説　five-stage hierarchy of needs ; hierarchy of needs five-stage model
欲求不満　frustration
欲求不満耐性　frustration tolerance
四つの食品群　four food groups
四つのP　Four P's : 4 P's
四つ這い　crawling
予防　prevention
予防医学　preventive medicine
予防隔離　protective isolation
•予防給付　preventive benefit
予防ケア　preventive care
予防サービス　preventive services
予防処置　preventive treatment
予防接種　vaccination
予防接種証明書　proof of vaccination ; proof of immunization
予防接種法　Vaccinations Act
世論調査　public opinion poll
四脚づえ　quad cane ; four-legged cane
四種混合ワクチン　diphtheria, tetanus, pertussis and polio vaccine : DTaP-IPV
四点歩行　four-point gait
四輪歩行車　four-wheel walker
四類感染症　category IV infection ; 4th-category infection

ら

癩 leprosy
来院時心停止 dead on arrival：DOA
来談者中心療法 client-centered therapy
来談面接 visitor's interview
ライチャード, S. Suzanne Reichard
ライフコース life course
ライフサイクル life cycle
ライブ・スーパービジョン live supervision
ライフステージ life stage；stages of life
*ライフレビュー life review；reminiscence
ラッサ熱 Lassa fever
ラポール形成 rapport building
*ラポール（ラポート） rapport
ランゲルハンス島 islets of Langerhans；
　pancreatic islets
乱視 astigmatism
卵巣 ovary
卵巣がん ovarian cancer
ランドリー laundry
ランドルト環 Landolt C；Landolt ring；Landolt
　broken ring
卵胞ホルモン estrogen

り

リアリティ・オリエンテーション reality orientation
リーダーシップ leadership
リーチャー reacher；grabber
リイ・モティベーション remotivation
リウマチ rheumatism；rheumatic disorder
リウマチ性多発筋痛症 polymyalgia
　rheumatica：PMR
リウマチ専門医 rheumatologist
理解促進研修・啓発事業 promotion of public
　awareness and understanding of
　developmental disabilities
理解・判断力の障害 impairment of judgment
　and comprehension deficits
理学療法 physical therapy；physiotherapy：
　PT
理学療法医 physiatrist；rehabilitation
physician
*理学療法士 physical therapist：PT
理学療法士及び作業療法士法 Physical
　Therapists and Occupational Therapists Act
罹患 incidence
罹患率 incidence rate
リクライニング型車いす reclining wheelchair
リクライニング・ティルト式普通型車いす
　reclining and tilting wheelchair
離婚 divorce
離婚証明書 divorce certificate
離床 out of bed
利殖商法 investment fraud
離職率 turnover rate
離人症 depersonalization disorder
リスク risk
リスクアセスメント risk assessment
リスク管理 risk control
リスクマネジメント risk management
リズム rhythm
理想体重 ideal body weight：IBW
離脱 disengagement
離脱症状 withdrawal symptom
離脱理論 disengagement theory
リチウム lithium
*立位 standing position
立位訓練 standing exercise
リッチモンド, M. Mary Ellen Richmond
立法者 lawmaker；legislator
離島等相当サービス equivalent services for
　islands and mountainous regions
利尿剤 diuretic
利尿作用 diuretic effect
リネン類 linens
リバース・モーゲージ reverse mortgage
リバーミード行動記憶検査 Rivermead
　Behavioural Memory Test：RBMT
*リハビリテーション rehabilitation
リハビリテーションアプローチ rehabilitation
　approach
*リハビリテーション医学 rehabilitation medicine
リハビリテーション・インターナショナル
　Rehabilitation International

リハビリテーション介護　rehabilitative care

リハビリテーション・カウンセラー　rehabilitation counselor

リハビリテーション看護　rehabilitation nursing

リハビリテーション機器　rehabilitation equipment

リハビリテーション計画　rehabilitation plan

リハビリテーション工学　rehabilitation engineering

リハビリテーション心理学　rehabilitation psychology

リハビリテーションセンター　rehabilitation center

リハビリテーション・ソーシャルワーカー　social worker in physical rehabilitation

リハビリテーションチーム　rehabilitation team

リハビリテーションプログラム　rehabilitation program

離被架　bed cradle

リビドー　libido

•リビング・ウィル　living will

リフォーム工事　home modification

リフォームヘルパー　home modification specialist

リフト　lift

リフトバス　wheelchair accessible bus

リフレーミング　reframing

利便性　accessibility

リポたんぱく質　lipoprotein

流行性　epidemic

流行性角結膜炎　epidemic keratoconjunctivitis：EKC

流行性耳下腺炎　mumps

流涎症　sialorrhea；polysialia；ptyalism

流唾症　ptyalism

•留置カテーテル　indwelling catheter

•流動食　liquid diet

•流動性知能　fluid intelligence

療育　health care and education

療育手帳　disability handbook

両価性（アンビバレンス）　ambivalence

両眼視機能　binocular function of the eyes

両脚支持期　double support period

良肢位　proper positioning

利用者主体　client-oriented；person-oriented

利用者負担　copayment

良性腫瘍　benign tumor

良性先天性筋緊張低下　benign congenital hypotonia

良性発作性頭位めまい症　benign paroxysmal positional vertigo：BPPV

（両）変形性膝関節症　(bilateral) knee osteoarthritis；(bilateral) osteoarthritis of the knee

両麻痺　diplegia

両面価値　ambivalence

療養　recuperation；convalescence

療養介護　convalescent care；recuperative care

療養型病床群　convalescent care beds；a group of beds for convalescent care

療養通所介護　day care services for persons requiring a higher level of care

療養の給付　medical benefit

療養費　medical expenses

療養病床　designated long-term care beds

料理道具　cooking utensil

利用料　fee；usage fee

緑黄色野菜　brightly colored fruits and vegetables

•緑内障　glaucoma

緑膿菌性肺炎　pseudomonas pneumonia

リラクセーション　relaxation

リロケーションダメージ　relocation stress；transfer trauma

理論　theory

理論最大一日摂取量　Theoretical Maximum Daily Intake：TMDI

リン　phosphorus

臨時的任用　temporary appointment

臨終　last hours of life

臨終期　last stages of life

臨床栄養アセスメント　clinical nutritional assessment

臨床家　clinician

臨床検査　clinical examination

臨床検査技師　clinical laboratory technologist and technician

臨床検査技師等に関する法律　Clinical Laboratory Technologists and Technicians Act

臨床工学技士　clinical engineering technologist

臨床工学技士法　Clinical Engineering Technologists Act

臨床試験　clinical trial

臨床心理技術　techniques of clinical psychology

臨床心理士　clinical psychologist

臨床的介入　clinical intervention

臨床的面接　clinical interview

臨床認知症評価尺度　Clinical Dementia Rating : CDR

臨床薬剤師　clinical pharmacist

リンパ（液）　lymph

リンパ球　lymphocytes

リンパ行性転移　lymphatic metastasis

リンパ節炎　lymphadenitis

隣保館　settlement house

倫理　ethics

倫理綱領　code of ethics

る

涙器　lacrimal apparatus

累積性疲労　cumulative fatigue

累積罹患率　cumulative incidence

ルウ　roux

れ

冷あん法　cold compress ; cold fomentation

冷汗　cold sweats

冷湿布　cold pack

霊性　spirituality

霊的幸福尺度　Spiritual Well-Being Scale : SWB

冷凍療法　cryotherapy

レイ複雑図形検査　Rey-Osterrieth Complex Figure Test : ROCF

冷滅菌　cold sterilization

レーザー手術　laser surgery

レーザー治療　laser therapy

暦年齢　chronological age

*レクリエーション　recreation

レクリエーション運動　recreation movement

レクリエーション援助者　recreation worker

レクリエーション援助体系　systematic process of recreational therapy

レクリエーション援助目標　objectives of recreational therapy

レクリエーション活動　recreational activity

レクリエーション（活動）援助　recreational therapy

レクリエーション活動の効果　benefits of recreational activities ; effects of recreational activities

レクリエーション行事　recreational event

レクリエーションサービスシステム　recreational services system

レクリエーションサービスの評価　evaluation of recreational services and programs

レクリエーション財　recreational activities

レクリエーション資源　recreation resources

レクリエーション指導　recreation guide

レクリエーション指導者　recreation worker

レクリエーション主体　person-centered recreational activity

レクリエーション相談　leisure counseling

レクリエーション組織　recreation organization

レクリエーションの意義　significance of recreation and leisure activities

レクリエーションの概念　concepts of recreation and leisure activities

レクリエーションの環境づくり　environment creation for recreation and leisure activities

レクリエーションの生活化　making recreational activities as a part of daily routine

レクリエーションの素材　recreational activities

レクリエーションの分類　types of recreational activities

レクリエーション費　recreation fees

レクリエーションプログラム　recreation program

レクリエーションプログラムサービス
recreational program services

レクリエーションマネジメントサービス
recreation management services

レクリエーション論　recreation and leisure studies

レクリエーションワーカー　recreation worker

レジデンシャル・ワーク　residential social work

レシピエント　recipient

レジャー　leisure

レジャー憲章　Charter for Leisure

レストホーム　rest home

レストレスレッグス症候群　restless legs syndrome : RLS

レスパイト・ケア　respite care

レスピレーター　respirator

レスポンデント行動　respondent behavior

レスポンデント条件づけ　respondent conditioning

レセプト　billing statement

劣性遺伝　recessive inheritance

劣等感　inferiority complex ; a sense of inferiority

劣等処遇の原則　principle of less eligibility

レトルト食品　boil-in-the-bag food

レビー小体型認知症　Lewy body dementia ; dementia with Lewy bodies : LBD

レビー小体病　Lewy body disease : LBD

レミニッセンス　reminiscence

*レム睡眠　rapid eye movement sleep : REM sleep

連携　collaboration ; cooperation

蓮華座（れんげざ）　lotus position

連合運動　associated movement

攣縮（れんしゅく）　spasm

連帯責任　joint and several liability

レントゲン線検査　x-ray

連絡　contact ; communication

ろ

ろう　deafness

ろうあ　deaf mutism

ろうあ児施設　facility for deaf-mute children

*老化　aging

老化の遺伝説　genetic theory of aging

老化の行動説　activity theory of aging

老化の離脱説　disengagement theory of aging

*老眼　presbyopia

老眼鏡　reading glasses for presbyopia

老健局　Health and Welfare Bureau for the Elderly

瘻孔（ろうこう）　fistula

労災保険　workers' accident compensation insurance

労災補償　industrial accident compensation

労作時狭心症　effort angina ; stable angina

老視　presbyopia

老人　elderly person

老人憩の家　senior center

老人介護支援センター　home care support center

老人休養ホーム　recreation and relaxation home

老人恐怖症　gerontophobia

老人居宅介護等事業　home-based care services for the elderly

老人居宅生活支援事業　home-based support services for the elderly

老人クラブ　senior citizens club

老人健康保持事業　health maintenance program for the elderly

老人週間　older people's week

老人性アルツハイマー型認知症　senile dementia of the Alzheimer's type : SDAT

老人性高血圧　hypertension in the elderly

老人性掻痒症（そうようしょう）　pruritus senilis

*老人性難聴　presbycusis ; senile deafness ; age-related hearing loss

老人性認知症　senile dementia : SD

老人性認知症疾患デイケア施設　adult day care center for people with dementia

老人性認知症疾患療養病棟　dementia special care unit

老人性白内障　senile cataract

老人世帯向公営住宅 public housing for elderly households

老人大学校 adult education and recreation classes

老人短期入所事業 short-term stay program for the elderly

老人短期入所施設 short-term care facility for the elderly

老人デイケア（センター） adult day care (center)

老人デイサービス事業 adult day services program

老人デイサービスセンター adult day services center

老人デイヘルスケア adult day health care

老人日常生活用具給付等事業 adaptive equipment loan program for the elderly ; technical aids loan program for the elderly

老人の日 Respect for the Aged Day

老人斑 senile plaques ; neuritic plaques

老人福祉 welfare of old people ; welfare of the elderly

老人福祉計画 welfare planning for the elderly

老人福祉施策 welfare policy for the elderly

老人福祉施設 welfare facility for the elderly

老人福祉施設付設作業所 welfare facility-based workshop

老人福祉指導主事 elderly welfare advisory officer

老人福祉センター welfare center for the elderly

老人福祉相談員 commissioned friendly visitor

老人福祉法 Social Welfare Services for the Elderly Act

老人ホーム elderly home

老人ホーム入所判定基準 admission standards for senior homes

老人保健 senior health

老人保健医療対策 geriatric health policy

老人保健事業 elderly health care program

老人保健制度 health care system for the elderly

老人保健福祉計画 health and welfare planning for the elderly

老人保健福祉圏域 elderly health and welfare services area

老人保健法 Health and Medical Services for the Elderly Act

老衰 senility

老性自覚 self-awareness of aging

労働安全衛生法 Industrial Safety and Health Act

労働環境 work environment

労働基準法 Labor Standards Act

労働組合 labor union

労働災害 industrial accident ; occupational injury ; work accident

労働時間 work hours

労働者災害補償保険法 Industrial Accident Compensation Insurance Act

労働者の心の健康の保持増進のための指針 Guidelines for Promoting Mental Health Care of Workers : Mental Health Guidelines

労働政策 labor policy

労働福祉 labour welfare

労働保険 workers' compensation insurance

労働力 labor force

労働力人口 working-age population

漏斗胸 pectus excavatum

朗読奉仕 reading service

朗読奉仕員 reading volunteer

老年医学 geriatrics

老年化指数 aging index

老年期 old-age ; late life

老年期うつ病 depression in the elderly ; geriatric depression

老年期うつ病評価尺度 Geriatric Depression Scale : GDS

老年期躁うつ病 bipolar disorder in late life ; geriatric bipolar disorder

老年社会福祉学 gerontological social work

老年者控除 tax deduction for seniors

老年症候群 geriatric syndrome

老年人口 population aged 65 and over ; older population

老年人口指数 ratio of the population aged 65

and over to the working-age population ;
ratio of the population aged 65 and over to
the population aged 15 to 64

老年人口比率　proportion of the population
aged 65 and over

•老年痴呆　senile dementia : SD

老年病　age-related disease

弄便（ろうべん）　scatolia ; fecal smearing

労務管理　labor management

老齢加算　supplemental payment for public
assistance recipients aged 70 and over

•老齢基礎年金　Basic Old-Age Pension

老齢厚生年金　Old-Age Employees' Pension

老齢年金　Old-Age Pension

老齢福祉年金　Old-Age Welfare Pension

老老介護　elder to elder care ; elderly care
provided by elderly

ローカル・オプティマム　local optimum

ロービジョン　low vision

ロールシャッハ・インクブロット・テスト
Rorschach Inkblot Test

ロールシャッハ・テスト　Rorschach Test

•ロールプレイ　role play ; role playing

六大栄養素　six major nutrients ; six essential
nutrients

肋軟骨炎（ろくなんこつえん）　costochondritis

肋間筋（ろっかん）　intercostal muscles

肋間神経痛　intercostal neuralgia

ロッキングチェアー型　rocking chair

ロフストランドクラッチ　Lofstrand crutch

ROM　range of motion

ROM検査(テスト)　range of motion testing :
ROM-T

わ

ワーカーズ・コレクティブ　workers' collective

ワーカビリティ　workability

ワーキングプア　working poor

ワークシェアリング　work sharing

ワークショップ　workshop

ワークハウス　workhouse

ワークライフバランス　work-life balance

ワイマール憲法　Weimar Constitution ;
Constitution of the German Reich

ワクチン　vaccine

和式便器　squat toilet

WAC法　Well-Aging Community Act : WAC
Act

WAB失語症検査　Western Aphasia Battery :
WAB

ワムネット　WAM NET ; welfare and medical
service network system

ワンセットプラン　one-set plan

第 **2** 部｜英和

A

Abbreviated Injury Scale：AIS　簡易損傷ス
　ケール
abdominal breathing　腹式呼吸
abdominalgia　腹痛
abdominal pain　腹痛
abdominal respiration　腹式呼吸
abdominal ultrasound　腹部超音波検査
abdominocentesis　腹部穿刺
abduction　外転
abduction gait　外転歩行
ability　能力
abiotic synthesis　非生物合成
abnormal behavior　異常行動
abnormal deformity　形態異常
abnormal eating　異食
abnormal eating habit　異食行為
abnormal gait　異常歩行
abnormal glucose metabolism　糖代謝異常
Abnormal Involuntary Movement Scale：AIMS
　異常不随意運動評価尺度
abrasion　擦り傷
abrasion resistance　摩耗抵抗
abscess　膿瘍
absence seizure　欠神発作；小発作
absolute muscle strength　絶対筋力
absolute poverty　絶対的貧困
absolute threshold of hearing　最小可聴値
absorption　吸収
absorption atelectasis　吸収性無気肺
absorption rate　吸収速度
absorption ratio　吸収率
abuse　虐待
academic achievement test　学力検査
acalculia　失算
acceptable daily intake：ADI　一日許容摂取量
acceptance　受容；受理
acceptance of disability　障害の受容
access　利便
accessibility　アクセシビリティ；利便性
accessory respiratory muscle　補助呼吸筋
accident　事故；災難

accidental extubation　事故抜管
accident evaluation　事故評価
accident insurance　災害補償
accountability　アカウンタビリティー；説明責任
acculturation　文化変容
acetabular fracture　寛骨臼骨折
acetate　酢酸塩
acetic acid　酢酸
Achilles tendon　アキレス腱
acid　酸
acid anhydride　酸無水物
acid-base balance　酸塩基平衡
acid-base regulation　酸塩基調節
acidemia　アシデミア
acidity　酸度
acidosis　酸血症；アシドーシス
acoustic trauma　音響外傷
acquired blindness　中途失明
acquired disability　後天性障害；中途障害
acquired disorder　後天性障害；中途障害
acquired hearing loss　中途聴覚障害
acquired immune deficiency syndrome：
　AIDS　後天性免疫不全症候群；エイズ
acquired impairment　後天性障害；中途障害
acromegaly　先端巨大症
action research　アクション・リサーチ；実践研究
active assisted exercise　自動介助運動
active carbon　活性炭素
active charcoal　活性炭
active exercise　自動訓練
active immunity　能動免疫
active life expectancy　活動的平均余命
active listening　傾聴
active movement　自動運動
active oxygen　活性酸素
active range of motion：AROM　自動可動域
active self-neglect　意図的自己放任
activities of daily living：ADL　日常生活活動
　（動作）
activities parallel to daily living：APDL　生活関
　連活動（動作）
activity　活動；アクティビティ
activity and participation　活動と参加

activity limitation　活動制限	adenoma　腺腫
activity services　アクティビティサービス	adhesive capsulitis　肩関節周囲炎
activity theory　活動理論	adipose tissue　脂肪組織
activity theory of aging　老化の行動説	adiposis dolorosa　有痛性脂肪症
actual expenditure　実支出	adjustment　適応；内的適応
actual income　実収入	adjustment disorder　適応障害
actual wage　実質賃金	adjustment mechanism　適応機制
actuarial table　生命表	administration　アドミニストレーション；投薬
acute　急性	administrative inspection　行政監査
acute brain syndrome　急性脳症候群	administrative reform　行政改革
acute colitis　急性腸炎(大腸)	administrator　施設長
acute coloenteritis　急性腸炎	admission　入所
acute coronary syndrome：ACS　急性冠症候群	admission decision　入所決定
acute cystitis　急性膀胱炎	adolescent depression　思春期うつ病
acute enteritis　急性腸炎(小腸)	adolescent emaciation　思春期やせ症
acute enterocolitis　急性腸炎	adolescent mental health　思春期精神保健
acute interstitial pneumonia　間質性肺炎	adolescent nausea　思春期拒食症
acute lung injury　急性肺傷害	adolescent psychology　青年期心理学
acute lymphoblastic leukemia　急性リンパ性白血病	adopted child　養子
acute lymphocytic leukemia：ALL　急性リンパ性白血病	adoption　養子縁組
acute lymphoid leukemia　急性リンパ性白血病	adrenal cortex　副腎皮質
acute myelocytic leukemia　急性骨髄性白血病	adrenalin　アドレナリン
acute myelogenous leukemia：AML　急性骨髄性白血病	adrenal medulla　副腎髄質
acute myeloid leukemia　急性骨髄性白血病	adult care home　老人ホーム
acute myocardial infarction　急性心筋梗塞	adult day care　老人デイケア
acute pancreatitis　急性膵炎	adult day health care　老人デイヘルスケア
acute poliomyelitis　急性灰白髄炎	adult education　成人教育
acute posthemorrhagic anemia　急性出血後貧血	adult guardian　成年後見人
	adult guardianship　成年後見制度
acute respiratory distress syndrome：ARDS　急性呼吸窮迫症候群	Adult Manifest Anxiety Scale　成人用顕現性不安尺度
adaptation　適応；外的適応	adult-onset　成人発症
adaptive clothing　介護服	adult-onset rheumatoid arthritis：AORA　成人発症関節リウマチ
adaptive equipment　補装具	adult protective services　成人保護サービス
adaptive sports　障害者スポーツ	adult respiratory distress syndrome　成人呼吸窮迫症侯群
addiction　依存症	adult T-cell leukemia：ATLL　成人 T 細胞白血病・リンパ腫
addictive drug　依存性薬物	
Addison's disease　アディソン病	advanced cardiovascular life support：ACLS　二次心肺蘇生法
adduction　内転	advanced life support：ALS　二次救命処置
adenocarcinoma　腺がん	advanced practice nurse　高度専門看護師

adverse drug reaction：ADR　薬剤副作用

adverse selection　逆選択

advisory council　諮問委員会

advocacy　アドボカシー；代弁的機能；擁護活動

advocate　代弁；代弁者

advocate services　権利擁護サービス

advocator　アドボケーター

against medical advice：AMA　医学指示拒否

age-adjusted death rate：AADR　年齢調整死亡率

aged care　高齢者ケア；高齢者介護

ageing　加齢

ageism　エイジズム；年齢差別

age-related disease　加齢性疾患

age-related hearing loss　加齢性難聴

age-related macular degeneration　加齢黄斑変性（症）

aggression　攻撃

aggressive behavior　攻撃的行動

aggressive casework　アグレッシブ・ケースワーク

aging　加齢

aging-associated cognitive decline：AACD　加齢関連認知低下

aging index　老年化指数

aging society　高齢化社会

agism　エイジズム；年齢差別

agnosia　失認（症）

agonal respiration　下顎呼吸

agonist　動筋

agoraphobia　広場恐怖

agraphia　失書

aid　援助；介助；扶助

Aid to the Permanently and Totally Disabled：APTD　完全・永続的重度障害者扶助

airborne bacteria　空中細菌

airborne infection　空気感染

airborne infection isolation：AII　空気感染隔離

airborne particle　空中塵埃

airborne precaution　空気予防策

airborne transmission　空気伝播

air bronchogram　気管支透亮像

air embolism　空気塞栓症

air permeability　通気

air pollution　空気汚染；大気汚染

airway　気道

airway burn　気道熱傷

airway cleaning　気道洗浄

airway closure　気道閉鎖

airway collapse　気道虚脱

airway maintenance　気道確保

airway management　気道管理

airway obstruction　気道閉塞

airway pressure　気道内圧

airway pressure-time curve　気道内圧時間曲線

airway resistance　気道抵抗

airway stenosis　気道狭窄

airway stent　気道ステント

akathisia　アカシジア；静座不能

akinesia　無動

albumin　アルブミン

albuminuria　たんぱく尿

alcohol abstinence　禁酒

alcohol abuse　アルコールの乱用

alcoholic　アルコール中毒

alcoholic beverage　アルコール飲料

alcoholic dementia　アルコール性認知症

alcoholic encephalopathy　アルコール性脳障害

alcoholic hallucinosis　アルコール幻覚症

alcoholic hepatitis　アルコール性肝炎

alcoholic hepatopathy　アルコール性肝障害

alcoholic liver disease　アルコール性肝疾患

alcoholic psychosis　アルコール精神病

Alcoholics Anonymous：AA　アルコホリックス・アノニマス

alcoholic self-help organization　断酒会

alcohol-induced encephalopathy　アルコール性脳障害

alcohol-induced liver injury　アルコール性肝障害

alcoholism　アルコール依存症

alcohol-related dementia　アルコール性認知症

alcohol-related liver disease　アルコール性肝疾患

alcohol-related psychosis　アルコール性精神病

alert safety system　警報安全システム

alexia 失読

algesia 痛覚

alimentary bolus 食塊（しょっかい）

alkalemia アルカリ血症

alkalosis アルカローシス

allergic asthma アレルギー性喘息（ぜんそく）

allergic bronchitis アレルギー性気管支炎

allergic contact dermatitis アレルギー性皮膚炎

allergic pruritus アレルギー性搔痒症

allergic reaction アレルギー反応

allergic rhinitis アレルギー性鼻炎

allergy アレルギー

allergy-like food poisoning アレルギー様食中毒

allowance 手当

Alma-Ata Declaration アルマ・アタ宣言

almshouse 救護施設；救貧院；養老院

altered consistency diet とろみ調整食品

altered states of consciousness 意識変容

alternate three-point gait 交互三点歩行

alternative medicine 代替医療；オルタナティブ・メディスン

alveolar air 肺胞気（はいほう）

alveolar-capillary barrier 肺胞・毛細血管障壁

alveolar dead space 肺胞死腔

alveolar edema 肺胞浮腫（ふしゅ）；肺胞水腫（すいしゅ）

alveolar epithelial cells 肺胞上皮細胞

alveolar gas exchange 肺胞ガス交換

alveolar hypoventilation 肺胞低換気

alveolar macrophage 肺胞マクロファージ

alveolar membrane 肺胞膜

alveolar pressure 肺胞内圧

alveolar space 肺胞腔

alveolar surface tension 肺胞表面張力

alveolar ventilation 肺胞換気

alveoli 肺胞

alveolus 肺胞

Alzheimer's disease アルツハイマー病

ambivalence アンビバレンス；両価性；両面価値

ambulation 歩行

ambulatory care 外来ケア；外来診療

amenity アメニティ

American Association of Intellectual and Developmental Disabilities：AAIDD 米国知的・発達障害学会

American Association on Mental Retardation：AAMR アメリカ精神遅滞協会

Americans with Disabilities Act：ADA 障害をもつアメリカ人法

amino acid アミノ酸

ammonia アンモニア

ammonia detoxification アンモニア解毒（げどく）

amnesia 健忘（けんぼう）(症)

amniocentesis 羊水診断（ようすい）

amniotic fluid test 羊水診断

amphetamine アンフェタミン

amputation 切断

amputation stump 断端

amylase アミラーゼ

amyloidosis アミロイドーシス

amylum でんぷん

Amyotrophic Lateral Sclerosis：ALS アミトロ；筋萎縮性側索硬化症（いしゅくせいそくさくこうかしょう）

anaerobe 嫌気性菌（けんきせいきん）

anaerobic exercise 無酸素訓練

anaerobic threshold：AT 嫌気性代謝閾値（いきち）；無酸素性作業閾値

anal speculum 肛門鏡

anal sphincter muscle 肛門括約筋（かつやく）

anal stage 肛門期

analysis 分析

analytical psychology 分析心理学

anaphylactic shock アナフィラキシーショック

anaplastic thyroid cancer 甲状腺未分化がん

anatomical position 解剖学的肢位

androgen アンドロゲン

androgen deprivation therapy：ADT アンドロゲン除去療法

anemia 貧血

anesthesia 麻酔；感覚消失

anesthetic 麻酔剤

aneurysm 動脈瘤（りゅう）

anger 怒り

angina attack 狭心症発作（ほっさ）

angina pectoris 狭心症

angiogram 血管造影

angioplasty 血管形成術

123

英和

A

angry men　慣慨(外罰)型

angular cheilitis　口角炎

animal assisted activity : AAA　動物介在活動

animal assisted therapy : AAT　アニマル・セラピー；動物介在療法

animal fat　動物性脂肪

animal protein　動物性たんぱく質

animal source foods : ASF　動物性食品

anionic surface active agent　陰イオン界面活性剤

Anisakis　アニサキス

ankle-foot orthosis : AFO　短下肢装具

ankylosing spondylitis : AS　強直性脊椎炎

ankylosis　強直；硬直

annual survey　年次調査

anomia　健忘失語

anorexia　拒食症

anorexia nervosa : AN　神経性無食欲症；神経性食欲不振症

anoscope　肛門鏡

anoscopy　肛門鏡検査

anosmia　嗅覚消失症

anosognosia　病態失認

anoxemia　無酸素血症

anoxia　無酸素症；低酸素症

antagonism　拮抗

antagonist　拮抗筋

antalgic gait　有痛性歩行；疼痛回避性歩行

antegrade colonic enema : ACE　順行性洗腸

anterior spinal artery syndrome
前脊髄動脈症候群

anterograde amnesia　前向(性)健忘

anthocyanin　アントシアニン

anthrophobia　対人恐怖

antianxiety medication　抗不安薬

antibacterial　抗菌

antibacterial agent　抗菌薬

antibacterial drug　抗菌薬

antibiotic　抗生剤

antibiotic resistant infection　抗生物質耐性菌感染

antibody　抗体

anticancer drug　抗がん剤

anticoagulant　抗凝固剤

antidepressant　抗うつ薬

antidiabetic　抗糖尿病薬

antidiuresis　抗利尿

antidote　解毒剤

antidromic conduction　逆方向性伝導

antiedemic　抗浮腫性

antiepileptic drug : AED　抗てんかん薬

antifungal　抗真菌性

antifungal antibiotic　抗真菌性抗生物質

antigen　抗原

antigen-antibody reaction　抗原抗体反応

antigenicity　抗原性

antigravity muscle　抗重力筋

antigravity position　抗重力姿勢

antihistamine　抗ヒスタミン剤

antiinflammatory drug　抗炎症薬

antimicrobial　抗細菌

antimicrobial resistance　抗菌薬抵抗性

antioxidant　酸化防止剤；抗酸化物

antioxidant agent　抗酸化薬

antioxidant therapy　抗酸化療法

antioxidant vitamin　抗酸化ビタミン

antiparkinson drug　抗パーキンソン病薬

antiparkinson medication　抗パーキンソン病薬

antiplatelet agent　抗血小板薬

antipsoriatic drug　抗乾癬薬

antipsychotic　抗精神病薬

antipsychotic medication　抗精神病薬

antipyretic medication　解熱剤

antiseizure drug　抗てんかん薬

antisepsis　生体消毒

antiseptic　防腐剤

antiseptic handrub　擦式手指消毒

antiserum　抗血清

antithrombotic drug　抗血栓薬

antithyroid medication　抗甲状腺薬

antiviral drug　抗ウイルス薬

anuria　無尿

anus　肛門

anxiety　不安症

anxiety disorder　不安障害

anxiety neurosis　不安神経症

124

anxiolytic　抗不安薬；精神安定剤

anxiousness　不安

aortic valve　大動脈弁

aortic valve stenosis　大動脈弁狭窄症（きょうさくしょう）

apex beat　心尖拍動（しんせんはくどう）

aphasia　失語（症）

aphonia　失声症

apical impulse　心尖拍動（しんせんはくどう）

aplastic anemia　再生不良性貧血

apnea　無呼吸

Apnea-Hypopnea Index : AHI　無呼吸低呼吸指数

apneusis　持続性吸息（きゅうそく）

apocrine sweat gland　アポクリン腺

apolipoprotein　アポリポたんぱく

appeal　異議申し立て；不服申立て

appetite　食欲

appetite center　食欲中枢

applicant　申請者

apraxia　失行

apraxia of speech　発語失行

aptitude test　適正検査

armored type　装甲（自己防衛）型

Arnold-Chiari malformation　アーノルド・キアリ奇形

Arnold's neuralgia　後頭神経痛

arrhythmia　不整脈（ふせいみゃく）

arterial blood　動脈血

arterial blood gas analysis　血液ガス分析

arterial blood pressure : ABP　動脈圧

arterial compliance　動脈コンプライアンス

arterial disease　動脈疾患

arterial embolism　動脈塞栓（そくせん）

arterial occlusive disease : AOD　動脈閉塞症（へいそくしょう）

arterial oxygen tension　動脈血酸素分圧

arterial partial pressure of oxygen : PaO2　動脈血酸素分圧

arterial pressure　動脈圧

arterial pulse　動脈拍動

arteriography　動脈造影

arteriole　細動脈（さい）

arteriosclerosis　動脈硬化（症）

arteriosclerosis obliterans　閉塞性動脈硬化症（へいそくせい）

arteriosclerotic heart disease : ASHD　動脈硬化性心疾患

artery　動脈

arthralgia　関節痛

arthritis　関節炎

arthrokinematic approach : AKA　関節運動学的アプローチ

articulation disorder　構音障害

artificial anus　人工肛門

artificial bladder　人工膀胱（ぼうこう）

artificial eye　義眼

artificial larynx　人工喉頭（こうとう）

artificial lens　人工レンズ

artificial limb　義肢（ぎし）

artificial respiration　人工呼吸

artificial respirator　人工呼吸器

artificial ventilator　人工呼吸器

art therapy　芸術療法

ascites　腹水（ふくすい）

asepsis　無菌

aseptic barrier　無菌的遮蔽（しゃへい）

aseptic technique　無菌操作

Ashworth Scale　アシュワース尺度

Asperger's syndrome : AS　アスペルガー症候群

aspergillosis　アスペルギルス症

asphyxia　窒息

asphyxiation　窒息

aspiration　吸息（きゅうそく）；吸入

aspiration cytology　吸引細胞診

aspiration pneumonia　嚥下性肺炎（えんげせい）；誤嚥性（ごえんせい）肺炎

aspirator　吸引器

aspirin therapy　アスピリン療法

assessment　アセスメント；評価

assessment item　評価項目

Assessment of Motor and Process Skills : AMPS　運動技能・プロセス技能評価

assessment sheet　アセスメントシート

assessment tool　アセスメントツール

assistance　援助；介助；扶助

assistance dog　介助犬

assistant　援助者；介助員

assistant administrator　副施設長	attention deficit hyperactivity disorder：ADHD
assistant director of nursing　副看護師長	注意欠陥・多動性障害
assisted coughing　咳嗽介助	atypical psychosis　非定型精神病
assisted living facility　アシステッド・リビング	audible pedestrian traffic signal　視覚障害者用
assisted suicide　自殺幇助	信号機
assistive appliance　補装具	audible traffic signal　視覚障害者用信号機
assistive bathing aid　入浴補助用具	audiogram　オーディオグラム
assistive device　支援機器；日常生活用具；福	audiology assessment　聴覚的評価
祉用具	audiometry evaluation　聴力検査
assistive equipment　福祉機器	auditory agnosia　聴覚失認
assistive exercise　介助訓練	auditory center　聴覚中枢
assistive technology：AT　補助技術	auditory environment　音環境
associated movement　連合運動	auditory hallucination　幻聴
asthenopia　眼精疲労	auditory impairment：HL　難聴
asthma　喘息	auditory nerve　聴神経
asthmatic attack　喘息発作	auditory perception　聴覚
astigmatism　乱視	auditory-verbal therapist　聴覚音声セラピスト
asymptomatic carrier　無症候性キャリア	auditory-verbal therapy：AVT　聴覚音声療法；
ataxia　運動失調症	オーディトリーバーバル法
ataxic dysarthria　麻痺性構音障害	aural hematoma　耳血腫
ataxic gait　失調性歩行	autism　自閉症
atheroma　アテローマ	autism spectrum disorder：ASD　自閉症スペク
atherosclerosis　アテローム性動脈硬化（症）	トラム障害
athetoid　アテトーゼ型	autoimmune hepatitis　自己免疫性肝炎
athetosis　アテトーゼ	autoimmunity　自己免疫
athletic injury　スポーツ外傷	autointoxication　自家中毒
atomic bomb survivor　被爆者	autolysis　自己消化
atonic constipation　弛緩性便秘	automated auditory brainstem response：
atopic asthma　アトピー性喘息	AABR　自動聴性脳幹反応
atopic cough　アトピー咳嗽	automated auditory brainstem response
atopic dermatitis　アトピー性皮膚炎	evaluation　自動聴性脳幹反応評価
atopy　アトピー	automated external defibrillator：AED
atrial fibrillation　心房細動	自動体外式除細動器
atrial septal defect：ASD　心房中隔欠損症	automatism　自動症
atrium　心房	autonomic dysfunction　自律神経機能障害
atrophic gastritis　萎縮性胃炎	autonomic dysreflexia　自律神経過反射
atrophic vaginitis　萎縮性膣炎	autonomic hyperreflexia　自律神経過反射
atrophy　萎縮	autonomic nerve　自律神経
attachment theory　愛着理論	autonomic nerve disorder　自律神経障害
attendance allowance　付添手当	autonomic nervous system　自律神経系
attendant　付添人	autonomic symptom　自律神経症状
attending physician　かかりつけ医	autonomic thought　自動思考
attention-deficit disorder　注意障害	autonomous affairs　自治事務

autonomy　オートノミー；自律

autophobia　単独恐怖症

autopsy　死体解剖；検死

autoreceptor　自己受容体

autoregulation　自己調節

autosomal abnormality　常染色体異常

autosomal dominant　常染色体優性

autosomal dominant disorder　常染色体優性
　遺伝病

autosomal dominant inheritance　常染色体優
　性遺伝

autosomal recessive　常染色体劣性

autosomal recessive disorder　常染色体劣性
　遺伝病

autosomal recessive inheritance　常染色体劣
　性遺伝

autosome　常染色体

average household size　平均世帯人員

average length of stay : ALOS　平均在院日数

average life span　平均寿命

average price of drugs　平均薬価

aversion therapy　嫌悪療法

aversive stimulus　嫌悪刺激

avoidance　逃避

avoidance conditioning　回避条件づけ

avoidance learning　回避学習

avolition　無為

axilla　腋窩

axillary artery　腋窩動脈

axillary crutch　松葉づえ；クラッチ

axillary hair　腋毛

axillary osmidrosis　腋臭

axillary temperature　腋窩温

axonal degeneration　軸索変性

Ayurvedic medicine　アユルベーダ医学

azotemia　高窒素血症

B

babbling　喃語

baby boom　ベビーブーム

baby boomer　ベビーブーマー

baby boom generation　ベビーブーム世代；団

塊の世代

backrest　バックレスト；背もたれ

bacteremia　菌血症

bacteria　細菌；感染菌

bacterial food poisoning　細菌性食中毒

bacterial pneumonia　細菌性肺炎

bactericidal action　殺菌作用

bacteriostatic action　静菌作用

bacterium　細菌

bacteriuria　細菌尿

balance　バランス

balance disorder　平衡（機能）障害

balloon catheter　バルーンカテーテル

balneotherapy　温泉療法

bandage　包帯

barrier precaution　バリア予防策

Barthel Index : BI　バーセル指数

basal body temperature　基礎体温

basal metabolic rate : BMR　基礎代謝量

basal metabolism　基礎代謝

basic human needs　人間の基本的欲求

basic needs　一次的欲求；基本的欲求

bath board　バスボード；入浴台

bath chair　入浴用いす

bathing　入浴

bathing services　入浴サービス

bathroom aid　入浴補助用具

Beck Depression Inventory : BDI　ベック抑うつ
　評価尺度

Becker muscular dystrophy : BMD　ベッカー型
　筋ジストロフィー

bed cradle　離被架

bed lift　ベッドリフト

bed mobility　起居動作

bedpan　差し込み便器

bedpan washer　便器洗浄機

bedridden period before death : BPbd　最終
　臥床期間

bedside commode　移動トイレ；便器付きいす；
　ポータブルトイレ

bedside rail　ベッド柵

bedside table　床頭台

Beers Criteria　ビアーズ基準

127

behavioral and psychological symptoms of dementia：BPSD　行動・心理症状；周辺症状；認知症に伴う行動障害と精神症状

behavioral assessment scale　行動評価スケール

behavioral disorder　行動障害

behavioral language　行動言語

behavioral observation　行動観察

behavioral science　行動科学

behavioral symptom　行動症状

behavioral theory　行動理論

behavior assessment　行動アセスメント

behaviorism　行動主義

behavior modification　行動変容法

behavior modification approach　行動変容アプローチ

behavior modification model　行動変容モデル

behavior pattern　行動パターン

behavior rehearsal　行動リハーサル

behavior therapy　行動療法

Behcet's disease　ベーチェット病

Behcet's syndrome　ベーチェット症候群

Bell's palsy　ベル麻痺

belongingness and love needs　社会的欲求

beneficence　善行；恩恵；慈善

beneficiary　受益者

benefit　給付

benefit fraud　不正受給

benefit in kind　現物給付

benefit period　給付期間

benign congenital hypotonia　良性先天性筋緊張低下

benign paroxysmal positional vertigo：BPPV　良性発作性頭位めまい症

benign prostatic hyperplasia：BPH　前立腺肥大症

benign prostatic hypertrophy　前立腺肥大症

benign tumor　良性腫瘍

benzalkonium chloride solution　ベンザルコニウム塩化物溶液

Berg Balance Scale：BBS　バーグバランス評価

beriberi　脚気

Bertolotti's syndrome　ベルトロッティ症候群

Beveridge Report　ベヴァリッジ報告

bilateral knee osteoarthritis　両変形性膝関節症

biliary tract cancer　胆道がん

biliary tract disease　胆道疾患

billing fraud　不正請求

billing period　請求対象期間

billing statement　請求書

Bill of Rights　権利章典

Binet Intelligence Test　ビネー式知能検査

Binswanger's disease　ビンスワンガー病

bioethics　生命倫理

biofeedback (therapy)　バイオフィードバック（療法）

biohazard sign　バイオハザードマーク

biological age　生物年齢

biological and physiological needs　生理的欲求；身体的欲求

biological clocks　体内時計

biological rhythm　生体リズム

biological therapy　生物学的治療法

biomechanics　生体力学

biomedical ethics　生命・医療倫理

biopsy　生検

biopsy forceps　生検鉗子

bipolar affective disorder　双極性感情障害

bipolar disorder　双極性障害；躁うつ病

bipolar I disorder　双極 I 型障害

bipolar II disorder　双極 II 型障害

birth certificate　出生証明書

birth rate　出生率

bitterness　苦味

bladder　膀胱

bladder fistula　膀胱瘻

bladder hypotonia　低緊張性膀胱

bladder training　膀胱訓練；排尿訓練

bleeding　出血

blended diet　ミキサー食

blenderized diet：BD　ミキサー食

blind interpreter　筆記通訳者；要約筆記者

blindness　盲

blister　水疱

blood　血液

blood bank　血液銀行

bloodborne infection　血液媒介感染

bloodborne pathogen　血液由来病原体	bowel movement　便通；便意；排便
bloodborne virus infection　血中ウイルス感染症	bowel obstruction　腸閉塞症
blood cell　血球	bowel training　排便訓練
blood donation　献血	Bowie-Dick Test　ボウィー・ディック・テスト
blood oxygen level　血液中酸素濃度	brachial artery　上腕動脈
blood plasma　血漿	Braden Scale for Predicting Pressure Sore Risk　褥瘡発生予測尺度
blood pressure　血圧	Braden Scale for Predicting Pressure Ulcer Risk　褥瘡発生予測尺度
blood pressure manometer　血圧計	bradycardia　徐脈
blood serum　血清	bradypnea　徐呼吸
bloodstream infection　血流感染	Braille　ブライユ式点字
blood sugar　血糖	Braille blocks　ブライユ式点字ブロック
blood sugar level　血糖値	Brailler　ブライユ式点字タイプライター；点字タイプライター
blood test　血液検査	brain death　脳死
blood transfusion　輸血	brain fog　意識混濁
blood urea nitrogen : BUN　血液尿素窒素	brain hemorrhage　脳出血
blunted affect　情意鈍麻；感情鈍麻	brain stem　脳幹
board and care home　ボード・アンド・ケアホーム	brainstorming technique　ブレーンストーミング法
body fluid　体液	brain tumor　脳腫瘍
body function　心身機能	brain waves　脳波
body image　身体像	brand name medication　先発薬品
body mass index : BMI　体格指数	breast cancer　乳がん
body mechanics　ボディメカニクス；生体力学	breathability　透湿性
body-powered prosthesis　能動義手	breathing　呼吸
body structure　身体構造	Brief Fatigue Inventory : BFI　簡易疲労一覧表
body temperature　体温	Brief Oral Health Status Examination : BOHSE　簡易口腔衛生検査
body wastes　排泄物	Brief Pain Inventory : BPI　簡易疼痛調査票
Boehmeria nivea　苧麻	brief therapy　ブリーフセラピー；短期療法
bolus　食塊	Broca's aphasia　ブローカ失語（症）
bone atrophy　骨萎縮	Broca's area　ブローカ野
bone density　骨密度	brokerage　仲介的機能
bone disease　骨疾患	bronchial asthma　気管支喘息
bone marrow　骨髄	bronchial drainage　気管支ドレナージ
bone metastasis　骨転移	bronchiolitis　細気管支炎
bone mineral density　骨塩量	bronchitis　気管支炎
borderline hypertension　境界域高血圧	bronchodilator　気管支拡張剤
Boston Naming Test : BNT　ボストン呼称テスト	bronchoscopy　気管支鏡
Bouchard's node　ブシャール結節	bronchus　気管支
bowel dysfunction　直腸機能障害	Brown-Sequard syndrome　ブラウン・セカール症候群
bowel function　腸機能	
bowel incontinence　便失禁	
bowel management　排便管理	

bruise 打撲；打撲傷

Brunnstrom stage ブルンストローム・ステージ

budget 予算

budgeting 予算編成

bulbar palsy 球麻痺

bulimia 過食症

bulimia nervosa 神経性大食症

bullying いじめ

bunion バニオン；腱膜瘤

buoyant effect 浮力作用

burden 負担

burial 埋葬

burn 熱傷；火傷

burnout syndrome バーンアウト・シンドローム；燃えつき症候群

bypass surgery バイパス手術

C

cadherin カドヘリン

caffeine カフェイン

calcitonin カルシトニン

calcium カルシウム

calcium deficiency カルシウム欠乏症

calculus 結石

caloric intake 摂取熱量

caloric restriction カロリー制限

calorie カロリー

campylobacter カンピロバクター

cancer がん

cancer gene がん遺伝子

cancerous growth 悪性腫瘍

cancer patient がん患者

cancer treatment がん治療

candida esophagitis カンジダ食道炎

cane つえ

canker sore 口内炎

cannabis 大麻草

cannula カニューレ

capability 能力

capsaicin カプサイシン

carbohydrate 炭水化物

carbon dioxide 二酸化炭素

carbon monoxide 一酸化炭素

carbon monoxide poisoning 一酸化炭素中毒

carcinogen 発がん物質

carcinogenesis 発がん

carcinomatous pain がん性疼痛

cardiac arrhythmia 心臓不整脈

cardiac dysrhythmia 心臓不整脈

cardiac nuclear medicine 心臓核医学

cardiac output 心拍出量

cardiac rehabilitation 心臓リハビリテーション

cardiac shock 心原性ショック

cardiac shunt 心シャント

cardiac surgery intensive care unit : CSICU 循環器外科集中治療室

cardiogenic cerebral embolism 心原性脳塞栓

cardiogenic pulmonary edema 心原性肺水腫

cardiology 循環器

cardiometabolic risk 心血管・代謝疾患リスク

cardiopulmonary cerebral resuscitation : CPCR 心肺脳蘇生法

cardiopulmonary function 心肺機能

cardiopulmonary resuscitation : CPR 心肺蘇生法

cardiothoracic ratio 心胸郭比

cardiotonic drug 強心薬

cardiovascular disease 循環器疾患；心血管疾患

cardiovascular system 循環器

care ケア；介護

caregiver 介護者

caregiver burden 介護者負担

Caregiver Burden Interview 介護負担質問票

Caregiver Burden Scale 介護負担尺度

caregiver burnout 介護者の燃え尽き症候群

caregivers' rights 介護者の権利

Caregiver Strain Index : CSI 介護者負担指標

caregiver stress 介護者ストレス

caregiving 介護

care pathway ケアパス

care plan ケアプラン

carer's allowance 介護者手当

carotene カロテン

carotenoid カロテノイド

carotid artery　頸動脈

carotid artery stenosis　頸動脈狭窄

carrier　保菌者

case aid　ケースエイド

case conference　ケースカンファレンス

case-control study　ケースコントロール研究；症例対照研究

case-fatality rate　致命率

case history　ケースヒストリー

case management　ケースマネジメント

case mix　ケースミックス

Case Mix Index : CMI　ケースミックス指数

case study　ケーススタディ；事例検討

casework　ケースワーク

case worker　ケースワーカー

cash benefit　現金給付；金銭給付

cast　ギプス

castration　去勢

castration anxiety　去勢不安

catalepsy　カタレプシー

cataplasm　湿布

cataract　白内障

catheter　カテーテル

catheter-associated bloodstream infection : CABSI　カテーテル関連血流感染

catheter-associated infection　カテーテル関連感染

catheterization　カテーテル留置法

catheter-related bacteremia　カテーテル由来菌血症

catheter-related bloodstream infection : CRBSI　カテーテル由来血流感染

catheter-related infection　カテーテル由来感染

cause of death : COD　死因

cellulitis　蜂巣織炎；蜂窩織炎

cellulose　セルロース

cemetery　墓地

cenesthopathy　体感症（セネストパチー）

census　センサス

Center for Disease Control and Prevention : CDC　疾病管理予防センター

Center for Epidemiological Studies Depression Scale : CES-D　抑うつ自己評価尺度

central auditory processing disorder : CAPD　中枢性聴覚処理障害

central catheter　中心カテーテル

central nerve　中枢神経

central nervous system : CNS　中枢神経系

central nervous system disease　中枢神経性障害

central nervous system disorder　中枢神経性障害

central parenteral nutrition　中心静脈栄養法

central retinal artery occlusion　網膜中心動脈閉塞症

central scotoma　中心暗点

central supply　中央供給

central venous pressure : CVP　中心静脈圧

cephalalgia　頭痛

cerebellum　小脳

cerebral anemia　脳貧血

cerebral arteriosclerosis　脳動脈硬化症

cerebral contusion　脳挫傷

cerebral cortex　大脳皮質

cerebral edema　脳浮腫

cerebral embolism　脳塞栓（症）

cerebral hemorrhage　脳（内）出血

cerebral infarction　脳梗塞

cerebral palsy : CP　脳性麻痺

cerebral thrombosis　脳血栓（症）

cerebrovascular dementia　脳血管性認知症

cerebrovascular disease : CVD　脳血管疾患；脳血管障害

cerebrum　大脳

certification　認定

certified child care worker : CCCW　保育士

certified health education specialist : CHES　認定健康教育士

certified nurse : CN　認定看護師

certified nurse midwife : CNM　認定看護助産師

cerumen　耳垢；耳あか

cerumen impaction　耳垢塞栓

cervical cancer　子宮頸がん

cervical cord injury　頸髄損傷

cervical dysplasia　子宮頸部異形成

cervical orthosis　頸椎装具

131

cervical radiculopathy 頸椎根症	children's home 児童養護施設
cervical spinal cord injury 頸髄損傷	chill 悪寒
cervical spine 頸椎	chiropractic カイロプラクティック
cervical spondylosis 変形性頸椎症	chlorhexidine gluconate solution クロルヘキシ
cervical traction 頸椎牽引	ジングルコン酸塩溶液
chamber pot 寝室用便器	chlorine bleach 塩素系漂白剤
Charcot joint シャルコー関節	cholera コレラ
charge nurse 主任看護師	cholestatic hepatitis 胆汁うっ滞性肝炎
charity 慈善	cholesterol コレステロール
Charity Organization Society : COS 慈善組織	chopped diet きざみ食
協会	chorea 舞踏病様運動
Charter for Leisure レジャー憲章	chromosomal abnormality 染色体異常
chemical digestion 化学的消化	chromosome 染色体
chemical food poisoning 化学物質食中毒	chronic bronchitis 慢性気管支炎
chemical indicator 化学的インジケータ	chronic disease 慢性疾患
chemical restraint 薬物拘束	chronic fatigue syndrome : CFS 慢性疲労症
chemical score ケミカルスコア	候群
chemoembolization 化学塞栓	chronic gastritis 慢性胃炎
chemotherapy 化学療法	chronic hepatitis 慢性肝炎
chest compression 非開胸心臓マッサージ；胸	chronic Illness 慢性病
部圧迫	chronic inflammatory demyelinating
chest pain 胸痛；胸部痛	polyneuropathy : CIPD 慢性炎症性脱髄性
chest physical therapy : CPT 肺理学療法	多発神経炎
chest respiration 胸式呼吸	chronic kidney disease : CKD 慢性腎臓病
chest X-ray : CXR 胸部エックス線	chronic lymphocytic leukemia : CLL 慢性リン
chewing 咀嚼	パ性白血病
chewing problem 咀嚼問題	chronic myelogenous leukemia : CML 慢性骨
Cheyne-Stokes psychosis チェーンストークス	髄性白血病
精神病	chronic obstructive pulmonary disease : COPD
Cheyne-Stokes respiration チェーンストークス	慢性閉塞性肺疾患
呼吸	chronic pain 慢性疼痛
chicken pox 水疱瘡	chronic pyelonephritis 慢性腎盂腎炎
chief complaint : CC 主訴	chronic renal failure : CRF 慢性腎不全
child abuse 児童虐待	chronic respiratory failure 慢性呼吸不全
child allowance 児童扶養手当；児童手当；子	chronic stage 慢性期
ども手当	chronic subdural hematoma 慢性硬膜下血腫
childhood autism 小児自閉症	chronic tension-type headache 慢性緊張型
childhood disintegrative disorder 小児期崩壊	頭痛
性障害	chronological age 生活年齢；実年齢；暦年齢
childhood disorder 児童期障害	cicatricial contracture 瘢痕拘縮
child neglect 育児放棄	circadian rhythm サーカディアンリズム；概日リ
child protective services 児童保護サービス	ズム
Children's Charter 児童憲章	circadian variation 日内変動

circular causality　循環的因果律

circular movement　分回し運動

circulatory system　循環器

circumduction　分回し運動

circumduction gait　分回し歩行

cirrhosis　肝硬変

citizen　市民

citizenship　市民権

city hospital　市立病院

Civic Code　民法典

civil law　民法；市民法

civil rights　公民権

Civil Rights movement　公民権運動

classical conditioning　古典的条件づけ

classless society　無階級社会

claudication　跛行

cleft lip and cleft palate　口唇・口蓋裂

client　クライエント

client-centered therapy　クライエント中心療法；来談者中心療法

climacteric disturbance　更年期障害

clinic　診療所

clinical criteria of brain death　脳死判定基準

Clinical Dementia Rating : CDR　臨床認知症評価尺度

clinical engineering technologist　臨床工学技士

clinical examination　臨床検査

clinical intervention　臨床的介入

clinical interview　臨床的面接

clinical laboratory technologist and technician　臨床検査技師

clinical nurse specialist : CNS　専門看護師

clinical nutritional assessment　臨床栄養アセスメント

clinical pathway　クリニカルパス

clinical pharmacist　臨床薬剤師

clinical psychologist : CP　臨床心理士

clinical psychology　臨床心理学

clinical trial　臨床試験

Clock Drawing Test : CDT　時計描画テスト

clock position　クロックポジション

closed-chest cardiac massage　非開胸心臓マッサージ

closed-ended question　閉じられた質問

closed fracture　閉鎖骨折

closed kinetic chain : KCK　閉運動連鎖

closed question　クローズド・クエスチョン

closed wound　非開放性損傷

Clostridium botulinum　ボツリヌス菌

Clostridium difficile　クロストリジウムディフィシル菌

Clostridium perfringens　ウエルシュ菌

Clostridium welchii　ウエルシュ菌

clothing allowance　被服手当

clouding of consciousness　意識混濁

clubfoot　内反尖足

cluster headache　群発頭痛

coated tongue　舌苔

cocaine　コカイン

cocaine addiction　コカイン型依存

cochlear implant　人工内耳

cochlear nerve　蝸牛神経

code of ethics　倫理綱領

co-dependency　共依存

cognition　認知

cognitive behavioral therapy : CBT　認知行動療法

cognitive disorder　認知障害

cognitive enhancement therapy　認知機能改善療法

cognitive-experiential self-theory : CEST　認知的・経験的自己理論

cognitive impairment　認識障害

cognitive needs　知的欲求

cognitive rehabilitation　認知リハビリテーション

cognitive remediation therapy : CRT　認知機能改善療法

cognitive status　認知状態

cognitive therapy　認知療法

cohort　コーホート

cohort isolation　集団隔離

co-insurance　共同保険

cold　感冒

cold sterilization　冷滅菌

cold stress　寒冷ストレス

cold sweats　冷汗	community center　コミュニティセンター
cold therapy　寒冷療法	community chest　共同募金
collaboration　連携	community chest campaign　共同募金活動
collagen　コラーゲン	community development　地域開発
collagen disease　膠原病	community diagnosis　地域診断
collective bargaining　団体交渉	community general hospital　地域一般病院
collective unconscious　集合的無意識	community health　地域保健
colon cancer　大腸がん	community health care　地域医療
colonoscope　結腸内視鏡	community hospital　地域病院
colonoscopy　結腸内視鏡検査	community nursing　地域看護
colon polyps　大腸ポリープ	community organization　コミュニティ・オーガ
color blindness　色盲	ニゼーション
color weakness　色弱	community participation　住民参加
colorectal cancer　大腸がん	community planning　地域計画
colorectal cancer screening　大腸がん検診	compensation　代償；補償
colorectal polyps　大腸ポリープ	competitive employment　競争的雇用
colostomy　コロストミー；結腸人工肛門	complaint　苦情
colostomy irrigation　洗腸法	complementary and alternative medicine：
coma　昏睡	CAM　補完代替医療
comatose　昏睡状態	complementary medicine　補完医療
commode　移動トイレ；便器付きいす；ポータブ	complete blood count：CBC　全血球計算
ルトイレ	complex　コンプレックス
communicable disease　伝染病	compliance　コンプライアンス
Communicable Diseases Prevention and	compliance rate　遵守率
Control Act　伝染病予防法	complication　合併症
communication　コミュニケーション	compound fracture　複雑骨折
communication aid　コミュニケーションエイド；	compressed recording　圧縮記録
意思伝達装置	compression　圧搾；圧迫
communication disorder　コミュニケーション障害	compression fracture　圧迫骨折
communication evaluation　コミュニケーション	compression fracture of the spine　脊椎圧迫
評価	骨折
communication skill　コミュニケーションスキル；	compromised host　易感染宿主
コミュニケーション能力	compromised patient　易感染患者
communication tool　コミュニケーション手段	compulsion　強迫行為
communicative ability　コミュニケーション能力	compulsive act　強迫行為
community　コミュニティ；地域；地域社会	compulsory education　義務教育
community-acquired infection　市中感染	computed tomography：CT　コンピュータ断層
community-based integrated care system	撮影
地域包括ケアシステム	computed tomography scan：CT scan　CTス
community-based rehabilitation：CBR　コミュ	キャン
ニティ・ベイスド・リハビリテーション；地域リハ	concentric contraction　求心性収縮
ビリテーション	condensation　結露
community care　コミュニティケア；地域ケア	conditioned reflex　条件反射

conditioned response　条件反応

conditioned stimulus　条件刺激

conditioning　条件づけ

conduct disorder　行為障害

conduction aphasia　伝導失語

conductive hearing loss　伝導性難聴；伝音性
難聴

cone　錐体

confabulation　作話

conference　カンファレンス

Conference on Aging　高齢化委員会

confidentiality　秘密保持；守秘

conflict　葛藤

confusion　錯乱

congenital anomaly　先天異常

congenital disease　先天性疾患

congenital disorder　先天性障害

congenital hip dislocation：CHD　先天性股関
節脱臼

congenital malformation　先天奇形

congenital muscular dystrophy：CMD　先天性
筋ジストロフィー

congenital nephrotic syndrome　先天性ネフ
ローゼ症候群

congestion　うっ血

congestive heart failure　うっ血性心不全

congregate home　集合ホーム

congregate housing center　集団住宅センター

congregate meal program　集団給食サービス

conjugal family　夫婦家族

conjunctivitis　結膜炎

consciousness　意識

conservatism　保守主義

conservator　後見人；保佐人

conservatorship　後見制度；後見；保佐

constipation　便秘

constitution　憲法

Constitution of the German Reich　ワイマール
憲法

Constitution of the World Health Organization
世界保健機関憲章

constructional apraxia　構成失行

constructive disability　構成障害

consultation　コンサルテーション；相談

consultation center　相談センター

consultation interview　相談援助面接

consumer　消費者

consumerism　消費者主義

consumer movement　消費者運動

Consumer Price Index：CPI　消費者物価指数

Consumer Product Safety Act　消費者安全法

consumer protection　消費者保護

consumer rights group　消費者権利グループ

consumption tax　消費税

contact infection　接触感染

contact reflection　接触反射

contaminated area　汚染区域；不潔区域

contaminated wound　汚染創

contamination　汚染

contextual factor　背景因子

contingency　随伴性

continuative passive motion：CPM　持続他動
運動

continuity theory　継続性理論

continuous ambulatory peritoneal dialysis：
CAPD　持続携帯式腹膜透析

continuous positive air pressure：CPAP　持続
的気道陽圧

continuous quality improvement　継続的改善
活動

continuous traction　持続牽引

continuum of care　継続ケア

contracture　拘縮

contracture prevention　拘縮予防

contrast bath　温冷交代浴

controlled emotional involvement　統制された
情緒的関与

contusion　打撲；打撲傷

convalescence　療養；回復

convalescent care　療養介護

convalescent carrier　回復期保菌者

convalescent home　回復期施設

Convention on the Rights of Persons with
Disabilities　障害者の権利に関する条約

conversion disorder：CD　転換性障害

convulsion　痙攣

coordination　協調	cream-skimming　クリーム・スキミング
coordination disorder　協調運動障害	creatinine　クレアチニン
coordination impairment　失調	cremation　火葬
coordinator　コーディネーター	Creutzfeldt-Jakob disease：CJD　クロイツフェ
copayment　利用者負担；一部負担金；自己負	ルト・ヤコブ病
担金	crime　犯罪
coping behavior　対処行動	criminal code　刑法典
coping strategy　対処戦略	criminal law　刑法
copycat medication　模倣薬	criminal psychology　犯罪心理学
corneal reflex　角膜反射	criminology　犯罪社会学
cornea transplant　角膜移植	crisis intervention　クライシス・インターベンショ
Cornell Medical Index：CMI　コーネル・メディ	ン；危機介入
カル・インデックス	critical　クリティカル
Cornell Scale for Depression in Dementia：	critical pathway：CP　クリティカルパス
CSDD　コーネル認知症抑うつ尺度	Crohn's disease　クローン病
coronary artery　冠状動脈；冠動脈	cross contamination　交差汚染
coronary artery disease：CAD　冠動脈疾患	cross infection　交差感染
coronary care unit：CCU　冠動脈疾患集中治	crotamiton　クロタミトン製剤
療室	crowding-out theory　クラウディング・アウト理
coronary heart disease：CHD　冠動脈性心疾患	論；閉め出し理論
corrected visual acuity　矯正視力	crude birth rate：CBR　粗出生率；普通出生率
corrective shoes　整形靴	crude death rate　粗死亡率
cortisol　コルチゾール	crude mortality rate　粗死亡率
cost-benefit　費用便益	crutch　松葉づえ；クラッチ
cost-benefit analysis：CBA　費用便益分析	crutch gait　松葉づえ歩行
cost containment　費用抑制	cryotherapy　冷凍療法
cost-effectiveness　費用対効果	crystal arthropathy　結晶関節症
costochondritis　肋軟骨炎	crystal induced arthritis　結晶誘発性関節炎
cost of living　生計費用	crystal lens　水晶体
cost-of-living adjustment：COLA　生計費調整	crystallized ability　結晶性能力
cough　咳	crystallized intelligence　結晶性知能
cough reflex：CR　咳反射	cultural assimilation　文化的同化
cough variant asthma：CVA　咳喘息	cultural barrier　文化的障壁
council　協議会	cultural pattern　文化様式
counseling　カウンセリング	cumulative effect　蓄積効果
counselor　カウンセラー	cumulative fatigue　累積性疲労
countertransference　逆転移	cumulative incidence　累積罹患率
couple therapy　カップル療法	cure　キュア
court-ordered psychological evaluation　精神	Cushing's syndrome　クッシング症候群
鑑定	custodial care　療護；養護
coxarthrosis　変形性股関節症	custodial facility　保護施設
cranial nerve　脳神経	customer satisfaction：CS　顧客満足
cranial nerve disorder　脳神経疾患	cyanosis　チアノーゼ

cyclothymia　循環気質

cyclothymic disorder　気分循環性障害

cyclothymic temperament　循環気質

cystitis　膀胱炎

cystocele　膀胱脱；膀胱瘤

cystometrography　膀胱内圧測定

cystometry　膀胱内圧測定

cystoscopy　膀胱鏡検査

D

dactylology　指文字

daily money management：DMM　日常的金銭管理

danger to others：DTO　他害行為

danger to self or others　自傷他害行為

dark adaptation　暗順応

date of birth　生年月日

day care　デイケア

day care services　通所介護

day laborer　日雇労働者

daylighting　採光

dead on arrival：DOA　来院時心停止

deaf-blindness　盲ろう

deaf mutism　ろうあ

deafness　ろう

death　死；死亡

death certificate　死亡診断書

death notification　死亡届

death rate　死亡率

death with dignity　尊厳死

Death with Dignity Act　尊厳死法

deceased　故人；死者；死亡者

decentralization　分権化；地方分権

decision-making　意思決定

Declaration of Alma-Ata　アルマ・アタ宣言

Declaration of Helsinki　ヘルシンキ宣言

Declaration of the Rights of the Child　児童権利宣言

Declaration on the Rights of Disabled Persons　障害者の権利宣言

declarative memory　陳述記憶

decompression　除圧

decongestant　充血除去剤

decubitus ulcer　褥瘡；圧迫潰瘍；床ずれ

deduction　控除

deductive reasoning　演繹推論

deep brain stimulation：DBS　脳深部刺激療法

deep sensation　深部感覚

deep vein thrombosis　深部静脈血栓症

defense mechanism　防衛機制；適応機制

deficiency　欠乏症；不適合

deficiency needs　一次的欲求；基本的欲求

deficient practice　不適合行為

deformity　形成不全；変形

degenerative disease　変性疾患

deglutition disorder　嚥下障害

deglutition pneumonia　嚥下性肺炎；誤嚥性肺炎

dehydration　脱水症

deinstitutionalization　脱施設（化）

delayed urination　遷延性排尿

delirium　せん妄

Delirium Rating Scale　せん妄評価尺度

delirium tremens：DTs　振戦せん妄

delusion　妄想

delusional disorder　妄想性障害

delusional jealousy　嫉妬妄想

delusion-like ideas　妄想様観念

delusion of grandeur　誇大妄想

delusion of guilt　罪業妄想

delusion of reference　関係妄想

delusion of self-accusation　罪業妄想

dementia　認知症

dementia care mapping：DCM　認知症ケアマッピング

dementia care pathway　認知症ケアパス

dementia of the Alzheimer's type：DAT　アルツハイマー型認知症

Dementia Rating Scale　認知症評価尺度

dementia special care unit　認知症ケア専門病棟

dementia wandering alarm　認知症老人徘徊感知機器

demerit goods　非価値財；負の価値財

demographic statistics　人口統計

demographic transition theory　人口転換論

demyelinating disease　脱髄疾患

demyelination　脱髄

denervation　脱神経

denial　否認

dental clinic　歯科診療所

dental disease　歯科疾患

dental floss　デンタルフロス；歯間歯磨き

dental hygienist　歯科衛生士

dental plaque　歯垢

dental technician　歯科技工士

dentist　歯科医師

dentistry　歯科

denture　入れ歯；義歯

Denver Developmental Screening Test：DDST
　デンバー式発達スクリーニング検査

dependence　依存

dependency ratio　従属人口指数

dependent　被扶養者

dependent population　従属人口

depersonalization disorder　離人症

depopulation　少子化；過疎化

depopulation and aging　少子・高齢化

depression　うつ；うつ病；単極性感情障害

depressive neurosis　抑うつ神経症

depressive state　抑うつ状態

depressurized room　陰圧室

Dercum disease　有痛性脂肪症

deregulation　規制緩和

dermatitis　皮膚炎

dermatologist　皮膚科医

dermatology　皮膚科学

dermatomyositis　皮膚筋炎

dermatophyte　皮膚糸状菌

dermatophytosis　皮膚糸状菌症

developmental age　発達年齢

developmental coordination disorder：DCD
　発達性協調運動障害

developmental delay　発達遅延

developmental disability　発達障害

developmental disorder　発達障害

developmental psychopathology　発達精神病
　理学

developmental quotient：DQ　発達指数

developmental task　発達課題

developmental test　発達検査

developmental theory　発達理論

development stage　発達段階

development theory　発達段階説

deviant behavior　逸脱行動

deviation　逸脱

device-related infection　器材関連感染

dexterity　巧緻性

diabetes mellitus：DM　糖尿病

diabetic coma　糖尿病性昏睡

diabetic exchange list　糖尿病交換表

diabetic food exchange list　糖尿病食品交換表

diabetic ketoacidosis：DKA　糖尿病性ケトアシ
　ドーシス

diabetic nephropathy　糖尿病性腎症

diabetic neuropathy　糖尿病性神経障害

diabetic retinopathy　糖尿病性網膜症

diagnosis　診断

diagnosis procedure combination：DPC　診断
　群分類

Diagnostic and Statistical Manual of Mental
　Disorders：DSM　精神障害の診断と統計の手
　引き

diagnostic imaging　画像診断

diagnostic laparoscopy：DL　診断的腹腔鏡
　検査

diagnostic related groups-prospective payment
　system：DRG-PPS　診断群別所定報酬額支
　払方式

dialysis　透析；人工透析；血液透析

dialysis therapy　透析療法

diaper　おむつ

diaphragm　横隔膜

diarrhea　下痢

diastolic pressure　拡張期血圧；最低血圧

dielectric heating　誘電加熱

diencephalon　間脳

dietary fiber　食物繊維

Dietary Guidelines　食生活指針

dietary habit　食習慣

dietary restriction　食事制限

dietary supplement　栄養剤；栄養補助食品

dietitian　管理栄養士

differential diagnosis　鑑別診断

diffuse alveolar damage：DAD　びまん性肺胞傷害

diffuse axonal injury：DAI　びまん性軸索損傷

digestion　消化

digestion and absorption　消化吸収

digestive disease　消化器疾患

digestive enzyme　消化酵素

digital examination　指診

digital removal of feces：DRF　摘便

dignity　尊厳

dilemma　ジレンマ

diminished capacity　心神耗弱

diminished responsibility　限定責任能力

diphtheria　ジフテリア

diplegia　両麻痺

direct care staff　介護職員

direct contact infection　直接接触感染

direct contact transmission　直接接触感染

direct language　直接言語

director of nursing　看護師長

direct tax　直接税

dirty utility room　不潔物収納室；汚物室

dirty wound　不潔創

disability　ディスアビリティ；障害；能力障害

disability allowance　障害手当金

disability certification　障害認定

disability insurance：DI　障害保険

disability organization　障害者団体

disability pension　障害年金

disability prevention　障害の発生予防

disability services　障害福祉サービス

disability standards for education　教育における障害基準

disability study　障害学

disabled person parking permit　障害者駐車許可証

disarticulation　関節離断

disaster　災害

disaster insurance　災害保険

disaster prevention and preparedness　防災

discharge　退院；退所

discharge against medical advice：DAMA　自主退院

discharge information　退所時情報

discharge management　退院調整

discharge planning　退院計画

disclosure　ディスクロージャー

discoloration　変色

discomfort index　不快指数

Discomfort Scale for Dementia of the Alzheimer's Type：DS-DAT　アルツハイマー型認知症不快評価尺度

discrimination　差別

discriminative stimulus　弁別刺激

disease　疾患；疾病

disease management：DM　疾患管理

disengagement　離脱

disengagement theory　離脱理論

disengagement theory of aging　老化の離脱説

disequilibrium syndrome　不均衡症候群

disinfectant　消毒剤

disinfection　消毒

disinhibition　脱抑制

disorder　疾患；疾病

disorder of environmental origin　環境由来疾患

disorganized thinking　滅裂思考

disorientation　失見当識；見当識障害；誤見当

displacement　置き換え

disposal　処理

disqualification criteria　欠格条項

disseminated intravascular coagulation：DIC　播種性血管内凝固症候群

dissociated sensory disturbance　解離性感覚障害

dissociative disorder：DD　解離性障害

dissociative identity disorder：DID　解離性同一性障害；多重人格障害

distal radius fracture　橈骨遠位端骨折

distance education　遠隔教育

distance learning　遠隔学習

distilled water　蒸留水

distractibility　転導性

distributive share　遺留分

district court　地方裁判所	droplet transmission　飛沫伝播
disturbance of consciousness　意識障害	drowsiness　傾眠；眠気
disuse atrophy　廃用性萎縮	drug　薬；薬剤
disuse muscle atrophy　廃用性筋萎縮	drug abuse　薬物乱用
disuse osteoporosis　廃用性骨粗鬆症	drug addiction　薬物依存；覚せい剤依存
disuse syndrome　廃用症候群；生活不活発病	drug allergy　薬物アレルギー
diuretic　利尿剤	drug-induced acute pancreatitis　薬剤性急性膵炎
diuretic effect　利尿作用	drug-induced chronic pancreatitis　薬剤性慢性膵炎
diversional occupational therapy　気晴らし的作業療法	drug-induced hepatitis　薬剤性肝炎
diversity　多様性	drug-induced liver disease　薬剤性肝疾患
diverticular disease　憩室疾患	drug-induced lupus　薬剤誘発性ループス
divorce　離婚	drug-induced osteoporosis　薬剤性骨粗鬆症
divorce certificate　離婚証明書	drug-induced pancreatitis　薬剤性膵炎
dizziness　めまい；立ちくらみ	drug-induced Parkinsonism　薬剤性パーキンソニズム
doctor's appointment　診療予約	drug-induced psychosis　薬剤性精神病
doctor's office　診療所	drug-induced Schizophrenia　薬剤性統合失調症
documentation　記録	
domestic violence：DV　ドメスティック・バイオレンス；家庭内暴力	drug intoxication　薬物中毒
domestic worker　家庭奉仕員	drug price controls　薬価規制
dominant inheritance　優性遺伝	drug price standards　薬価基準
donation　寄付	drug rash　薬疹
donor　ドナー	dry heat sterilization　乾熱滅菌
Do Not Attempt Cardiopulmonary Resuscitation：DNACPR　蘇生処置拒否	dry mouth　ドライマウス
	Duchenne muscular dystrophy：DMD　デュシェンヌ型筋ジストロフィー
Do Not Attempt Resuscitation：DNAR　蘇生処置拒否	duck-like walk　動揺性歩行
	dumping syndrome　ダンピング症候群
Do Not Resuscitate：DNR　蘇生処置拒否	duodenal ulcer　十二指腸潰瘍
dopamine　ドーパミン	Dupuytren's contracture　デュピュイトラン拘縮
dorsalis pedis artery　足背動脈	durable medical equipment：DME　耐久医療機器
dorsiflexion　背屈	
dose modification　投与量の調整	duty of confidentiality　守秘義務
double-bind theory　ダブルバインド仮説；二重拘束説	dysarthria　構音障害
	dysarthria training　構音訓練
double stance phase　同時定着時期	dysautonomia　自律神経失調
double support period　両脚支持期	dyscalculia　失算
Down's syndrome　ダウン症候群	dyschezia　排便障害
drain　ドレーン	dysentery　赤痢
drama therapy　ドラマセラピー	dysesthesia　異常知覚
dressing dyspraxia　着衣失行	dysexecutive syndrome　遂行機能障害症候群
droplet infection　飛沫感染	
droplet precaution　飛沫予防策	

dysgraphia　書字障害
dyskinesia　ジスキネジア
dyslipidemia　脂質異常症
dysphagia　嚥下障害
dysphagia diet　嚥下困難者用食品
dysplasia　形成不全
dyspnea　呼吸困難
dysthymia　気分変調性症
dysthymic disorder　気分変調性症
dystonia　ジストニア
dysuria　排尿障害

E

early ambulation　早期離床
early detection　早期発見
early intervention　早期介入
early morning awakening　早朝覚醒
early-onset Alzheimer's disease　早発性アルツ
　ハイマー病
early-onset dementia：EOD　若年性認知症；
　早発性認知症
Early Speech Perception Test　初期発話知覚テ
　スト
early-stage cancer　早期がん
earnings test　所得調査
ear, nose and throat evaluation　耳鼻咽喉検査
ear, nose and throat specialist　耳鼻咽喉科医
earwax　耳垢
earwax blockage　耳垢塞栓
easy fatigability　易疲労性
eating abnormality　異食
eating disorder　摂食障害
eating habit　食習慣
Eaton-Lambert syndrome　イートン・ランバート
　症候群
eccentric contraction　遠心性収縮
eccrine gland　エクリン腺
echocardiogram　心エコー図
echocardiography　心エコー
echographia　反響書字
echokinesis　反響動作；反響運動
echolalia　反響言語

echologia　反響言語
echomatism　反響動作
echomimia　反響表情
echopathy　反響症
echophenomenon　反響症状；反響現象
echophrasia　反響言語
echopraxia　反響動作
ecological approach　エコロジカルアプローチ
ectopic kidney　異所性腎
ectopic pregnancy　子宮外妊娠
ectopic rhythm　異所性リズム
ectopic sebaceous gland　異所性皮脂腺
ectopic ureter　異所性尿管
ectopic ureterocele　異所性尿管瘤
eczema　湿疹；皮膚炎
edema　浮腫
edentulism　無歯症
education　教育
educational rehabilitation　教育リハビリテーション
education benefit　教育給付
effort angina　労作時狭心症
ego　エゴ；自我
ego analysis　自我分析
ego-consciousness　自我意識
ego identity　自我同一性
eicosapentaenoic acid：EPA　エイコサペンタエ
　ン酸
elasticity　弾力性
elbow bathing　肘浴
elder　高齢；年長；年上
elder abuse　高齢者虐待
elder abuse prevention　高齢者虐待防止
elder care　高齢者ケア；高齢者介護
elderly　高齢者
elderly care　高齢者ケア；高齢者介護
elderly-onset rheumatoid arthritis：EORA
　高齢発症関節リウマチ
elderly population　高齢者人口
elder neglect　高齢者ネグレクト
electric aspirator　電動吸引器
electric records　電子記録
electric wheelchair　電動車いす
electrocardiogram：EKG　心電図検査

electroconvulsive therapy：ECT　電撃療法；電気ショック療法；電気けいれん療法

electrodiagnosis：EDX　電気診断法

electroencephalogram：EEG　脳波図

electroencephalography：EEG　脳波検査

electromyogram：EMG　筋電図

electromyography　筋電図検査

electron-beam computed tomography：EBCT　電子ビームCT

electronic endoscopy　電子内視鏡検査

electronic health records：HER　電子カルテ；電子健康記録

electrostimulation　電気刺激

electrotherapy　電気療法

elevation　補高；挙上

Elizabethan Poor Law　エリザベス救貧法

embolism　塞栓

embryonic stage　胎芽期

embryopathy　胎芽病

emergency alarm system　緊急通報装置

emergency assistance：EA　緊急扶助

emergency call　緊急通報

emergency call system　緊急通報システム

emergency care and resuscitation　救急蘇生

emergency contact information　緊急連絡先

emergency medical services　救急医療

emergency medical technician：EMT　救急救命士

emergency room：ER　救急救命室；救急外来

emergency treatment　救急処置；応急手当

emerging and re-emerging infectious diseases　新興・再興感染症

emerging infectious disease　新興感染症

emollient　軟化剤

emotion　情動

emotional abuse　精神的虐待；情緒的虐待

emotional care　心理的ケア；心のケア

emotional disturbance　情緒障害

emotional incontinence　感情失禁；情動失禁

empathetic attitude　共感的態度

empathic understanding　共感的理解

empathy　共感

emphysema　気腫

emphysematous pyelonephritis　気腫性腎盂腎炎

empiric therapy　経験的治療

employee satisfaction：ES　従業員満足度

Employment Act　雇用法

employment insurance　雇用保険

employment rate　雇用率

employment verification letter　在職証明書

empowerment　エンパワメント

empowerment approach　エンパワメントアプローチ

empty nest syndrome　空の巣症候群

encephalitis　脳炎

encoding　記銘

encoding deficit　記銘力障害

endocrine　内分泌

endocrine disorder　内分泌疾患

endocrine organ　内分泌器官

endocrinologist　内分泌医

endocrinology　内分泌学

end-of-life　終末期

end-of-life care　エンド・オブ・ライフケア；終末期ケア；終末期介護

endogenous　内因

endogenous infection　内因性感染

endogenous mental disorder　内因性精神障害

endogenous psychosis　内因性精神病

endoscope　内視鏡

endoscopy　内視鏡検査

endotracheal anesthesia　気管内麻酔

end-stage kidney disease　末期腎不全

end-stage renal disease：ESRD　末期腎不全

endurance　持久性

enema　浣腸

energy expenditure　エネルギー消費

energy metabolism　エネルギー代謝

energy requirement　エネルギー必要量

energy storing prosthetic foot　エネルギー蓄積足部

Engel's coefficient　エンゲル係数

Engel's law　エンゲルの法則

enmeshment　纏綿状態

enteral tube：ET　外部チューブ

enterocele 小腸瘤

enterohemorrhagic Escherichia coli：EHEC
　腸管出血性大腸菌

enterotoxin エンテロトキシン

enterovirus エンテロウイルス

entrapment neuropathy 絞扼神経障害

enuresis 遺尿症

environmental factor 環境因子

environmental hazards 環境危険物質

environmental hormone 環境ホルモン

environmental pollution 環境汚染

environmental rights 環境権

environmental surveillance 環境サーベイランス

enzyme 酵素

epidemic 流行性

epidemic keratoconjunctivitis：EKC 流行性角
　結膜炎

epidemiological study 疫学調査

epidemiology 疫学

epidural analgesia 硬膜外鎮痛法

epidural hematoma 硬膜外血腫

epiglottis 喉頭蓋

epilepsy てんかん

epileptic seizure てんかん発作

epinephrine エピネフリン

epiphysis cerebri 松果体

episodic memory エピソード記憶

epistaxis 鼻出血

epithelial tissue 上皮組織

e-prescription 電子処方

equal rights 平等権

equinovarus foot 内反尖足

equity 公平

erectile dysfunction：ED 勃起不全

erection 勃起

erector spinae 脊柱起立筋

ergometer エルゴメーター

ergonomics エルゴノミクス

erosion びらん

erythema 発赤；紅斑

erythrocyte sedimentation rate：ESR 赤血球
　沈降速度

erythropoietin エリスロポエチン

es エス

Escherichia coli：E. coli 大腸菌

esophageal cancer 食道がん

esophageal manometry 食道内圧検査

esophageal motility disorder 食道運動障害

esophageal phase 食道相

esophagus 食道

esotropia 内斜視

essential amino acid 必須アミノ酸

essential hypertension 本態性高血圧

estate tax 遺産税

esteem needs 自我の欲求

estimated daily intake 推定一日摂取量

Estimated Energy Requirement：EER 推定エ
　ネルギー必要量

estrogen エストロゲン；卵胞ホルモン

estrogen replacement therapy：ERT エストロ
　ゲン補充療法

ethanol disinfectant エタノール消毒液

ethics 倫理

ethnic discrimination 民族差別

ethnic minority 少数民族

ethnicity エスニシティ

ethylene oxide gas sterilization エチレンオキサ
　イドガス滅菌

eugenic protection 優性保護

eugenics 優生学

eurhythmia 整脈

euthanasia 安楽死

evacuation site 避難場所

evaluation エバリュエーション；評価

evidence エビデンス；根拠；証拠

evidence-based care：EBC 根拠にもとづくケア

evidence-based medicine：EBM 根拠にもとづ
　く医療

evidence-based nursing：EBN 根拠にもとづく
　看護

excessive daytime sleepiness：EDS 日中過
　睡眠

excrement 便

excretion 排泄

executive function disorder：EFD 実行機能障
　害；遂行機能障害

exercise capacity　運動許容量

exercise load　運動負荷

exercise prescription　運動処方

exercise strength　運動強度

exercise tolerance test：ETT　運動負荷テスト

exfoliative cytology　剥離細胞診

existential therapy　実存的療法

exogenous　外因（性）

exogenous hormone　外因性ホルモン

exogenous infection　外因性感染

exogenous psychosis　外因性精神障害

exotropia　外斜視

expert　専門家

expiration date　消費期限；賞味期限

expiration reflex：ER　呼息反射

explicit memory　陳述記憶

expressions of desires　意思の伝達

extended family　拡大家族；複合家族

extended spinal stenosis　広範脊柱管狭窄症

extension　伸展

extension contracture　伸展拘縮

external frame of reference　外的照合枠

external respiration　外呼吸；呼吸運動

external rotation　外旋

extinction phenomenon　消去現象

extrapyramidal symptoms：EPS　錐体外路症状

extraversion　外向性

extraversion-introversion test　向性検査

extremities　四肢

extrinsic asthma　外因型喘息

eye disease　眼病

eye drops　点眼液

eye pressure　眼（内）圧

F

face sheet　フェイス・シート

face-to-face interview　対面法

facial paralysis　顔面神経麻痺

facility　施設

fainting　失神

fall　転倒

fallen arches　扁平足

fall incident　転倒事故

fall prevention　転倒予防

fall risk　転倒危険度

familial adenomatous polyposis：FAP　家族性大腸ポリポーシス

family　家族；家庭

family-based care　家族中心ケア

family caregiver　家族介護者

Family Caregiver Burden Scale　家族介護負担感尺度

family caregiving　家族介護

family casework　ファミリー・ケースワーク；家族ケースワーク

family caseworker　家族ケースワーカー

family counselor　家庭相談員

family doctor　家庭医

family history　家族歴

family identity　ファミリー・アイデンティティ

family life cycle　ファミリー・ライフサイクル；家族周期

family of orientation　出生家族；定位家族

family of procreation　生殖家族；創設家族

family-oriented care　家族指向ケア

family relationship　家族関係

family social work　ファミリー・ソーシャルワーク；家族ソーシャルワーク

family social worker　家族ソーシャルワーカー

family structure　家族構成；世帯構造

family support　ファミリー・サポート；家族支援

family support center　ファミリーサポートセンター；家族支援センター

family system　家族システム

family systems approach　家族システムズアプローチ

family system theory　家族システム理論

family therapy　家族療法

family welfare　家族福祉

fasciitis　筋膜炎

fasting blood sugar　空腹時血糖

fat　脂肪

fatal familial insomnia　致死性家族性不眠症

fatigue　疲労

fat-soluble vitamin　脂溶性ビタミン

fatty acid　脂肪酸

favorable tax treatment　税制優遇措置

fecal examination　糞便検査

fecal impaction　宿便

fecal incontinence：FI　便失禁

fecal occult blood test：FOBT　便潜血検査

fecal sampling　採便

fecal smearing　糞便塗抹

feces　便

fee-for-service：FFS　出来高払い

Feeling Tone Questionnaire：FTQ　感情気分質問票

feminism　フェミニズム

feminist social work　フェミニスト・ソーシャルワーク

feminist theory　フェミニズム理論

femoral neck fracture　大腿骨頸部骨折

fermentation　発酵

festinating gait　突進現象；小刻み歩行

festination　加速歩行

fetal alcohol spectrum disorder　胎児性アルコール・スペクトラム障害

fetal alcohol syndrome　胎児性アルコール症候群

fetal disorder　胎児期障害

fetal mortality rate　死産率

fetal stage　胎児期

fever　発熱

fever of unknown origin：FUO　不明熱

fiber　繊維

fiberscope　ファイバースコープ

fiduciary abuse　経済的虐待

filial piety　親孝行

financial abuse　経済的虐待

finger agnosia　手指失認

fingerspelling　指文字

fire-retardant material　難燃剤

first aid　応急手当；救急処置

fistula　瘻孔

fixation　固着

fixed dystonia　固定ジストニア

flaccid　弛緩

flaccidity　弛緩

flaccid paralysis　弛緩性麻痺

flail joint　動揺関節

flame-resistant material　防炎素材

flame sterilization　火炎滅菌

flashback　フラッシュバック

flat affect　感情鈍麻；情意鈍麻

flat foot　扁平足

flax　亜麻

flexibility　柔軟性

flexibility exercise　柔軟体操

flexion　屈曲

flexion contracture　屈曲拘縮

flight of ideas　観念奔逸

flu　感冒；インフルエンザ

fluid　水分

fluid balance　水分バランス

fluid intake　水分摂取

fluid intelligence　流動性知能

fluoroscopy　X線透視検査

flu shot　インフルエンザワクチン

flu virus　インフルエンザウイルス

focal　巣状

focal infection　病巣感染

focal neurologic deficit　巣症状

focal neurologic sign　巣症状

folic acid　葉酸

folk medicine　民間療法

folliculitis　毛嚢炎

follow-up　フォロー・アップ

food allergen labeling　アレルギー表示

food allergy　食物アレルギー

food-borne infection　食物媒介感染

food composition table　食品成分表

food contamination　食品汚染

food exchange lists　食品交換表

food groups　食品群

food guide pyramid　フードガイドピラミッド

food inspector　食品衛生監視員

food intake　摂食

food poisoning　食中毒

food-related disorder　食物関連障害

food sanitation　食品衛生

英和

A
B
C
D
E
F
G
H
I
J
K
L
M

145

Food Sanitation Act　食品衛生法

food sanitation supervisor　食品衛生管理者

foot bath　足浴

foot drop　尖足

forced crying　強制泣き

forced laughing　強制笑い

forceps　鉗子

forceps biopsy　鉗子生検

forearm crutch　エルボークラッチ

forensic autopsy　司法解剖

forgetfulness　物忘れ

formal care　フォーマルケア

formal network　フォーマルネットワーク

formal service　フォーマルサービス

formulary　処方集

for-profit organization　営利団体

four-point cane　四脚づえ

four-point gait　四点歩行

four-wheel walker　四輪歩行車；歩行車

Fowler's position　ファーラー位

fracture　骨折

fracture of upper end of the humerus
　上腕骨近位端骨折

frailty　虚弱

Frankel Classification　フランケル分類

fraud　詐欺

free association technique　自由連想法

free trial scam　無料商法

freezing of gait：FOG　すくみ足歩行

frequent bowel movements　頻便

friction　摩擦

friendly society　友愛組合

friendly visiting　友愛訪問

friendly visitor　友愛訪問員

frontal lobe　前頭葉

frontal lobe dysfunction　前頭葉障害

frontal lobe syndrome　前頭葉症状

frontotemporal dementia：FTD　前頭側頭型認
　知症

frontotemporal lobar degeneration：FTLD
　前頭側頭葉変性症

front wheel folding walker　折りたたみ前輪歩
　行器

front wheel walker　前輪歩行器

frostbite　凍傷

frozen gait　すくみ足

frozen shoulder　凍結肩；肩関節周囲炎

fructose　果糖

frustration　フラストレーション；欲求不満

frustration tolerance　フラストレーション耐性；
　欲求不満耐性

full denture　総入れ歯

fulminant hepatitis　劇症肝炎

function　機能

Functional Activities Questionnaire：FAQ
　機能的活動質問票

functional age　機能年齢

functional approach　機能的アプローチ

functional assessment　機能評価

Functional Assessment Inventory：FAI　機能評
　価票

Functional Assessment of Cancer Therapy：
　FACT　がん治療機能評価

Functional Assessment of Chronic Illness
　Therapy：FACIT　慢性疾患療法機能評価

functional autonomy　機能的自律

functional cardiac disorder　心臓機能障害

functional component　機能性成分

functional constipation　機能性便秘

functional differentiation　機能分化

functional electrical stimulation：FES　機能的
　電気刺激

functional incontinence　機能性尿失禁

functional independence　機能的自立

functional independence measure：FIM　機能
　的自立度評価法

functionalism　機能主義

functional localization　機能局在

functional maintenance　機能維持

functional mental disorder　機能性精神障害

functional neurological symptom disorder
　転換性障害

functional occupational therapy　機能的作業
　療法

functional position　機能肢位

functional prognosis　機能予後

functional reconstruction　機能再建

functional recovery　機能回復

functional residual capacity　機能的残気量

functional respiratory disorder　呼吸（器）機能障害

Functional Status Questionnaire : FSQ　機能状態質問票

functional training　機能訓練

fundamental human rights　基本的人権

fundamental position　基本肢位

fungal endophthalmitis　真菌性眼内炎

fungal infection　真菌感染

fungemia　真菌血症

G

gait　歩行；歩容

gait analysis　歩行分析

gait apraxia　歩行失行

gait assessment　歩行機能評価

gait cycle　歩行周期

gait disability　歩行障害

gait pattern　歩行パターン

gait speed　歩行速度

gait training　歩行訓練；歩行練習

gait velocity　歩行速度

galactose　ガラクトース

gallstone　胆石

gangrene　壊疽

gargling　うがい

gas exchange　ガス交換

gas gangrene　ガス壊疽

gasping respiration　下顎呼吸

gastrectomy　胃切除術

gastric cancer　胃がん

gastric juice　胃液

gastric lavage　胃洗浄

gastric tube feeding　胃ろう経管栄養

gastric ulcer　胃潰瘍

gastritis　胃炎

gastroduodenal ulcer　胃・十二指腸潰瘍

gastroenterologist　消化器内科医

gastroesophageal reflex disease : GERD　胃食道逆流症

gastrointestinal bleeding　消化管出血

gastrointestinal hormone　消化管ホルモン

gastrointestinal physiology　消化管生理学

gastrostomy　胃ろう

gastrostomy tube　胃ろうチューブ

gauze　ガーゼ

gender　ジェンダー；性別

gender difference　性差

gender discrimination　性差別

gender dysphoria　性同一性障害

gender-equal society　男女共同参画社会

gender identity disorder : GID　性同一性障害

gender-related development index : GDI　ジェンダー開発指数

gender role　性役割

gene　遺伝子

gene mutation　遺伝子の突然変異

general bed　一般病床

general health education　一般健康教育

general hospital　一般病院；総合病院

general household survey : GHS　一般世帯調査；総合世帯調査

generalized anxiety disorder : GAD　全般性不安障害

generalized dementia　全般性認知症

general practitioner : GP　一般医

general system theory　一般システム論

generation　世代

generatively　生殖性

generic drug　ジェネリック医薬品；後発医薬品

generic social work　ジェネリックソーシャルワーク

genetically modified organism : GMO　遺伝子組み換え食品

genetic diagnosis　遺伝子診断

genetic disorder　遺伝（子）病

genetics　遺伝学

genetic testing　遺伝子検査

genetic theory of aging　老化の遺伝説

genital hygiene　陰部洗浄

genital stage　性器期

genital ulcer　陰部潰瘍

genogram　ジェノグラム

genomic imprinting　遺伝刷り込み

genuineness　真実性

genuine stress incontinence　完全尿失禁；真性腹圧性尿失禁

geriatric dentistry　高齢者歯科学分野

Geriatric Depression Scale：GDS　老年期うつ病評価尺度

geriatrician　高齢者専門医

geriatric medicine　老人医学

geriatric nursing　老人看護

geriatrics　老年医学

geriatric syndrome　老年症候群

gerontological social work　老年社会福祉学

gerontology　老年学

gerontophobia　老人恐怖症

Gerstmann syndrome　ゲルストマン症候群

gestational diabetes　妊娠糖尿病

giant cell arteritis　巨細胞性動脈炎

gingiva　歯肉

glass eye　義眼

glaucoma　緑内障

global aging　世界的老化

global aphasia　全失語

Global Assessment of Functioning：GAF　全体的機能評価

Global Assessment Scale：GAS　全体的評価尺度

globalization　グローバリゼーション

glomerular filtration rate：GFR　糸球体濾過量

glossopharyngeal breathing：GPS　舌咽呼吸

glossopharyngeal neuralgia　舌咽神経痛

glossoptosis　舌根沈下

glucocorticoid　糖性グルココルチコイド

glucosamine　グルコサミン

glucose　ブドウ糖

glucose anhydride　グルコース無水物

glucose level　糖値

glucose tolerance test：GTT　ブドウ糖負荷試験

glucosuria　尿糖

glutaraldehyde　グルタルアルデヒド

gluteus maximus muscle　大臀筋

glycemic index：GI　グリセミック・インデックス（指数）

glycogen　グリコーゲン

glycosuria　尿糖

goiter　甲状腺腫

gonad　性腺

gonarthrosis　変形性膝関節症

goniometer　関節角度計

gout　痛風

gouty arthritis　痛風性関節炎

grab bar　移動バー

grand mal seizure　大発作

Graves' disease　グレーブス病

graveyard　墓地

Great Depression　世界大恐慌

greater trochanter　大転子部

Gresham's law　グレシャムの法則

grief　悲嘆

grief care　グリーフケア

grief reaction　悲嘆反応

grievance　苦情

grievances and complaints resolution　苦情解決

grip strength　握力

gross domestic product：GDP　国内総生産

gross national product：GNP　国民総生産

gross national welfare：GNW　国民総福祉

group　集団

group approach　グループ・アプローチ

group counseling　グループ・カウンセリング

group dynamics　グループ・ダイナミックス；集団力学

group exercise　グループ運動

group home　グループホーム

grouping　グルーピング

group interview　グループ・インタビュー

group psychotherapy　集団精神療法

group supervision　グループ・スーパービジョン

group therapy　集団療法

group work　グループワーク

growth hormone　成長ホルモン

growth needs　二次的欲求

guarantor　保証人

guardian　後見人；保佐人；保護者

guardianship　後見；後見制度；保佐

guide dog　盲導犬

Guillain-Barre syndrome：GBS　ギラン・バレー症候群

gum disease　歯周病

gustation　味覚

gustatory hallucination　幻味

gynecologist　婦人科医

gynecology　婦人科；婦人科学

H

habilitation　ハビリテーション

haemostasis　止血

Haglund's deformity　ハグルンド奇形

halitosis　口臭

hallucination　幻覚

hallux valgus　外反母趾

Hamilton Rating Scale for Depression　ハミルトンうつ病評価尺度

hand antisepsis　手指消毒

handicap　ハンディキャップ；社会的不利

handrail　ハンドレール；手すり

hand washing　手洗い

handwriting　ハンドライティング

Hansen's disease　ハンセン病

Hansen's disease control policy　ハンセン病対策

hard of hearing　難聴

Harris-Benedict equation　ハリス・ベネディクト算定式

Hartnup disease　ハートナップ病

Hartnup disorder　ハートナップ病

Hashimoto's disease　橋本病

Hashimoto's thyroiditis　橋本甲状腺炎

hay fever　アレルギー性鼻炎；花粉症

hazardous material　危険物；危険有害物質

headache　頭痛

head injury　頭部外傷；外傷性脳損傷；脳外傷

head tilt/chin lift maneuver　頭部後傾法

health　健康

health behavior　保健行動

health behavior theory　健康行動理論

health belief model　健康信念モデル

health care　医療；医療的ケア

health-care proxy　医療委任状

health check-up　健康チェック

health education　衛生教育；健康教育

health examination　健康診査

health indicator　健康指標

health insurance　健康保険；医療保険

health insurer　医療保険者

health maintenance　健康維持

Health Maintenance Organization：HMO　健康維持組織

health management　健康管理

health observation　健康観察

health policy　医療政策

health professional　医療専門職

health promotion　ヘルスプロモーション；健康増進

health-related quality of life　健康関連QOL

health-related services　医療関連サービス

health risk management　健康危機管理

health service area　医療圏

healthy carrier　健康保菌者

healthy life expectancy：HALE　健康寿命

healthy person　健常者

healthy volunteer　健康ボランティア；健常人

hearing　聴力

hearing aid　補聴器

hearing and balance disorder　聴覚・平衡機能障害

hearing assessment　聴覚的評価

hearing dog　聴導犬

hearing impairment　聴覚障害

hearing level　聴力レベル

hearing loss　聴覚障害；難聴

hearing test　聴力検査

hearing therapist　聴能訓練士

heart　心臓

heartbeat　心拍

heartburn　胸やけ

heart catheterization　心臓カテーテル法

heart disease　心疾患；心臓病

heart failure　心不全

heart rate　心拍数

149

heat burn 高温やけど	hereditary disease 遺伝病
heat exhaustion 熱疲労	hereditary nonpolyposis colorectal cancer：
heat rash あせも	HNCC 家族性非ポリポーシス大腸がん
heat retention うつ熱	herniated disc 椎間板ヘルニア
heat-shock response ヒートショック	heroin ヘロイン
heat stroke 日射病；熱中症	heroin addictive ヘロイン依存
heat therapy 温熱療法	heroin dependence ヘロイン依存
Heberden's nodes ヘバーデン結節	herpes zoster 帯状疱疹
heel strike 踵接地	heterotopic bone formation 異所性骨化
Heimlich maneuver ハイムリッヒ法	hiatal hernia 食道裂孔ヘルニア
Helicobacter pylori：H. pylori ヘリコバクター・	hiatus hernia 食道裂孔ヘルニア
ピロリ	hiccups しゃっくり
Heller's syndrome ヘラー症候群	hidden cultural barrier 隠れた文化的障壁
hematemesis 吐血	hierarchical society 階級社会
hematochezia 血便	hierarchy of needs ニーズの階層
hematocrit ヘマトクリット	hierarchy of needs theory 欲求階層説
hematology 血液学	high deductible health insurance plan：HDHP
hematoma 血腫	高免責額医療保険
hematuria 血尿	high-density lipoprotein 高比重リポたんぱく質
hemianopia 半盲	high-density lipoprotein cholesterol HDLコレ
hemiparesis 不全片麻痺	ステロール
hemiplegia 片麻痺	higher order brain dysfunction 高次脳機能
hemi walker ウォーカーケイン；歩行器型つえ	障害
hemocyte 血球	higher order brain function 高次脳機能
hemodialysis 人工透析；血液透析	high-Fowler's position 長座位
hemoglobin：Hb ヘモグロビン；血色素	high-functioning autism：HFA 高機能自閉症
hemolytic anemia 溶血性貧血	highly advanced medical technology：HAMT
hemophilia 血友病	高度先進医療
hemophilic arthropathy 血友病性関節症	high molecular absorbent 高分子吸水体
hemoptysis 喀血	high-touch surface 高頻度接触面
hemorrhage in ocular fundus 眼底出血	hip fracture 股関節骨折
hemorrhagic bullae 出血性水疱	hoarding 異物収集；収集癖
hemorrhagic stroke 出血性卒中	holistic medicine ホリスティック医療；全人的
hemorrhaging 大出血	医療
hemostasis 止血	Holter monitor ホルターモニター
hemp 麻	home care 在宅ケア；在宅介護；訪問介護
Hendrich Fall Risk Assessment Tool ヘンドリッ	home care assessment 在宅ケアアセスメント
ク転倒危険度評価ツール	home care medicine 在宅医療
hepatic cirrhosis 肝硬変	home care physician 在宅医
hepatitis 肝炎	home dialysis 在宅透析療法
hepatologist 肝臓専門医	home health 訪問看護；在宅看護
hepatology 肝臓病学	home health care 訪問看護ケア
herbal medicine 漢方薬	home health nurse 訪問看護師

home mechanical ventilation　在宅人工呼吸療法

home modification　住宅改修

homeostasis　ホメオスタシス；恒常性

home oxygen therapy：HOT　在宅酸素療法

home parenteral nutrition：HPN　在宅中心静脈栄養

home repair scam　家屋修理詐欺

home safety　住宅安全

home treatment　在宅治療

homosexuality　同性愛

honey-thickened liquid diet　濃厚はちみつ状液体食

hormone replacement therapy：HRT　ホルモン補充療法

hormones　ホルモン

Horner syndrome　ホルネル症候群

horticultural therapy　園芸療法

hospice　ホスピス

hospice care　ホスピス・ケア

hospital　病院

hospital accreditation　病院機能評価

hospital-acquired infection　院内感染；病院感染

hospital-acquired pneumonia　病院感染肺炎

hospital-based services　病院基盤型サービス

hospital bed　特殊寝台

hospital bed control　病床規制

hospital environment　病院環境

Hospital Infection Control Practice Advisory Committee：HICPAC　病院感染管理実践諮問委員会

hospital information system　病院情報システム

hospital insurance：HI　入院保険

hospitalism　ホスピタリズム

hospitalization　入院

hospital stay　在院

hospital transfer　転院

hospital volunteer　病院ボランティア

housebound syndrome　閉じこもり症候群

human immunodeficiency virus：HIV　ヒト免疫不全ウイルス

human lymphocyte antigen　ヒト白血球抗原

human poverty index：HPI　人間貧困指数

human resources　人的資源

human rights　人権

human rights advocacy　権利擁護

Human Rights Watch：HRW　ヒューマン・ライツ・ウォッチ

hunchback　円背；後弯

Huntington's chorea　ハンチントン（舞踏）病

Huntington's disease　ハンチントン（舞踏）病

hydronephrosis　水腎症

hydrostatic pressure　静水圧作用

hydrotherapy　水治療法

hygiene　衛生

hygienics　衛生学

hygroscopic fiber　吸湿性繊維

hyperactivity　多動

hyperacusis　聴覚過敏

hyperalgesia　温痛覚過敏

hyperalimentation　高カロリー輸液

hypercapnia　高炭酸ガス血症

hypercholesterolemia　高コレステロール血症

hyperemia　充血

hyperesthesia　感覚過敏

hyperextension　過伸展

hyperglycemia　高血糖症

hyperkalemia　高カリウム血症

hyperkeratosis　過角化症

hyperkinesia　運動亢進

hyperkinetic disorder　多動性障害

hyperlipidemia　高脂血症

hyperopia　遠視

hypersalivation　唾液分泌過多

hypertension　高血圧（症）

hyperthermia　高体温

hyperthyroidism　甲状腺機能亢進症

hypertonia　緊張亢進

hypertonic dehydration　水分欠乏性脱水；高張性脱水症

hypertriglyceridemia　高トリグリセリド血症；高中性脂肪血症

hypertrophic cardiomyopathy：HCM　肥大型心筋症

hypertrophic osteoarthropathy：HOA　肥大性骨関節症

hypertrophic pulmonary osteoarthropathy：HPOA　肥大性肺性骨関節症

hypertrophic pyloric stenosis：HPS　肥厚性幽門狭窄症

hypertropia　上斜視

hyperuricemia　高尿酸血症

hyperventilation attack　過呼吸発作

hypesthesia　感覚鈍麻

hypnotherapy　催眠療法

hypnotic　睡眠剤；睡眠薬

hypnotic drug　睡眠剤；睡眠薬

hypochondria　心気症

hypochondriacal delusion　心気妄想

hypochondriasis　心気症

hypodermic injection　皮下注射

hypoglycemia　低血糖症状

hypokalemia　低カリウム血症

hypokinesia　寡動；運動機能低下症

hypokinesis　運動機能低下症

hyponatremia　低ナトリウム血症

hyponatremic dehydration　食塩欠乏性脱水；低張性脱水

hypoproteinemia　低たんぱく血症

hypostatic pneumonia　沈下性肺炎

hypotension　低血圧

hypothalamus　視床下部

hypothermia　低体温症

hypothyroidism　甲状腺機能低下症

hypotonia　緊張低下

hypotonic dehydration　食塩欠乏性脱水；低張性脱水

hypotropia　下斜視

hypouresis　乏尿

hypovolemic shock　循環血液量減少性ショック

hypoxemia　低酸素血症

hysteria　ヒステリー

I

iatrogenesis　医原病

iatrogenic　医原性

ice bag　氷のう

ice pillow　氷枕

id　イド

ideal body weight：IBW　理想体重；基準体重

idea of reference　関係妄想

ideational apraxia　観念失行

identification　同一化；同一視；身分証明書

identity　アイデンティティ

identity crisis　同一性危機

identity theft　個人情報の窃盗

ideomotor apraxia　観念運動失行

idiopathic generalized epilepsy　一次性（本態性）てんかん

idiopathic thrombocytopenic purpura：ITP　特発性血小板減少性紫斑病

ileal conduit urinary diversion　回腸導管

ileostomy　イレオストミー；回腸人工肛門

ileus　イレウス；腸閉塞

illness anxiety disorder：IAD　病気不安症；心気症

immune system　免疫システム

immunity　免疫

immunodeficiency　免疫不全

immunoglobulin：Ig　免疫グロブリン

immunosuppressant drug　免疫抑制剤

immunotherapy　免疫療法

impaired fasting glucose：IFG　空腹時高血糖

impaired glucose tolerance：IGT　耐糖能異常

impaired renal function　腎臓機能障害

impairment　インペアメント；機能障害

impetigo　膿痂疹

implantable cardioverter defibrillator：ICD　植込み型除細動器

implanted pacemaker　埋込式ペースメーカー

implicit memory　非陳述記憶

inaction　無為

inapparent aspiration　不顕性誤嚥

inapparent infection　不顕性感染

incidence　罹患

incidence rate　罹患率

incident report　インシデント報告書；事故報告書

inclusion　インクルージョン；包括性

income security　所得保障

income tax　所得税

income test　所得テスト

incomplete quadriplegia　不全四肢麻痺

incontinence　失禁

incontinence care　失禁ケア

incubation period　潜伏期

incubatory carrier　潜伏期保菌者

incurable disease　難治性疾患

independence　自立

independent living　自立生活

independent living skill　自立生活スキル

indicator　指標

indirect contact infection　間接接触感染

indirect contact spread　間接接触伝播

indirect contact transmission　間接接触感染

indirect language　間接言語

indiscrimination　無差別

individualism　個人主義

individualization　個別化

individualized care　ケアの個別化；個別ケア；
　個別介護

individualized care plan　個別援助計画

Individual Retirement Accounts : IRA　個人退
　職年金勘定

indoor climate　室内気候

indoor relief　収容保護；院内救助

induction heating　誘導加熱

inductive reasoning　帰納推理

industrial accident　労働災害

industrial accident compensation　労災補償

indwelling catheter　留置カテーテル

infant mortality rate　乳児死亡率

infection　感染

infection control　感染対策；感染制御

infection prevention　感染予防

infectious disease　感染症；伝染病

infectious enteritis　感染性腸炎

infectious gastroenteritis　感染性胃腸炎

infectious waste　感染性廃棄物

infective endocarditis　感染性心内膜炎

inflamed gum　歯肉炎

inflammation　炎症

influenza　インフルエンザ

influenza vaccine　インフルエンザワクチン

influenza virus　インフルエンザウイルス

informal care　インフォーマルケア

informal resources　インフォーマル資源

information disclosure　情報公開

information management　情報管理

information network　情報ネットワーク

information system　情報システム

information technology : IT　情報技術

informed choice　インフォームド・チョイス

informed consent : IC　インフォームド・コンセント

infrared light therapy　赤外線療法

ingrown toenail　陥入爪

inhalation　吸息；吸入

inhaler　吸入薬

inheritance　相続

inheritance tax　相続税

inherited metabolic disorder　先天性代謝異常

inhibition　制止

inhibition of thought　思考制止

inhibitor　阻害因子

initial intake　初期面接

injection　注射

injury　傷害；損傷

in-kind benefit　現物給付

inpatient　入院患者

inpatient care　入院医療

inpatient hospice　入院型緩和ケア

insanity　心神喪失

insensible perspiration　不感蒸泄

insight　洞察

insight therapy　洞察療法

insomnia　不眠（症）

inspection　監査

inspection fraud　点検商法

inspector　監査官

institution　施設

institutional care　施設ケア

institutionalism　施設主義

institutionalization　施設収容

instrumental activities of daily living : IADL
　手段的日常生活動作

instrumental conditioning　道具的条件づけ

insulin　インスリン；インシュリン

insulin-dependent diabetes mellitus : IDDM
　インスリン依存性糖尿病

insulin self-injection　インスリン自己注射

insurance　保険

insurance benefit　保険給付

insurance doctor　保険医

insurance premium　保険料

insured event　保険事故

intake　インテーク

integrated delivery system : IDS　統合医療供
　給システム

integrated education　統合教育

integrated health care delivery system　医療複
　合体

integration　インテグレーション；統合化

integumentary　外皮

integumentary system　外皮系

intellectual age　知能年齢

intellectual disability　知的障害；知能障害

intellectual level　知的水準

intelligence　知能

intelligence quotient : IQ　知能指数

intelligence test　知能検査

intensive care management　集中的ケアマネジ
　メント

intensive care unit : ICU　集中治療室

intercostal muscles　肋間筋

intercostal neuralgia　肋間神経痛

interdisciplinary team : IDT　多職種チーム

interest group　利益団体

interface reflection　界面反射

interferon　インターフェロン

intergenerational care　世代間ケア

intergenerational conflict　世代間紛争

intergenerational relations　世代間関係

intermediate facility　中間施設

intermittent claudication　間欠性跛行

intermittent urethral catheterization　間欠導尿

internal bleeding　内出血

internal medicine　内科

internal respiration　内呼吸

internal rotation　内旋

International Bill of Human Rights　国際人権
　憲章

International Classification for Standards :
　ICS　国際規格分類

International Classification of Diseases : ICD
　国際疾病分類

International Classification of Functioning,
　Disability and Health : ICF　国際生活機能
　分類

International Classification of Impairments,
　Disabilities and Handicaps : ICIDH　国際障
　害分類

International Council on Social Welfare : ICSW
　国際社会福祉協議会

International Covenant on Civil and Political
　Rights : ICCPR　市民的及び政治的権利に関
　する国際規約

International Covenant on Economic, Social
　and Cultural Rights　社会的及び文化的権利
　に関する国際規約

International Covenant on Human Rights
　国際人権規約

International Human Rights Organization :
　IHRO　国際人権擁護団体

International Labour Organization : ILO　国際
　労働機関

International Organization for Standardization :
　ISO　国際標準化機構

International Psychogeriatric Association :
　IPA　国際老年精神学会

International Standard : IS　国際規格

international symbol of accessibility : ISA
　障害者のための国際シンボルマーク

International Women's Year : IWY　国際婦人年

International Year of Biodiversity : IYB　国際生
　物多様性年

International Year of Chemistry : IYC　国際化
　学年

International Year of Disabled Persons : IYDP
　国際障害者年

International Year of Older Persons : IYOP
　国際高齢者年

International Year of Sanitation : IYS　国際衛

生年

International Year of the Child : IYC　国際児童年

International Year of the Family : IYF　国際家族年

interpersonal relationship　対人関係

interpersonal skills　対人関係スキル

interprofessional collaboration　多職種連携

interprofessional education　多職種連携教育

intertrochanteric fracture　転子間骨折

intervention　インターベンション；介入

intervertebral disc herniation　椎間板ヘルニア

interview　インタビュー；面接

intestinal juice　腸液

intestinal obstruction　腸閉塞症

intestinal stoma　消化管ストーマ

intestinal tube feeding　腸ろう経管栄養

intestine　腸

intoxication　酩酊

intradermal injection　皮内注射

intramuscular : IM　筋肉内

intramuscular injection　筋肉内注射

intraocular lens : IOL　眼内レンズ

intraocular pressure　眼（内）圧

intratracheal injection　気管内注入

intravascular catheter　血管内留置カテーテル

intravascular catheter-related infection　血管内留置カテーテル関連感染症

intravenous : IV　点滴

intravenous drip　点滴静脈内注射

intravenous hyperalimentation : IVH　高カロリー輸液療法

intravenous injection　静脈内注射

intravenous therapy : IV therapy　点滴治療

intrinsic　内因

intrinsic asthma　内因型喘息

intrinsic sphincter deficiency : ISD　内因性括約筋不全

introversion　内向性

investment fraud　利殖商法

involuntary admission　強制入所

involuntary hospitalization　強制入院

involuntary movement　不随意運動

involuntary psychiatric hold　精神鑑定措置入院

involuntary psychiatric hospitalization　精神鑑定措置入院

involutional depression　退行期うつ病

involutional melancholia　退行期うつ病

iodine　ヨウ素

iron (deficiency)　鉄分（欠乏症）

iron deficiency anemia　鉄欠乏性貧血

irrational belief　非合理的信念

irrigation　イリゲーション

irritable bowel syndrome　過敏性腸症候群

irritant dermatitis　刺激性皮膚炎

ischemia　虚血

ischemic colitis　虚血性大腸炎

ischemic heart disease : IHD　虚血性心疾患

ischemic stroke　虚血性発作

islets of Langerhans　ランゲルハンス島

isokinetic contraction　等運動性収縮

isokinetic exercise　等運動性運動

isolation　隔離

isolation hospital　隔離病院

isolation precaution　隔離予防策

isolation room　隔離病室

isolation unit　隔離病棟

isolophobia　単独恐怖症

isometric contraction　等尺性収縮

isometric exercise　等尺性訓練

isotonic contraction　等張性収縮

isotonic exercise　等張性訓練

itch mite　ヒゼンダニ

J

Janz syndrome　ヤンツ症候群

jaundice　黄疸

jaw thrust　下顎押し出し法

job coach　ジョブコーチ；職場適応援助者

job seeker　求職者

job seeker's benefit　求職者給付

joint　関節；継手

joint and several liability　連帯責任

joint contracture　関節拘縮

joint dislocation　関節脱臼

joint family　複合家族

joint motion　関節運動

joint prosthesis　関節補綴

joint replacement　関節置換術

joint stiffness　関節拘縮

judgmental attitude　審判的態度

Jungian psychology　ユング心理学

justice　正義；公正；公平

juvenile diabetes　若年性糖尿病

juvenile idiopathic arthritis　若年性特発性リウマチ

juvenile myoclonic epilepsy：JME　若年性ミオクローヌスてんかん

juvenile Parkinsonism　若年性パーキンソン病

juvenile polyps　若年性ポリープ

juvenile rheumatoid arthritis　若年性関節リウマチ

K

Katz ADL index　カッツ ADL インデックス

Kegel exercise　ケーゲル訓練（法）

Kenny Self-Care Evaluation　ケニー式セルフケア評価

keratosis　角化症

keratotic lesions　角化症病変

kernicterus　核黄疸

kidney　腎臓

kidney cancer　腎がん

kidney disease　腎疾患

kidney failure　腎機能障害；腎不全

kidney function　腎機能

kidney stone　腎結石

kidney transplantation　腎移植

kinematic analysis　運動学的分析

kinesthesia　運動感覚

kinesthetic sense　運動覚

Klebsiella pneumonia　クレブシエラ肺炎

Kluver-Bucy syndrome　クリューバービューシー症候群

knee-ankle-foot orthosis：KAFO　長下肢装具

knee osteoarthritis　変形性膝関節症

knee pad　膝当て

knee replacement　膝関節置換術

Korsakoff's amnesic syndrome　コルサコフ健忘症候群

Korsakoff's psychosis　コルサコフ精神病

Korsakoff's syndrome　コルサコフ症候群

kyphosis　円背；後弯

L

labile hypertension　動揺性高血圧症

labor force　労働力

labor policy　労働政策

labor union　労働組合

labyrinthitis　内耳炎

lacrimal apparatus　涙器

language　言語

language capability　言語能力

laparoscopy　腹腔鏡検査

laryngeal cancer　喉頭がん

laryngeal carcinoma　喉頭がん

laryngotracheitis　喉頭気管炎

laser surgery　レーザー手術

laser therapy　レーザー治療

Lassa fever　ラッサ熱

late effect　後遺症

late life　老年期

late marriage　晩婚

latency period　潜伏期

latent autoimmune diabetes in adults：LADA　成人潜在性自己免疫性糖尿病

latent infection　潜伏感染

late-onset Alzheimer's disease　遅発性アルツハイマー病

late-onset disability　中途障害

lateral position　側臥位

lavage cytology　洗浄細胞診

laxative　緩下剤；下剤

leadership　リーダーシップ

lead poisoning　鉛中毒

lean body mass：LBM　除脂肪体重

learned helplessness　学習性無力感

learned helplessness theory　学習性無力感理論

learning 学習

learning ability 学習能力

learning disability : LD 学習障害

learning disorder : LD 学習障害

learning theory 学習理論

leave benefit 休業給付

leave of absence : LoA 休暇

left atrium 左心房

left lateral recumbent position : LLR position
左側臥位

left-right disorientation 左右失認

legal assistance 法律支援

legal guardian 法定後見

legal guardianship 法定後見制度

legal representative 法定代理人

leisure レジャー；余暇

length of stay : LOS 入院期間；入所期間

leprosy 癩；ハンセン病

lethargy 無気力

leukemia 白血病

leukocytes 白血球

Lewy body dementia : LBD レビー小体型認
知症

Lewy body disease : LBD レビー小体病

liaison critical pathway 地域連携パス

libido リビドー

licensed practical nurse : LPN 准看護師

licensed vocational nurse : LVN 准看護師

Life Assessment Scale for Mental Illness :
LASMI 社会生活評価尺度

life course ライフコース

life expectancy 平均余命

life history 生活歴

life insurance 生命保険

life insurance premium 生命保険料

lifelong education 生涯教育

lifelong learning 生涯学習

lifelong pension 終身年金

lifelong sports 生涯スポーツ

life model 生活モデル

life-prolonging treatment 延命治療

life review ライフレビュー；回想

life space crisis intervention 生活空間危機
介入

life space interview 生活場面面接

life span 寿命

life-span development 生涯発達

life stage ライフステージ

life structure 生活構造

lifestyle ライフスタイル；起居様式；生活習慣

lifestyle disease 生活習慣病

lifestyle-related disease 生活習慣病

life-support (equipment) 生命維持（装置）

life-sustaining (equipment) 生命維持（装置）

life-sustaining treatment 延命治療

life table 生命表

lifting platform 段差解消機

light and dark adaptation 明暗順応

light-headedness 立ちくらみ

limb kinetic apraxia 肢節運動失行

limbs 四肢

limited assistance 部分介助；一部介助

Linum usitatissimum 亜麻

lipid 脂質

lipid storage disease 脂質蓄積症

lipoprotein リポたんぱく質

lipreading 読唇（術）

liquid diet 流動食

lithium リチウム

liver 肝臓

liver cancer 肝がん

liver disease 肝疾患

liver function test : LFT 肝機能検査

liver spots 肝斑

live supervision ライブ・スーパービジョン

living donor kidney transplantation 生体腎
移植

living donor liver transplantation 生体肝移植

living environment 生活環境；住環境

living trust 生前信託

living will リビング・ウィル；尊厳死宣言書

livor mortis 死斑

local autonomy 地方自治

local government 地方自治体

locked facility 閉鎖施設

locked-in syndrome : LIS 閉じこめ症候群

locked unit　閉鎖病棟

locomotive syndrome　ロコモティブシンドローム；運動器症候群

locomotor movements　移動動作

Lofstrand crutch　ロフストランドクラッチ

logotherapy　ロゴセラピー

long-distance care　遠距離介護

long-distance medicine　遠距離医療

longevity　長寿

longevity science　長寿科学

long-term care　長期ケア；長期介護；介護

long-term care facility　介護施設

long-term care model　介護モデル

long-term care ombudsman　介護オンブズマン

long-term care services　介護サービス

long-term goal　長期目標

long-term memory　長期記憶

long-term stay　長期入所

lordosis　前弯

loss of appetite　食欲不振；食欲低下

lotus position　蓮華座

Lou Gehrig's disease　ルー・ゲーリッグ病；筋萎縮性側索硬化症

low back pain　腰痛

low-density lipoprotein　LDLコレステロール

lower esophageal sphincter：LES　下部食道括約筋

lower esophageal sphincter dysfunction　下部食道括約筋機能障害

lower extremity　下肢

lower extremity lymphedema　下肢リンパ浮腫

lower extremity orthosis　下肢装具

lower gastrointestinal　下部消化管

lower-limb prosthesis　義足

lower motor neuron　下位運動ニューロン

lower social stratum　下層社会

low-fat diet　低脂肪食

low income　低所得

low income assistance program　低所得者対策

low income class　低所得層

low income household　低所得世帯

low salt diet　減塩食

low sodium diet　減塩食

low-temperature sterilization　低温滅菌

low-wage labor　低賃金労働

lumbago　腰痛

lumbar compression fracture　腰椎圧迫骨折

lumbar herniated disc　腰椎椎間板ヘルニア

lumbar spinal cord injury　腰髄損傷

lumbar vertebrae　腰椎

lung cancer　肺がん

lung capacity　肺活量

lung disease　肺疾患

lung transplantation　肺移植

luxation　脱臼

lying position　臥位

lymph　リンパ（液）

lymphadenitis　リンパ節炎

lymphatic metastasis　リンパ行性転移

lymphocytes　リンパ球

lysosomal storage diseases　ライソゾーム病

M

macrocytic anemia　大球性貧血

macular degeneration　黄斑部変性症；網膜黄斑部変性症

mad-cow disease　狂牛病

magnesium　マグネシウム

magnetic resonance angiography：MRA　磁気共鳴血管撮影

magnetic resonance imaging：MRI　磁気共鳴断層撮影

magnification device　拡大読書器

mail order business　通信販売

mail survey　郵送調査法

major depression　大うつ病；単極性うつ病

Major Diagnostic Category：MDC　主要診断群

malacia　軟化症

maladjusted behavior　不適応行動

maladjustment　不適応

malformation　形成不全

malignancy　悪性

malignant neoplasm　悪性新生物

malignant rheumatoid arthritis　悪性関節リウ

マチ

malignant tumor　悪性腫瘍

mallet finger　マレット指

malnutrition　栄養失調；栄養不良

malocclusion　咬合異常；不正咬合

malposition　不良肢位

malposture　不良姿勢

malpractice　不正行為

mammogram　マンモグラム

mammography　マンモグラフィ

managed care　マネジドケア

managed health care　マネジドヘルスケア

mandatory retirement　定年退職

mania　マニア，躁病

manic-depressive illness　双極性感情障害；躁うつ病

Manifest Anxiety Scale　顕在性不安尺度

mannerism　衒奇症

manual height adjustable wheelchair　手動リフト式普通型車いす

Manual Muscle Testing：MMT　徒手筋力テスト

manual therapy　徒手療法

manual wheelchair　手動車いす

marijuana　マリファナ；大麻

marital deduction　配偶者控除

marital property agreement　夫婦財産契約

marital relationship　夫婦関係

marital therapy　夫婦療法

market mechanism　市場メカニズム

marriage　結婚

marriage certificate　婚姻証明書

masked depression　仮面うつ病

mask-like face　仮面様顔貌

Maslow's hierarchy of needs　マズローの欲求段階

massage　マッサージ

massage therapist　マッサージ師；あん摩師

massage therapy　マッサージ療法

mastication　咀嚼

masticatory disorder　咀嚼障害

masticatory disturbance　咀嚼障害

masticatory myositis　咀嚼筋炎

material abuse　物質的虐待

material culture　物質文化

maternity allowance　出産手当

maternity assistance　出産扶助

maternity leave　産前産後休暇；産休

maternity neurosis　育児ノイローゼ

maternity nurse　助産師

mature　円熟型

maximal gait velocity　最大歩行速度

maximum gait speed　最大歩行速度

maximum muscle strength　最大筋力

maximum oxygen consumption：VO2 max　最大酸素摂取量

maximum oxygen uptake　最大酸素摂取量

maximum resting pressure：MRP　最大静止圧

maximum squeeze pressure：MSP　最大随意収縮圧

maximum tolerable volume：MTV　最大耐容量

McGill Pain Questionnaire：MPQ　マクギル疼痛質問表

meal　食事

meal delivery service　配食サービス；食事宅配サービス

meal management　食事管理

meal planning　食事計画

meal preparation　食事準備

meal services　食事サービス

meals-on-wheels　配食サービス；食事宅配サービス

means test　ミーンズ・テスト；資力調査；資産調査

measles　麻疹

mechanical digestion　機械的消化

mechanical soft diet　機械的軟食

mechanical ventilator　人工呼吸器

medial heel whip　内側ホイップ

Medicaid　メディケイド［低所得者医療扶助制度］

medical bathtub　特殊浴槽

medical benefit　医療給付

medical care　医療；医療的ケア

medical certificate of cause of death　死体検案書

medical device　医療機器；医療器具；医療器材

medical equipment 医療機器；医療器具；医療器材	melanocyte メラノサイト；メラニン細胞
medical error 医療事故	melena 下血
medical ethics 医療倫理	memorial hospital 記念病院
medical expenses 医療費；療養費	memory 記憶
medical facility 医療提供施設	memory disorder 記憶障害
medical history 既往歴；治療歴	memory disturbance 記憶障害
medical leave 傷病休暇	memory impairment 記憶障害
medically underserved area 無医地区；医療過疎地域	Memory Impairment Screen：MIS 記憶障害検査
medical malpractice (suit) 医療過誤（訴訟）	memory recall 想起
medical malpractice insurance 医療過誤保険	memory retention 記銘力
medical malpractice liability insurance 医療過誤補償保険	memory retrieval 想起
medical marijuana 医療大麻	Meniere's disease メニエール病
medical model 医学モデル	meningeal leukemia 髄膜白血病
medical model of disability 障害の医学モデル	meningitis 髄膜炎
medical nutrition therapy：MNT 食事療法	menopausal depression 更年期うつ病
medical practice 医業；医行為	menopausal disorder 更年期障害
medical records 医療記録	menopause メノポーズ；閉経；更年期
medical rehabilitation 医学的リハビリテーション；更生医療	mental abuse 精神的虐待
medical resources 医療資源	mental age：MA 精神年齢
medical social work 医療ソーシャルワーク	mental capacity assessment 意思能力評価
medical social worker：MSW メディカル・ソーシャルワーカー；医療ソーシャルワーカー	mental disorder 精神障害
medical staff 医療職員	mental fog 意識混濁
medical thermometer 体温測定計	mental health メンタルヘルス；精神保健
medical waste 医療廃棄物	Mental Health Act 精神保健法
Medicare メディケア［老人・障害者医療保険制度］	mental health assessment 心理判定
medication 薬；薬剤	mental health care メンタルヘルスケア；こころのケア
medication compliance 服薬遵守	mental health counselor 精神保健カウンセラー
medication error 誤薬；投薬過誤	mental health services 精神保健サービス
medication interaction 薬物相互作用	mental hospital 精神（科）病院
medication management 服薬管理	mental hygiene 精神衛生
medication restriction 投与制限	mental illness 精神障害；精神病
Medigap メディギャップ［メディケア補足保険制度］	mental preparation 心理的準備
medulla oblongata 延髄	mental retardation：MR 精神（発達）遅滞
medullary thyroid cancer 甲状腺髄様がん	meralgia paresthetica 知覚過敏性大腿痛
megaloblastic anemia 巨赤芽球性貧血	mercury poisoning 水銀中毒
meiosis 減数分裂	merit goods メリット財；価値財
	merosin-deficient congenital muscular dystrophy メロシン欠損型先天性筋ジストロフィー
	mesencephalon 中脳
	metabolic disorder 代謝疾患；代謝異常

metabolic equivalent of task：MET　メッツ；代謝当量

metabolic syndrome　メタボリックシンドローム

metabolism　（新陳）代謝

metacognition　メタ認知

metastasis　転移

methicillin-resistant Staphylococcus aureus：MRSA　メチシリン耐性黄色ブドウ球菌

micturition center　排尿中枢

micturition disorder　排尿障害

midbrain　中脳

middle-of-the-night insomnia　中途覚醒

midwife　助産師

migraine headache　片頭痛

mild cognitive impairment：MCI　軽度認知機能障害

miliary tuberculosis　粟粒結核症

minced diet　ミンチ食

mineral　ミネラル；無機質

mineral deficiency　ミネラル欠乏症

mineral supplementation　ミネラル補給

minimal brain dysfunction：MBD　微細脳機能障害

minimal erythema dose：MED　最小紅斑量

Mini-Mental State Examination：MMSE　ミニメンタルステート検査

minimum cost of living　最低生活費

Minimum Data Set：MDS　ミニマムデータセット

minimum wage　最低賃金

Mini Nutritional Assessment：MNA　簡易栄養状態アセスメント

mini stroke　ミニ脳卒中

Minnesota Multiphasic Personality Inventory：MMPI　ミネソタ多面人格目録

minor　未成年

minority　マイノリティ；少数派

minority group　少数派グループ

minutes　議事録

miosis　縮瞳

mirror writing　鏡像書字

misdiagnosis　誤診

misuse syndrome　誤用症候群

mite　ダニ

mitochondrial disease　ミトコンドリア病

mixed dementia　混合型認知症

mixed hearing loss　混合性難聴

mobility　可動性；移動性

model　モデル

modeling　モデリング

models of disability　障害モデル

modernization　近代化；現代化

modernization theory　近代化論

Modified Ashworth Scale　改訂アシュワース尺度

modified Barthel index　改訂バーセル指数

modified consistency diet　とろみ調整食品

Modified Water Swallowing Test：MWST　改訂水飲みテスト

modular prosthetic limb　モジュラー義肢

modular wheelchair　モジュラー型車いす

module　モジュール

moist heat sterilization　湿熱滅菌

moist heating　湿性温熱

monetary needs　貨幣的ニード

money management　金銭管理

monitoring　モニタリング

monophobia　単独恐怖症

monoplegia　単麻痺

monosaccharide　単糖類

monosaccharide anhydride　単糖無水物

monthly premium　月額保険料

mood　気分

mood disorder　気分障害

morale　モラール

moral hazard　モラルハザード

morbidity compression　傷病平均年数の圧縮

morbilli　麻疹

morgue　遺体安置所

morphine　モルヒネ

morphine addiction　モルヒネ型依存

mortality rate　死亡率

mortality table　生命表

motherhood　母性

mother-to-child transmission　母子感染

motion analysis　動作分析

motion control　運動制御

motivation　意欲；動因；動機

motive　意欲；動因；動機

motor age　運動年齢

motor-age test　運動年齢検査

motor aphasia　運動性失語（症）

motor apraxia　運動失行

motor assessment　運動評価

motor control　運動制御

motor development　運動発達

motor developmental evaluation　運動発達
　評価

motor function　運動機能

motor impairment　運動障害

motor impersistence　運動維持困難症

motor learning　運動学習

motor nerve　運動神経

motor neuron (disease)　運動ニューロン（疾患）

motor paralysis　運動麻痺

mourning　喪

mouth-to-mouth breathing　口対口人工呼吸

mouth-to-nose breathing　口対鼻人工呼吸

movement analysis　運動分析

movement-related functional limitation　運動
　制限

moxibustion　きゅう；きゅう療法

moxibustion therapist　きゅう師

mucocutaneous lymph node syndrome
　川崎病

mucopolysaccharidosis : MPS　ムコ多糖症

muffled voice　含み声

Multidimensional Functional Assessment
　多次元的機能評価

Multidimensional Poverty Index : MPI　多次元
　貧困指数

multidrug resistance : MDR　多剤耐性

multidrug resistant tuberculosis : MDR-TB
　多剤耐性結核

multi-infarct dementia : MID
　多発梗塞性認知症

Multilevel Assessment Instrument　多段階評価

multimodal therapy : MMT　多面的療法

Multiphasic Environmental Assessment
　Procedure : MEAP　包括的環境要因調査票

multiple cerebral infarction　多発性脳梗塞

multiple disabilities　重複障害

multiple organ dysfunction syndrome : MODS
　多臓器不全症候群

multiple organ failure　多臓器不全

multiple personality disorder : MPD　多重人格
　障害

multiple sclerosis : MS　多発性硬化症

multiple system atrophy : MSA　多系統萎縮症

multi-point cane　多点つえ

multipotent　多分化能

mumps　おたふくかぜ；流行性耳下腺炎

municipal court　自治体裁判所

muscle　筋肉

muscle biopsy　筋生検

muscle contracture　筋拘縮症

muscle cramp　筋痙攣

muscle endurance　筋持久力

muscle fatigue　筋疲労

muscle fiber type　筋線維タイプ

muscle hypertonia　筋緊張亢進

muscle hypertrophy　筋肥大

muscle hypotonia　筋緊張低下

muscle maintenance　筋力維持

muscle reeducation　筋再教育

muscle relaxation　筋弛緩

muscle strength　筋力

muscle strengthening exercise　筋力強化訓練

muscle strength measurement　筋力測定

muscle tonus　筋緊張

muscular atrophy　筋萎縮

muscular dystrophy　筋ジストロフィー

muscular strengthening　筋力強化

muscular strength testing : MMT　筋力テスト

muscular weakness　筋力低下

musculoskeletal disease　筋骨格疾患

musculoskeletal system　筋骨格系

music therapy　音楽療法

mutism　無言（症）

mutual aid　相互扶助

myalgic encephalomyelitis　筋痛性脳脊髄炎

myasthenia gravis : MG　筋無力症；重症筋無
　力症

mycosis　真菌症

myelodysplastic syndrome　骨髄異形成症候群

myelopathy　脊髄症

myocardial infarction　心筋梗塞

myocardial ischemia　心筋虚血

myoclonic seizure　ミオクロニー発作

myoclonus epilepsy　ミオクローヌスてんかん

myodesopsia　飛蚊症

myofascial pain syndrome : MPS　筋筋膜性疼痛症候群

myofascial release　筋膜リリース

myopia　近視

myositis　筋炎

myositis ossificans　骨化性筋炎

myotonic dystrophy　筋強直性ジストロフィー

N

narcissistic caregiver　自己愛性介護者

narcissistic personality disorder　自己愛性人格障害

narcotic　麻薬

narcotic addiction　麻薬中毒

narrative approach　ナラティブ・アプローチ

narrative recording　叙述体

narrative therapy　ナラティブ・セラピー

nasal : NAS　経鼻

nasal bleeding　鼻出血

nasal cannula : NC　酸素（経鼻）カニューレ；鼻カニューレ

nasal flaring　鼻翼呼吸

nasal tube feeding　経鼻経管栄養

national census　国勢調査

National Fertility Survey　出生動向基本調査

national income : NI　国民所得

nationalism　ナショナリズム

national minimum　ナショナル・ミニマム

national minimum standards　国家最低基準

national minimum wage　国家最低賃金

National Nursing Home Survey　全米ナーシングホーム調査

National Pension　国民年金

national responsibility　国家責任

natural disaster　自然災害

naturally occurring retirement community　自然発生的退職者コミュニティ

nausea　吐き気；嘔気

near-infrared　近赤外線

near-sightedness　近視

nebulizer　ネブライザー

neck distortion　頸椎捻挫

necrosis　壊死

nectar liquid diet　ネクター状液体食

needle biopsy　針生検

needle puncture　針穿刺

needs　ニーズ；欲求

needs assessment　ニーズ・アセスメント

needy　（生活）困窮者

negative pressure pulmonary edema　陰圧性肺水腫

negative punishment　負の罰

negative reinforcement　負の強化

negative symptom　陰性症状

negativism　拒絶症

neglect　ネグレクト；介護放棄；放棄・放任

Neonatal Behavior Assessment Scale : NBAS　新生児行動評価

neonatal mortality rate　新生児死亡率

neonate　新生児

nephrectomy　腎摘除

nephritic syndrome　ネフローゼ症候群

nephritis　腎炎

nephrologist　腎臓内科医

nephropathy　腎症

nephrosis　ネフローゼ

nerve block　神経ブロック

nerve entrapment　神経絞扼

nervous tissue　神経組織

networking　ネットワーキング

neuralgia　神経痛

neuritic plaques　老人斑

neurocirculatory asthenia　神経循環無力症

neurodegenerative disease　神経変性疾患

neurodevelopmental approach　神経発達的アプローチ

neurogenic bladder　神経因性膀胱

neurogenic muscle atrophy　神経原性筋萎縮

neurogenic pulmonary edema　神経原性肺水腫

neurogenic shock　神経原性ショック

neurological examination　神経学的検査

neurological status　神経学的状態

neurological symptom　神経症候

neuromuscular disease　神経筋疾患

neuromuscular facilitation technique　神経筋促通法

neuromuscular junction　神経筋接合部

neuro-oncologist　神経腫瘍医

neuropathic pain　神経原性疼痛

neuropathy　ニューロパチー；神経障害

neurophysiological approach　神経生理学的アプローチ

neuropsychiatric symptoms of dementia　行動・心理症状；周辺症状；認知症に伴う行動障害と精神症状

neuropsychological disorder　高次脳機能障害

neuropsychological evaluation　神経心理学的評価

neuropsychological test　神経心理学的検査

neurosis　ノイローゼ；神経症

neurotic disorder　神経症性障害

neutral fat　中性脂肪

neutral position　中立位

Newborn Screening Test　先天性代謝異常検査

new daily persistent headache : NDPH　新規発症持続性連日性頭痛

new flu virus strains　新型インフルエンザウイルス株

New Poor Law　新救貧法

nidus　病巣

night blindness　夜盲症

nil per os : NPO　絶食

nitrate　硝酸塩

nitrogen dioxide　二酸化窒素

nitroglycerin : NG　ニトログリセリン

no added salt : NAS　無塩

no added salt diet : NAS diet　無塩食

nocardiosis　ノカルジア症

nocturia　夜尿症

nocturnal awakening　中途覚醒

non-cash benefit　現物給付

nondeclarative memory　非陳述記憶

non-esterified fatty acid : NEFA　遊離脂肪酸

non-governmental organization : NGO　非政府組織

non-insulin-dependent diabetes mellitus : NIDDM　インスリン非依存型糖尿病

nonjudgmental attitude　非審判的態度

non-maleficence　無危害

non-monetary need　非貨幣的ニード

non-prescription drug　非処方箋薬

nonprofit organization　非営利組織

non-rapid eye movement sleep : NREM sleep　ノンレム睡眠

non-slip mat　ノンスリップマット

non-slip rug　滑り止めマット

nonsubstitutability　非代替性

nontuberculous mycobacterial infection　非結核性抗酸菌症

nonverbal communication　非言語的コミュニケーション

noradrenaline : NA　ノルアドレナリン

normal blood pressure　正常血圧

normal curve　正規曲線

normal flora　正常細菌叢

normal gait　正常歩行

normalization　ノーマライゼーション

normal pressure hydrocephalus　正常圧水頭症

normal temperature　平熱

normal value　正常値

normocytic anemia　正球性貧血

norovirus　ノロウイルス

Norwegian scabies　角化型疥癬

nosocomial infection　院内感染；病院感染

notarial deed　公正証書

notary public　公証人

notification of death　死亡届

novel infectious disease　新感染症

novel influenza　新型インフルエンザ

nuclear family　核家族

Numeric Rating Scale : NRS　数値評価スケール

nurse　看護師

英和

nurse aide　看護助手

nursing　看護

nursing home　ナーシングホーム

Nursing Home Reform Act　ナーシングホーム改革法

nursing hours per patient per day：nhppd　一患者一日あたりの看護時間

nursing notes　看護日誌；介護日誌

nursing process　看護過程

nursing records　看護記録；介護記録

nursing shortage　看護師不足

nursing staff　看護職員

nutrient　栄養素

nutrient function claims　栄養機能食品

nutrient intake　栄養摂取量

nutrition　栄養

nutritional assessment　栄養評価

nutritional education　栄養指導

nutritional requirement　栄養必要量

nutritional screening　栄養スクリーニング

nutritional status　栄養状態

nutritional supplement　栄養剤；栄養補助食品

nutrition care management　栄養ケアマネジメント

nutrition care plan　栄養ケア計画

nutrition claim　栄養表示

nutrition disorder　栄養障害

nutrition fact label　栄養表示

nutrition improvement　栄養改善

nutrition labeling　食品表示

nutrition management　栄養管理

nutrition support team：NST　栄養サポートチーム

nutrition therapy　食事療法

nyctalopia　夜盲症

nycturia　夜尿症

nystagmus　眼振；眼球振盪

O

obesity　肥満

obesity hypoventilation syndrome：OHS　肥満低換気症候群

obesity index　肥満指数

objective fact　客観的事実

objective information　客観的情報

observation　観察

observation unit　経過観察病棟

obsession　強迫観念

obsessive-compulsive disorder：OCD　強迫性障害

obstructive sleep apnea syndrome：OSAS　閉塞性睡眠時無呼吸症候群

occipital neuralgia　後頭神経痛

occult blood test　潜血試験

occupancy rate　占床率

occupational assistance　生業扶助

occupational disease　職業病

occupational exposure　職業曝露

occupational group insurance　職域保険

occupational infection　職業感染

occupational injury　労働災害

occupational therapist：OT　作業療法士

occupational therapy aide　作業療法士助手

occupational therapy：OT　作業療法

ocular albinism　白子眼

odynophagia　嚥下痛

Oedipus complex　エディプス・コンプレックス

Oedipus phase　エディプス期

off-the-job-training：OFF-JT　職場外訓練

ointment　軟膏

old-age　老年期

Old-Age and Survivors Insurance：OASI　老齢遺族保険

Older Americans Act：OAA　アメリカ高齢者法

older people's week　老人週間

oldest-old　オールデスト・オールド；85歳以上の高齢者

old-old　オールド・オールド；75〜84歳の高齢者

olfaction　嗅覚

olfactory hallucination　幻嗅

oliguria　乏尿

ombudsman　オンブズマン

ombudsperson　オンブズパーソン

Omnibus Budget Reconciliation Act：OBRA
　包括予算調整法

oncogene　発がん遺伝子；腫瘍遺伝子

one-parent family　単親家庭；ひとり親家庭；欠
　損家庭

online education　通信教育

on-site interview　訪問面接

on-the-job-training：OJT　職場訓練

onychia　爪炎

onychocryptosis　陥入爪

onychodystrophy　爪ジストロフィー

onychogryphosis　爪甲鉤弯症

onychomycosis　爪真菌症

open-ended question　開かれた質問

open facility　開放施設

open fracture　開放骨折

open wound　開放性損傷

operant conditioning　オペラント条件づけ

operating room：OR　手術室

operation room registered nurse：OR RN
　手術室看護師

opiate addiction　アヘン中毒

opiate dependence　アヘン依存

opinion survey　意識調査

opportunistic infection　日和見感染症

optic nerve atrophy　視神経萎縮

optometrist　検眼医；眼鏡士

oral cancer　口腔がん

oral care　口腔ケア

oral cavity　口腔

oral disease　口腔疾患

oral health　口腔衛生

oral health assessment　口腔保健アセスメント

oral health care　口腔ケア

oral hygiene　口腔清掃行動

oral intake　経口摂取

oral liquid medication　内服用水剤

oral medication　内服薬

oral propulsive phase　口腔相

oral rehydration therapy　経口補液療法

oral stage　口唇期

oral status　口腔状態

oral temperature　口腔温

oral thermometry　口腔検温

organ donation　臓器提供

organic brain disease：OBD　脳器質(性)疾患

organic brain disorder　脳器質(性)疾患

organic constipation　器質性便秘

organic labeling　有機食品表示

organic mental disorder　器質性精神障害

organic psychosis　器質精神病

organic solvent abuse　有機溶剤依存

organization　組織

Organization for Economic Cooperation and
　Development：OECD　経済協力開発機構

organ transplantation　臓器移植

orientation　オリエンテーション；見当識

Orientation-Memory-Concentration Test　見当
　識・記憶・集中テスト

orphanage　児童養護施設

orthopedic impairment　肢体不自由；体幹機能
　障害

orthopedics　整形外科

orthopedic shoes　整形靴

orthopnea　起座呼吸

orthoptic exercise　視能訓練

orthoptist：ORT　視能訓練士

orthosis　装具

orthostatic dizziness　起立性調節障害

orthostatic hypotension　起立性低血圧

orthostatic vertigo　起立性調節障害

osteoarthritis：OA　変形性関節症

osteomalacia　骨軟化症

osteopenia　骨減少性

osteoporosis　骨粗鬆症

osteoporosis-related test　骨粗鬆症検診

ostomate　オストメイト

otitis media　中耳炎

otolaryngologist　耳鼻咽喉科医

ototoxicity　耳毒性

ototoxic substance　聴器毒性物質

Ottawa Charter for Health Promotion　オタワ
　憲章

outbreak　アウトブレイク；集団発生

Outcome and Assessment Information Set：
　OASIS　オアシス[在宅ケアアセスメント表]

outdoor recreational activity　野外レクリエーション

out of bed　離床

out-of-pocket　自己支払い；自費支払い

outpatient　通院患者

outpatient care　外来ケア；外来診療

outpatient rehabilitation　外来リハビリテーション；通所リハビリテーション

ovarian cancer　卵巣がん

ovary　卵巣

overbed table　オーバーベッドテーブル

overcompensation　過補償

overeating　過食

overflow incontinence　溢流性尿失禁

overgrowth　過重成長

overpopulation　過密人口

overprotection　過保護

over-the-counter medication : OTC　市販薬

overuse syndrome　過用症侯群

overwork weakness　過用性筋力低下

oxidation　酸化

oxygen　酸素

oxygen concentrator　酸素濃縮器

oxygen consumption　酸素消費

oxygen intake　酸素摂取

oxygen therapy　酸素療法；酸素吸入

P

pacemaker　ペースメーカー

paid time off : PTO　有給休暇

paid volunteer　有償ボランティア

pain　疼痛

pain control　疼痛管理

pain disorder　疼痛性障害

pain management　疼痛マネジメント；疼痛管理

pain medication　疼痛薬

pain relief medication　疼痛薬

palatine tonsil　口蓋扁桃

palatine uvula　口蓋垂

palliative care　緩和ケア

palliative medicine　緩和医療

palmar flexion　掌屈

palpation　触診

palpitation　動悸

pancreas　膵臓

pancreatic cancer　膵臓がん

pancreatic islets　ランゲルハンス島

pancreatic juice　膵液

pancreatitis　膵炎

panic disorder　パニック障害；恐慌性障害

pantothenic acid　パントテン酸

papillary thyroid cancer　甲状腺乳頭がん

paradoxical directive　逆説的指示

paradoxical incontinence　奇異性尿失禁

paradoxical intention　逆説的志向

paradoxical sleep　逆説睡眠

paraffin bath　パラフィン浴

parallel bar　平行棒

paralysis　麻痺

paramedical staff　パラメディカルスタッフ

paranoia　パラノイア；偏執病

paranoid　妄想

paranoid reaction　妄想反応

paraparesis　不全対麻痺

paraphasia　錯語

paraplegia　対麻痺；下半身麻痺

parasites　寄生虫

parasitic disease　寄生虫病

parasympathetic nerve　副交感神経

parental authority　親権

parent-child relationship　親子関係

parenteral feeding　非経口栄養

parenteral nutrition　静脈栄養法

parent group　親の会

parenting　子育て

paresis　不全麻痺

Parkinson's disease : PD　パーキンソン病

Parkinson's syndrome　パーキンソン症候群

parotid gland　耳下腺

participation　参加

participation restriction　参加制約

partner dog　介助犬

passive exercise　他動運動

passive immunity　受動免疫

passive range of motion　他動可動域

pasteurization　低温殺菌

pathogen　病原体

pathogenic Escherichia coli　病原大腸菌

pathogenic organism　病原体

pathological aging　病的老化

pathological fracture　病的骨折

pathology test　病理検査

patient　患者

patient advocacy　患者擁護

patient-centered medicine　患者中心医療

patient-centered therapy　患者中心療法

patient-controlled analgesia：PCA　自己調節
鎮痛法

Patient Protection and Affordable Care Act：
PPACA　医療保険改革法；患者の保護と手頃
な医療法

patient records　患者記録

patient safety　患者の安全

patient satisfaction survey　患者満足度調査

Patient's Bill of Rights　患者の権利章典

Patient Self-Determination Act　患者の自己決
定法

patients' rights　患者の権利

patient support group　患者会

patient survey　患者調査

Pavlovian conditioning　古典的条件づけ

pay-as-you-go system　賦課方式

payroll tax　給与税

pectin　ペクチン

pectus excavatum　漏斗胸

pediatric　小児科

pediatric advanced life support：PALS　小児に
対する二次救命心肺蘇生法・処置

pediatric home care　小児在宅ケア

pediatric home health care　小児在宅医療

pediatrician　小児科医

peer counseling　ピア・カウンセリング

peer group　ピアグループ

peer group supervision　ピアグループスーパー
ビジョン

peer relationship　仲間関係

peer supervision　ピアスーパービジョン

peer support　ピアサポート

pelvic band　骨盤帯

pelvic floor muscle exercises　骨盤底筋訓練法

pelvic floor muscles　骨盤底筋群

pelvic floor relaxation　骨盤底弛緩

pelvic fracture　骨盤骨折

pension　年金

pensionable age　年金支給開始年齢

pension benefit　年金給付

pensioner　年金受給者

pension fund　年金基金

peptic ulcer　消化性潰瘍

perception　知覚

percussion　叩打法

percutaneous infection　経皮感染

performance IQ：PIQ　動作性IQ

peri care　陰部清拭

perinatal mortality rate　周産期死亡率

perineal care　陰部清拭

periodic health evaluation：PHE　定期的健康
診断

periodic leg movement　周期性四肢運動

periodic leg movement disorder：PLMD　周期
性四肢運動異常症

periodic limb movement disorder：PLMD
周期性四肢運動障害

periodontal disease　歯周病；歯周疾患

periodontitis　歯周炎

periodontium　歯周組織

peripheral arterial disease：PAD　末梢動脈
疾患

peripheral arterial occlusive disease：PAOD
末梢動脈閉塞性疾患

peripheral edema　末梢浮腫

peripheral nerve　末梢神経

peripheral nerve disorder　末梢神経性障害

peripheral nerve palsy　末梢神経麻痺

peripheral neuropathy：PN　末梢神経障害

peripheral parenteral nutrition：PPN　末梢静脈
栄養法

peripheral vascular disease　末梢血管疾患

peripheral vision　視野；周辺視野

peristalsis　蠕動運動

peritoneal dialysis：PD　腹膜透析

pernicious anemia　悪性貧血	photoaging　光老化
peroneal nerve paralysis　腓骨神経麻痺	photophobia　羞明
persecutory delusion　被害妄想	photoreceptor　視細胞
personal care aide　日常生活介護者	physiatrist　理学療法医
personal development　自己開発	physical abuse　身体的虐待
personal factor　個人因子	physical activity level : PAL　身体活動レベル
personal hygiene　個人衛生；整容；保清	physical addiction　身体依存
personality　パーソナリティ；人格；性格	physical aggression　身体的攻撃
personality change　人格変化	physical barrier　物理的障壁
personality disorder　パーソナリティ障害；人格	physical care　身体介護
障害	physical disability　身体障害
personality test　人格検査；性格検査	physical energy　体力
personality traits　気質	physical examination (diagnosis)　健康診査
personality trait theory　性格の特性論	（診断）
personality type theory　性格の類型論	physical function　身体機能
personal protective equipment : PPE　個人防	physical medicine　物理医学
護用装備	physical performance test : PPT　身体機能
personal social services　パーソナル・ソーシャ	検査
ル・サービス；対人社会サービス	physical restraint　身体拘束
personal space　パーソナル・スペース	physical strength　体力
person-centered care　パーソンセンタードケア	physical therapist : PT　理学療法士
pervasive developmental disorder : PDD	physical therapy : PT　理学療法
広汎性発達障害	physician　医師；医者
pes planus　扁平足	physician-assisted suicide　医師自殺幇助
phagocytosis　食（菌）作用	physician referral services　医師紹介サービス
phallic stage　男根期	physician rounds　回診
phantom limb　ファントム・リブ；幻肢	physiological aging　生理的老化
phantom limb pain　幻肢痛	physiotherapy　物理療法
phantom smell　幻嗅	Pick's disease　ピック病
phantosmia　幻嗅	pineal body　松果体
pharmaceutical inspection　薬事監視	pineal gland　松果腺
pharmaceutical inspector　薬事監視員	pituitary gland　下垂体；脳下垂体
pharmacist　薬剤師	placebo effect　プラセボ効果
pharmacotherapy　薬物療法	plain weave　平織
pharmacy　薬局	plantar flexion　底屈
pharyngeal phase　咽頭相	plasma glucose　血漿グルコース
pharynx　咽頭	plasticity　可塑性
phenylketonuria : PKU　フェニールケトン尿症	platelet　血小板
philanthropy　フィランソロピー：博愛事業	platform crutch　肘台付つえ
phlebitis　静脈炎	play therapy　プレイセラピー；遊戯療法
phobia　恐怖症	pleasure principle　快楽原則
phone scams　電話勧誘販売	pneumococcal meningitis　肺炎球菌性髄膜炎
phosphorus　リン	pneumococcal pneumonia　肺炎球菌性肺炎

英和

N
O
P
Q
R
S
T
U
V
W
X
Y
Z

pneumococcal vaccination　肺炎球菌ワクチン

pneumonia　肺炎

podiatric medicine　足病（そくびょう）

podiatrist　足病医

podiatry　足病学

point gait　動作歩行

policy　政策

policymaker　政策立案者

poliomyelitis：polio　ポリオ；灰白髄炎（かいはくずいえん）

pollakiuria　頻尿

polyarticular gout　多関節性痛風

polycythemia　多血症

polymyalgia rheumatica：PMR　リウマチ性多発筋痛症

polymyositis　多発性筋炎

polyneuropathy　多発ニューロパチー

polyp　ポリープ

polypharmacy　多剤処方（たざい）；多剤併用

polysaccharides　多糖類

polysialia　唾液分泌過多（だえき）；流涎症（りゅうぜんしょう）

polysynaptic reflex　多シナプス反射

polyunsaturated fatty acid：PUFA　多価不飽和（ふほうわ）脂肪酸（しぼうさん）

polyurethane　ポリウレタン

polyuria　多尿

poor　貧困者

poor eye sight　弱視

poor family　貧困家庭

population aging　高齢化

population census　全数調査

population dynamics　人口動態

population estimates　人口推計

population explosion　人口爆発

population movement　人口移動

population projection　将来推計人口

portable bathtub　ポータブル浴槽；移動浴槽；簡易浴槽

portable wheelchair ramp　可搬型スロープ

position　体位

position change　体位変換

positioning　ポジショニング；体位設定

positioning device　体位変換器

positive discrimination　肯定的差別

positive finding　陽性所見

positive mold　陽性モデル

positive punishment　正の罰

positive reinforcement　正の強化

positive symptom　陽性症状

positron emission tomography：PET　ポジトロン・エミッション・トモグラフィー；陽電子放射断層撮影法

post-disability personality　障害後性格

post evaluation　事後評価

post-fall syndrome　転倒後症候群

postherpetic neuralgia：PHN　帯状疱疹後神経痛（たいじょうほうしん）

post-infection cough　感染後咳（がい）そう

post-injury personality　障害後性格

postmortem care　死後のケア；死後の処置

postmortem lividity　死斑（しはん）

post nasal drip syndrome：PNDS　後鼻漏（こうびろう）候群

postoperative infection　術後感染

postpartum infection　産褥感染症（さんじょく）

post-polio syndrome：PPS　ポリオ後症候群

post-transfusion hepatitis　輸血後肝炎

post-traumatic neurosis　外傷神経症

posttraumatic stress disorder：PTSD　心的外傷後ストレス障害

postural drainage　体位ドレナージ

postural exercise　姿勢訓練

postural hypotension　起立性低血圧

postural reaction　姿勢反応

postural reflex　姿勢反射

postural reflex impairment　姿勢反射障害

posture　姿勢

post-viral fatigue syndrome　ウイルス感染後疲労症候群

potassium　カリウム

poultice　湿布

poverty　貧困

poverty index　貧困指数

poverty level　貧困水準

poverty study　貧困調査

powdered medication　散剤

practice examination　実技試験

practice manual　業務マニュアル

precancerous condition　前がん状態

preconscious　前意識

pre-disability personality　障害前性格

preemie　未熟児

pre-evaluation　事前評価

preimplantation genetic diagnosis　着床前診断

pre-injury personality　障害前性格

prejudice　偏見

premature atrial contraction：PAC　心房期外
　収縮

premature infant　未熟児

premature ventricular contraction：PVC　心室
　期外収縮

prenatal diagnosis　出生前診断

prenatal infection　胎内感染

preoperative anxiety　術前不安

prepaid group practice：PGP　前払い型グルー
　プ診療

prerequisite criteria　必要前提基準

presbycusis　老人（加齢）性難聴

presbyopia　老眼；老視

prescription　処方箋

presenile dementia　初老期認知症

pressure　圧迫

pressure group　圧力団体

pressure sore　褥瘡；圧迫潰瘍；床ずれ

pressure ulcer　褥瘡；圧迫潰瘍；床ずれ

Pressure Ulcer Scale for Healing：PUSH
　褥瘡治癒過程スケール

pressurized room　陽圧室

presyncope　意識消失発作

prevalence　有病

prevalence rate　有病率

prevention　予防

preventive care　予防ケア

preventive medicine　予防医学

primary afferent fiber　一次求心性線維

primary aging　一次的老化

primary bacteremia　原発性菌血症

primary biliary cirrhosis　原発性胆汁性肝硬変

primary blood stream infection　原発性血流
　感染

primary care　プライマリ・ケア

primary caregiver　主介護者

primary care physician：PCP　プライマリ・ケ
　ア医

primary delusion　一次妄想

primary doctor　主治医

primary health care：PHC　プライマリ・ヘルス・
　ケア

primary impairment　一次障害

primary motive　一次的動機

primary poverty　第一次貧困

primary prevention　一次予防

primary process　一次過程

primary stimulus　原刺激

prime mover　主動筋

primitive reflex　原始反射

privacy　プライバシー

privacy protection　プライバシー保護

private health insurance　民間医療保険

private hospital　私立病院；民間病院

private insurance　民間保険

private long-term care insurance　民間介護
　保険

private pension　民間年金

private room　個室

problem behavior　問題行動

problem-oriented recording：POR　問題志向
　記録

problem solving approach　問題解決アプ
　ローチ

problem solving process　問題解決過程

procedural memory　手続き記憶

process　プロセス

process recording　プロセス・レコード

productive　プロダクティブ

productive age population　生産年齢人口；労
　働力人口

productive aging　プロダクティブ・エイジング

professional ethics　職業倫理

professionalism　専門性

progeria　早老症

progesterone　黄体ホルモン

progesterone therapy　プロゲステロン療法

prognosis　予後	proximal humerus fracture　上腕骨近位端骨折
prognosis and prediction　予後予測	proximal tibia fracture　脛骨近位部骨折
programmed theory　プログラム説	proxy decision maker　意思決定代理者
progressive bulbar palsy　進行性球麻痺	pruritus　かゆみ
progressive muscular dystrophy：PMD　進行性筋ジストロフィー	pruritus senilis　老人性掻痒症
progressive myoclonus epilepsy：PME　進行性ミオクローヌスてんかん	pseudobulbar paralysis　仮性球麻痺
	pseudodementia　仮性認知症
progressive systemic sclerosis：PSS　全身性進行性硬化症	pseudomonas pneumonia　緑膿菌性肺炎
projection　投影；投射	psychiatric disorder　精神障害
projective techniques　投影法	psychiatric hospital　精神（科）病院
projective test　投影検査	psychiatric medication　精神薬
proliferation　増殖	psychiatric occupational therapy　精神科作業療法；精神障害作業療法
pronation　回内	psychiatric rehabilitation　精神医学的リハビリテーション
prone position　腹臥位	
proof of immunization　予防接種証明書	psychiatric social work　精神医学的ソーシャルワーク
proof of vaccination　予防接種証明書	
proper positioning　良肢位	psychiatric social worker：PSW　精神医学的ソーシャルワーカー
property tax　資産税	
proportional mortality indicator：PMI　50歳以上死亡割合	psychiatrist　精神科医
	psychiatry　精神医学
proportional mortality rate：PMR　死因別死亡割合	psychic trauma　心的外傷
	psychoanalysis　精神分析
proprietary medicine　専売医薬	psychoanalyst　精神分析家
proprioception　固有感覚	psychoanalytical psychotherapy　精神分析的心理療法
proprioception deficit　固有受容性欠陥	
prosopagnosia　相貌失認	psychoanalytic therapy　精神分析療法
prostate　前立腺	psychodrama　サイコドラマ；心理劇
prostate cancer　前立腺がん	psychodrama therapy　心理劇療法
prostate disease　前立腺疾患	psychodynamics　心理力動論
prostate specific antigen：PSA　前立腺特異抗原	psychogenesis　心因
	psychogenic pollakiuria　心因性頻尿
prostatic hypertrophy　前立腺肥大症	psychogenic psychosis　心因性精神障害
prostatitis　前立腺炎	psychogenic reaction　心因反応
prosthesis　義肢	psychological abuse　心理的虐待
prosthetic　補綴	psychological addiction　精神依存
prosthetist and orthotist：PO　義肢装具士	psychological assessment　心理評価；心理判定
protective isolation　予防隔離	
protein　たんぱく質	psychological care　心理的ケア
protein energy　たんぱく質エネルギー	psychological intervention techniques　心理学的援助技術
protein-energy malnutrition：PEM　たんぱく質・エネルギー低栄養状態	psychological needs　心理的欲求；人格的欲求
	psychological preparation　心理的準備

psychological process　心理過程

psychological test　心理検査；心理テスト

psychological therapy　心理療法；精神療法

psychopathic personality　精神病質

psychopathy　精神病質

psychosexual development　心理・性的発達理論

psychosexual stages　心理・性的段階

psychosis　精神病

psychosocial assessment　心理社会評価

psychosomatic disorder：PSD　心身症

psychotherapy　心理療法；精神療法

psychotic behavior　精神病的行動

psychotropic　向精神薬

psychotropic medication　向精神薬

ptyalism　唾液分泌過多；流唾症

public aid　公的扶助；公助

public assistance　公的扶助；公助

public assistance recipient　公的扶助受給者；被保護者

public health　公衆衛生

public health center　保健所

public health nurse：PHN　保健師

Public Health Services Act　公衆衛生法

public hospital　公立病院

public housing　公営住宅

public intervention　公的介入

public opinion poll　世論調査

public pension　公的年金

public policy　公共政策

public responsibility　公的責任

public services　公的サービス

public transportation　公共交通機関

puerperal fever　産褥熱

puerperal infection　産褥感染症

puffer fish poisoning　フグ中毒

pulmonary artery　肺動脈

pulmonary aspiration　誤嚥

pulmonary atelectasis　無気肺

pulmonary atresia　肺動脈閉鎖症

pulmonary disease　肺疾患

pulmonary edema　肺水腫

pulmonary embolism：PE　肺塞栓

pulmonary emphysema　肺気腫

pulmonary function tests：PFTs　肺機能検査

pulmonary rehabilitation　呼吸リハビリテーション

pulmonary tuberculosis　肺結核

pulse　脈拍

pulse oximeter　パルスオキシメーター；経皮酸素飽和度モニター

pupillary light reflex　瞳孔対光反射

pureed diet　ペースト食

pureed solid　ピューレ状

pure tone audiometry：PTA　純音聴力検査

purposeful expression of feelings　意図的な感情表現

purposeful wandering　意図的徘徊

pursed lip breathing　口すぼめ呼吸

pyelitis　腎盂炎

pyelography　腎盂造影

pyelonephritis　腎盂腎炎

pyorrhea alveolaris　歯槽膿漏

pyramidal tract　錐体路

pyramid cane　歩行器型つえ；ウォーカーケイン

pyrexia　発熱

pyuria　膿尿

Q

quad cane　四脚づえ

quadriceps femoris　大腿四頭筋

quadriplegia　四肢麻痺

quality control：QC　品質管理活動

quality improvement：QI　改善活動

quality indicator　クオリティインジケータ

quality measure　クオリティメジャー

quality of care　ケアの質

quality of death：QoD　死の質

quality of life：QOL　クオリティ・オブ・ライフ；生活の質；人生の質

quarantine　検疫

quasi-medical practice　医業類似行為

quaternary prevention　四次予防

questionnaire　質問紙法；質問紙；調査票

R

rabies　狂犬病

race discrimination　人種差別

racism　人種差別主義

radial artery　橈骨動脈

radial artery aneurysm　橈骨動脈瘤

radiation　放射線

radiation therapy　放射線治療

radiculopathy　神経根症

radiography　X線撮影

radiologic technologist　診療放射線技師

radiology test　X線検査

rage　狂気；怒り

ramie　苧麻

ramp　傾斜路

random sampling　無作為抽出法

range of motion：ROM　関節可動域

range of motion testing：ROM-T　関節可動域
テスト

rapid eye movement sleep：REM sleep　レム
睡眠

rapport　ラポール；ラポート；信頼関係

rat-bite disease　鼠咬症

rational emotive behavior therapy　理性感情行
動療法

rationalization　合理化

reaction formation　反動形成

reaction time　反応時間

reactive psychosis　反応性精神病

reading glasses　読書眼鏡

reality orientation：RO　リアリティ・オリエンテー
ション；現実見当識

reality orientation training：ROT　現実見当識
訓練

reality principle　現実性の原理

reasonable accommodation　合理的配慮

reassessment　再アセスメント

receptive attitude　受容的態度

recertification　再認定；再指定

recessive inheritance　劣性遺伝

recipient　レシピエント；受給者

reciprocal walker　交互型四脚歩行器；交互式
歩行器

reciprocating gait orthosis：RGO　交互歩行
装具

reclining and tilting wheelchair　リクライニング・
ティルト式普通型車いす

reclining wheelchair　リクライニング型車いす

recognition　再認

recommended dietary allowance：RDA　栄養
所要量

recreation　レクリエーション；娯楽

recreational activity　レクリエーション活動

recreational therapy　レクリエーション療法

recreation program　レクリエーションプログラム

rectal cancer　直腸がん

rectal examination　直腸診

rectal prolapse　直腸脱

rectocele　直腸瘤

recuperation　療養

recuperative care　療養介護

red blood cell：RBC　赤血球

redistribution　再分配

re-emerging infectious disease　再興感染症

re-emerging influenza　再興型インフルエンザ

referral fee　紹介料

referral services　紹介サービス

referred pain　関連痛

reflection of feeling　感情の反射

reflex incontinence　反射性尿失禁

reflex movement　反射運動

reflex sympathetic dystrophy：RSD　反射性交
感神経性ジストロフィー

regenerative medicine　再生医療

registered dietitian　管理栄養士

registered nurse　登録看護師

regression　退行

regressive behavior　退行行動

regular diet　普通食；常食

rehabilitation　リハビリテーション；更生

rehabilitation approach　リハビリテーションアプ
ローチ

rehabilitation counselor　リハビリテーションカウ
ンセラー

rehabilitation engineering　リハビリテーション

工学

Rehabilitation International：RI　リハビリテーション・インターナショナル；国際リハビリテーション協会

rehabilitation medicine　リハビリテーション医学

rehabilitation nursing　リハビリテーション看護

rehabilitation psychology　リハビリテーション心理学

rehabilitative care　リハビリテーションケア

rehydration　水分補給

reimbursement　償還払い；払い戻し

Reiter's syndrome　ライター症候群

relative　親族

relative metabolic rate：RMR　エネルギー代謝率

relaxation　リラクセーション；気晴らし

relocation stress　転居ストレス

remaining sense　残存感覚

reminiscence　レミニッセンス；回想

reminiscence therapy　回想法

remission　寛解（かんかい）

remote care　遠隔ケア

remote medicine　遠隔医療

remote memory　遠隔記憶

remotivation　リイ・モティベーション；再動機づけ

renal disease　腎疾患

renal failure　腎機能障害；腎不全

renal function　腎機能

renal insufficiency　腎機能障害；腎不全

renewal　更新

renewal application　更新申請

repetitive behavior　多動

repetitive saliva swallowing test：RSST　反復唾液嚥下（だえきえんげ）テスト

replacement level fertility　人口置換水準

repression　抑圧

reproductive gland　生殖腺

rescue breathing　人工呼吸

resident　住民；入居者；入所者

resident bacteria　常在菌

resident flora　常在菌

residents' rights　入所型施設利用者の権利

residual function　残存機能

residual functional capacity　残存能力

residual sensory function　残存感覚機能

residual urine　残尿

resistance　耐性（たいせい）；抵抗

resonance　共鳴

Resource-Based Relative Value Scale：RBRVS　診療報酬支払相対評価スケール方式

respiration　呼吸

respirator　レスピレーター

respiratory disease　呼吸器疾患

respiratory disorder　呼吸障害

respiratory dysfunction　呼吸器機能障害；呼吸機能障害

respiratory failure　呼吸不全

respiratory infection　呼吸器感染

respiratory isolation　気道感染隔離

respiratory organ　呼吸器

respiratory paralysis　呼吸麻痺（まひ）

respiratory therapy　呼吸療法

respite　レスパイト；休息

respite care　レスパイト・ケア

respondent behavior　レスポンデント行動

respondent conditioning　レスポンデント条件づけ

responsibility　責任

rest angina　安静時狭心症

rest home　レストホーム

resting energy expenditure：REE　安静時エネルギー消費量

resting tremor　安静時振戦（しんせん）

restless legs syndrome：RLS　レストレスレッグス症候群；むずむず脚症候群

restraint　拘束（こうそく）

restricted diet　制限食

restricted mobility　運動制限

retina　網膜（もうまく）

retinal detachment　網膜剥離（はくり）

retinal hemorrhage　網膜出血

retinoblastoma　網膜芽細胞腫（がさいぼうしゅ）

retinopathy　網膜症

retirement　引退；定年；退職

retirement allowance　退職手当

retirement community　退職者コミュニティ

175

retirement earnings test　退職所得調査

retirement home　退職者ホーム

retrograde amnesia　逆向健忘

retroperitoneal hematoma　後腹膜血腫

Rett syndrome　レット症候群

return policy　返品特約

reversed isolation　逆隔離

reverse mortgage　リバース・モーゲージ

Revised Children's Manifest Anxiety Scale
　改訂版児童用顕在性不安尺度

Revised Wechsler Adult Intelligence Scale：
　WAIS-R　改定版ウェクスラー成人知能検査

Revised Wechsler Memory Scale：WMS-R
　改定版ウェクスラー記憶検査

Rey-Osterrieth Complex Figure Test：ROCF
　レイ複雑図形検査

rheumatic disorder　リウマチ性疾患

rheumatism　リウマチ

rheumatoid arthritis：RA　関節リウマチ

rheumatologist　リウマチ専門医

rhinitis　鼻炎

rhythm　リズム

right atrium　右心房

righting reaction　立ち直り反応

right lateral recumbent position：RLR
　position　右側臥位

rights　権利

right ventricle　右心室

rigidity　固縮

rigor mortis　死後硬直

risk　リスク

risk assessment　リスクアセスメント

risk control　リスク管理

risk factor　危険因子

risk management　リスクマネジメント；危機管理

risk prevention　危険防止

Rivermead Behavioural Memory Test：RBMT
　リバーミード行動記憶検査

rod　桿体

role　役割

role behavior　役割行動

role conflict　役割葛藤

role perception　役割認知

role playing　ロールプレイ；役割演技

role theory　役割理論

Rorschach Inkblot Test　ロールシャッハ・インク
　ブロット・テスト

rotator cuff injury　腱板損傷

roundback　円背；後弯

routes of infection　感染経路

routes of transmission　感染経路

rubbing board　洗濯板

rubella　風疹

rubeola　麻疹

S

saccharide　糖質

sacrum　仙骨

safety needs　安全の欲求

safety net　セーフティネット；安全ネット

saliva　唾液

salivary function　唾液機能

salivary secretion　唾液分泌

salmonella　サルモネラ菌

salmonella food poisoning　サルモネラ食中毒

salty taste　塩味

sample survey　標本調査

sampling　標本抽出

sampling error　標本誤差

sandplay therapy　箱庭療法

sanitization　サニテーション

saponated cresol solution　クレゾール石鹸液

sarcoidosis　サルコイドーシス

sarcopenia　サルコペニア

Sarcoptes scabiei　ヒゼンダニ

satiety center　満腹中枢

satisfaction　満足

satisfaction survey　満足度調査

scabies　疥癬

scam　詐欺

scapulohumeral rhythm　肩甲上腕リズム

scar contracture　瘢痕拘縮

scarlatina　猩紅熱

scarlet fever　猩紅熱

scatolia　弄便

schizoaffective disorder　統合失調感情障害

schizophrenia　統合失調症

school absenteeism　不登校

school counselor　スクールカウンセラー

school infirmary　保健室

school nurse　養護教諭

school social worker　スクールソーシャルワーカー

sciatica　坐骨神経痛

science　科学

scientific evidence　科学的根拠

scoliosis　側弯

screening　スクリーニング；検診

seasonal work　季節労働

seating aid　座位補助具

seating position　椅座位

sebum　皮脂

secondary aging　二次的老化；病的老化

secondary delusion　二次妄想

secondary health care　二次医療

secondary hypertension　二次性高血圧

secondary impairment　二次障害

secondary infection　二次感染

secondary medical service area　二次医療圏

secondary motive　二次的動機

secondary physician　副主治医

secondary poverty　第二次貧困

secondary prevention　二次予防

secondary process　二次過程

secondhand smoke　受動喫煙

second opinion　セカンドオピニオン

Seddon's classification　セドンの分類

seeing-eye dog　盲導犬

seizure　発作

selective dissemination of information：SDI
　選択的情報提供

selective optimization with compensation：
　SOC　選択的最適化論

self-actualization　自己実現

self-advocacy movement　セルフアドボカシー
　運動；自己擁護運動

self-assisted exercise　自己他動運動

self-awareness　自己覚知

self-care　セルフケア

self-catheterization　自己導尿

self-concept　自己概念

self-control theory　自己コントロール理論

self-determination　自己決定

self-digestion　自己消化

self-disclosure　自己開示

self-disturbance　自我障害

self-efficacy　自己効力感

self-employment　自営業

self-esteem　自尊心

self-evaluation　自己評価

self-expression　自己表現

self-harm：SH　自傷行為

self-hater　自責（内罰）型

self-hatred　自己嫌悪

self-help　セルフヘルプ；自助

self-help group：SHG　自助グループ

self-identity　自己同一性

self-improvement　自己改善

self-infection　自己感染

self-injection　自己注射

self-injury　自傷行為

self-loathing　自己嫌悪

self-mutilation　自傷行為

self-neglect　自己放任

self-propelled wheelchair　自走式普通型車いす

Self-Rating Depression Scale：SDS　自己評価
　式抑うつ性尺度

self-responsibility　自己責任

semantic dementia：SD　意味性認知症

semantic memory　意味記憶

semi-Fowler's position　セミファーラー位

semi-private room　二人部屋；準個室

senile cataract　老人性白内障

senile dementia：SD　老年痴呆；老人性認知症

senile dementia of the Alzheimer's type：SDAT
　老人性アルツハイマー型認知症

senile plaques　老人斑

senility　老衰

senior　高齢者；年長者；上級

senior center　シニアセンター；高齢者センター

senior health　老人保健

senior housing　シニア住宅；高齢者住宅

177

sensation 知覚；感覚	sex discrimination 性差別
sense 感覚	sex gland 性腺
sensitivity test 感受性試験	sex hormone 性ホルモン
sensorineural deafness 感音難聴	sex-linked disease 伴性遺伝病
sensorineural hearing loss：SNHL 感音性難聴	sexual abuse 性的虐待
sensory aphasia 感覚性失語（症）	sexual assault nurse examiner：SANE 性暴力被害者支援看護職
sensory disturbance 感覚障害	sexual division of labor：SDL 性別役割分業
sensory enhancement 感覚強化法	sexual dysfunction 性機能障害
sensory function 感覚機能	sexual harassment セクシュアルハラスメント
sensory impairment 知覚障害	sexuality セクシュアリティ
sensory integration 感覚統合	sexually transmitted disease：STD 性行為感染症
sensory memory 感覚記憶	
sensory nerve 感覚神経	sexual minority 性的マイノリティ
sensory paralysis 感覚麻痺；知覚麻痺	sexual orientation disturbance：SOD 性指向障害
sensory substitution 感覚代行	
sensory substitution device：SSD 感覚代行機器	sexual preference disorder 性嗜好障害
	sexual violence 性的暴力
Sentence Completion Test：SCT 文章完成テスト	sharps injury 鋭利物損傷
	shelter 救護施設；救貧院；養老院
separated by death 死別	shingles 帯状疱疹
separation 分離	shoe horn brace：SHB 靴べら式装具
separation anxiety 分離不安	short leg brace 短下肢装具
separation anxiety disorder 分離不安障害	shortness of breath：SOB 息切れ；呼吸困難
sepsis 敗血症	short-sightedness 近視
septicemia 敗血症	short stump 短断端
septic shock 敗血症性ショック	short-term care facility 短期ケア施設
sequela 後遺症	short-term goal 短期目標
serotonin セロトニン	short-term memory 短期記憶
serous otitis media：SOM 滲出性中耳炎	shot 注射
serum albumin level 血清アルブミン値	shoulder dislocation 肩関節脱臼
serum cholesterol 血清コレステロール	shoulder-hand syndrome 肩手症候群
serum hepatitis 血清肝炎	shoulder impingement syndrome 肩インピンジメント症候群
service area サービス提供圏	
service dog 介助犬；補助犬	shoulder subluxation 肩関節亜脱臼
settlement セツルメント	shuffling gait 小刻み歩行
settlement house 隣保館	Shy-Drager syndrome：SDS シャイ・ドレーガー症候群
severance package 退職手当	
severance pay 退職手当	sialorrhea 流涎症；唾液分泌過多
severe acute respiratory syndrome：SARS 重症急性呼吸器症候群	sibling conflict きょうだい間葛藤
	sibling rivalry きょうだい間競争
sex 性別	sick leave 傷病休暇；疾病休暇
sex chromosome 性染色体	Sickness Impact Profile：SIP 疾病影響プロ

ファイル

sickness insurance　疾病保険

side effect　副作用

siderail　サイドレール

sigmoid colon　S状結腸

sigmoidoscopy　S状結腸鏡検査

significant change　著変

sign language　手話

silent aspiration　不顕性誤嚥

silent infection　不顕性感染

simple fracture　単純骨折

Sims' position　シムス位

single-hand manual drive wheelchair　片手駆動式普通型車いす

single-parent family　単親家庭；ひとり親家庭；欠損家庭

single-use device：SUD　単回使用器材

sinobronchial syndrome：SBS　副鼻腔気管支症候群

sinopulmonary infection　経気道感染

sinus headache　副鼻洞性頭痛

sitting balance　座位バランス

sitting exercise　座位訓練

sitting position　座位

sit-to-stand exercise　立ち上がり運動

situational reflection　状況反射

Sjogren's syndrome　シェーグレン症候群

skeletal muscle　骨格筋

skeleton　骨格

skilled nursing facility：SNF　スキルドナーシングホーム；高度看護施設

skin　皮膚

skin antiseptic　皮膚消毒

skin cancer　皮膚がん

skin disease　皮膚疾患

skin disorder　皮膚障害

skin pruritus　皮膚掻痒症

skin rash　発疹

skin redness　発赤

skin tear　皮膚損傷

sleep apnea　睡眠時無呼吸

sleep apnea syndrome：SAS　睡眠時無呼吸症候群

sleep disorder　睡眠障害

sleeping pill　睡眠薬

sleep-onset insomnia　入眠障害

sleep-related breathing disorder　睡眠関連呼吸障害

slight fever　微熱

sling　スリング；三角巾

slope　スロープ

small cell lung cancer：SCLC　小細胞肺がん

small intestinal polyps　小腸ポリープ

small intestine　小腸

small intestine dysfunction　小腸機能障害

smallpox　痘そう

smoke detector　煙感知器

social action　ソーシャルアクション；社会活動法

social activity　社会活動

social adequacy　社会的適用

social administration　ソーシャルアドミニストレーション；社会福祉管理

social allowance　社会手当

social anxiety disorder：SAD　社会恐怖

social assistance　社会扶助

social barrier　社会的障壁

social capital　ソーシャル・キャピタル；社会資本

social care　社会的介護

social case work　ソーシャルケースワーク；個別援助活動

social cognitive theory　社会認知理論

social consciousness　社会意識

social diagnosis　社会診断

social education　社会教育

social facilitation　社会的促進

social functioning ability：SFA　社会生活力

social group　社会集団

social inclusion　ソーシャル・インクルージョン；社会的包摂；社会的受容

social insurance　社会保険

social interaction　社会的相互作用

socialism　社会主義

social isolation　社会的隔離

socialization　社会化

social medicine　社会医学

social model　社会モデル

social models of disability　障害の社会モデル

social movement (theory)　社会運動（論）

social needs　社会ニーズ；社会的要求

social network　社会的ネットワーク

social participation　社会参加

social phobia　社会恐怖

social planning　ソーシャルプランニング；社会計画

social policy　社会政策

social psychiatry　社会精神医学

social reform　社会改良

social rehabilitation　社会リハビリテーション

social resources　社会資源

social rights　社会権

social risk　社会的危険

social risk management　ソーシャルリスクマネジメント

social role　社会的役割

social role theory　社会的役割論

social role valorization：SRV　社会的役割の実現

social science　社会科学

social security　社会保障

Social Security Act　社会保障法

social security benefit　社会保障給付

social security tax　社会保障税

social services　ソーシャルサービス；社会福祉；福祉サービス

social skill　ソーシャルスキル

social skills training：SST　ソーシャル・スキルズ・トレーニング；社会生活技能訓練

social structure　社会構造

social support　ソーシャルサポート；社会的支援

social support network　ソーシャル・サポート・ネットワーク；社会的支援ネットワーク

social survey　社会踏査

social welfare　社会福祉

social withdrawal　引きこもり

social work　ソーシャルワーク；社会福祉

social worker：SW　ソーシャルワーカー

social work research　ソーシャルワーク・リサーチ；社会福祉調査法

socioemotional selectivity theory：SST　社会情動的選択理論

sociology　社会学

sociometry　ソシオメトリー

sodium　ナトリウム

sodium hypochlorite solution　次亜塩素酸ナトリウム溶液

sodium intake　塩分摂取

soft diet　ソフト食；軟菜食

soft palate　軟口蓋

soil-borne infection　土壌感染

solo practitioner　単独開業医

solution-focused approach　解決志向的アプローチ

somatic nervous system　体性神経

somatic sensation　体性感覚

somnipathy　睡眠障害

somnolence　傾眠；眠気

sopor　昏眠

sound amplifier　音声増幅器

source isolation　感染源隔離

source of infection　感染源

sour taste　酸味

spasm　攣縮

spastic　痙性；痙直型

spastic diplegia　痙直型両麻痺

spasticity　痙縮

spastic paralysis　痙性麻痺

spastic paraparesis　痙性対麻痺

spastic quadriplegia　痙直型四肢麻痺

spastic torticollis　痙性斜頸

spatial agnosia　空間失認

spatial perception　空間認知

special care unit　認知症専門病棟

special therapeutic diet　特別治療食

specific developmental disorder：SDD　特異的発達障害

specimen collection　検体収集

speech and language disorders　言語障害

speech and language training　言語訓練

speech center　言語中枢

speech clarity　言葉の明瞭性

speech disorder　音声障害；音声機能障害

speech function　言語機能

speech-generating device　携帯用会話補助
　装置

speech impairment　音声障害；音声機能障害

speech-language-hearing rehabilitation　言語
　聴覚リハビリテーション

speech-language-hearing therapist　言語聴
　覚士

speech-language-hearing therapy　言語聴覚
　療法

speech organ　音声器官

speechreading　読話

speech therapist : ST　言語療法士

speech therapy : ST　言語療法

sphincter　括約筋

sphincter disturbance　括約筋障害

spina bifida　二分脊椎

spinal compression fracture　脊椎圧迫骨折

spinal cord　脊髄

spinal cord injury : SCI　脊髄損傷

spinal nerve　脊髄神経

spinal orthosis　体幹装具

spinal reflex　脊髄反射

spinal stenosis　脊柱管狭窄症

spinal tap　脊椎穿刺

spinal X-ray　脊椎 X 線

spine　脊柱

spinocerebellar ataxia : SCA　脊髄小脳失調症

spinocerebellar degeneration : SCD　脊髄小脳
　変性症

spiritual care　スピリチュアルケア

spirituality　霊性

spiritual pain　スピリチュアルペイン

Spiritual Well-Being Scale : SWB　霊的幸福
　尺度

spleen　脾臓

splint　副子

spondylolysis　脊椎分離症

spondylosis deformans　変形性脊椎症

sponge bath　スポンジバス；清拭

spore　芽胞

sports injury　スポーツ外傷

spousal abuse　配偶者虐待

spouse　配偶者

sprain　捻挫

spray　散布

sputum　喀痰

sputum suction　喀痰吸引

squamous cell carcinoma　扁平上皮がん

stability　安定性

stable angina　労作時狭心症

staff development　職員研修

staffing　職員配置

stair lift　階段昇降機

standard deduction　基礎控除；標準控除

standardization　標準化

standardized care　ケアの標準化

standardized mortality ratio : SMR　標準化死
　亡比

Standard Language Test of Aphasia : SLTA
　標準失語症検査

standard of living　生活水準

standard precautions　標準予防策

standing exercise　立位訓練；起立訓練

standing position　立位

staphylococcal pneumonia　黄色ブドウ球菌性
　肺炎

Staphylococcus　ブドウ球菌

Staphylococcus aureus　黄色ブドウ球菌

stasis dermatitis　うっ滞性皮膚炎

stated needs　顕在的ニーズ

static population　人口静態

steam sterilization　蒸気滅菌

stem family　直系家族

step length　歩幅

stereotype　ステレオタイプ

stereotyped behavior　常同行動

stereotypical behavior　常同行動

stereotypy　常同症

sterilant　滅菌剤

sterility assurance　滅菌保証；無菌保証

sterility assurance level : SAL　滅菌保証レベル；
　無菌性保証水準

sterility testing　無菌試験

sterilization　殺菌；滅菌；消毒

steroid　ステロイド

stigma　スティグマ

stimulation　刺激

stoma　ストーマ；人工肛門

stomach cancer　胃がん

stomatitis　口内炎

stool　便

stool examination　糞便検査

stool specimen　検便

strained back　ギックリ腰

strength　ストレングス

strengths perspective　ストレングス視点

Streptococcus pneumoniae　肺炎レンサ球菌

stress　ストレス

stress incontinence　腹圧性尿失禁

stress inoculation training　ストレス免疫訓練

stress management　ストレスマネジメント

stress model　ストレスモデル

stressor　ストレッサー

stress reaction　ストレス反応

stretcher　ストレッチャー

stretching exercise　ストレッチ体操；伸張運動

stride length　ストライド長

stride width　歩隔

stroke　脳卒中

Stroke Impairment Assessment Set：SIAS　脳卒中機能障害評価法

stroking　撫擦法

stump pain　断端痛；断端神経痛

stupor　昏迷

subacute care facility　亜急性ケア施設

subarachnoid hemorrhage：SAH　くも膜下出血

subchorionic hematoma　絨毛膜下血腫

subconscious mind　潜在意識

subcortical vascular dementia　皮質下血管性認知症

subcutaneous：Sub-Q　皮下

subcutaneous bleeding　皮下出血

subdural hematoma　硬膜下血腫

subjective happiness　主観的幸福感（幸福度）

Subjective Happiness Scale　主観的幸福感尺度

subjective information　主観的情報

subjective needs　主観的ニーズ

subjective well-being：SWB　主観的幸福感（幸福度）

sublimation　昇華

sublingual gland　舌下腺

subluxation　亜脱臼

submandibular gland　顎下腺

subsidy　補助金

substance abuse　薬物乱用；物質乱用

substance-induced psychosis　物質誘発性精神病

substitutability　代替性

substituted judgment　代理判断

substitute function　代替機能

subungual hematoma　爪下血腫

successful aging　サクセスフル・エイジング；幸福な老い

succession　相続

suction biopsy　吸引生検

suctioning　吸引

suction machine　吸引器

sudden deafness　突発性難聴

sudden death　突然死

sudden hearing loss　突発性難聴

sudden sensorineural hearing loss　突発性感音難聴

suffocation　窒息

suicidal ideation　希死念慮

suicide　自殺

suicide prevention　自殺予防

summary recording　要約記録

sundowning　日暮れ時兆候

sundown syndrome　夕暮れ症候群

sun stroke　日射病；熱中症

superannuation fund　年金基金

superego　スーパー・エゴ；超自我

superficial sensation　表在感覚

superinfection　菌交代症

superstition　迷信

supervisee　スーパーバイジー

supervision　スーパービジョン

supervisor　スーパーバイザー

supination　回外

supine position　仰臥位；背臥位

supplementary benefit　補足給付

support　サポート；支持
support bar　支持棒
support group　サポートグループ；支援グループ
supportive occupational therapy　支持的作業
　療法
suppository　座薬
supraglottic swallow　息こらえ嚥下
surfactant　界面活性剤
surgery　手術
surgical mask　サージカルマスク；外科用マスク
surgical wound　手術創
surgical wound infection　手術創感染
surrogate decision　代理決定
surveillance　サーベイランス，監視
survey　監査
surveyor　監査官
survivors' benefit　遺族給付
survivors' pension　遺族年金
swallowing　嚥下
swallowing difficulty　嚥下困難
swallowing disorder　嚥下障害
swallowing function　嚥下機能
swallowing reflex　嚥下反射
swallowing training　嚥下訓練
swan neck deformity　スワンネック変形
sweat glands　汗腺
sweating disorder　発汗障害
sweepstakes and lottery scam　当選商法
sweet taste　甘味
swelling　腫脹
swing phase　遊脚期
swing-through gait　大振り歩行
swing-to gait　小振り歩行
symbiosis society　共生社会
symbolic barrier　象徴的障壁
sympathetic muscle nerve activity　筋交感神
　経活動
sympathetic nerve　交感神経
sympathetic skin response　交感神経皮膚反応
sympathy　同情
symptom　症状
symptomatic anemia　症候性貧血
symptomatic epilepsy　症（候）性てんかん

symptomatic therapy　対症療法
syncope　意識喪失
syndrome　症候群
syphilis　梅毒
systemic lupus erythematosus : SLE　全身性
　紅斑性狼瘡
systems perspective　システム的視点
systems theory　システム理論
systolic blood pressure　最高血圧；収縮期
　血圧
systolic pressure　収縮期圧

T

tablet　錠剤
tachycardia　頻脈
tachypnea　頻呼吸
tactile hallucination　幻触
tactual form recognition　形態認知
talipes calcaneus　踵足変形
talipes valgus　外反足
tannin　タンニン
tap water　水道水
tardive dyskinesia　遅発性ジスキネジア
targeted surveillance　対象限定サーベイランス
tarry stool　タール便
task analysis　課題分析
task-centered approach　課題中心アプローチ
task performance ability　課題遂行能力
taste buds　味蕾
tax　税金
tax deduction　税控除
tax-exempt household　非課税世帯
Taylor's Manifest Anxiety Scale : TMAS　テイ
　ラー顕現性不安尺度
T-cane　T字づえ
team-based approach　チームアプローチ
team-based care　チームケア
team-based health care　チーム医療
team conference　チームカンファレンス
teamwork　チームワーク
technical aid　日常生活用具；福祉用具；補助具
telemarketing scams　電話勧誘販売

telecommunications relay service：TRS　代理
電話

temperament　気質

temporary　一時性；一時的

temporary aid　一時扶助

temporary assistance　一時扶助

temporary disability allowance　障害一時金

temporary employment　一時雇用

tenodesis　腱固定

tenodesis effect　テノデーシス作用

tension-type headache　緊張型頭痛

terminal care　ターミナルケア

terminal sterilization　最終滅菌

tertiary education　三次教育

tertiary prevention　三次予防

testament　遺言；遺言書

testator　遺言者

testicle　睾丸

testis　精巣

testosterone　テストステロン

tetanus　破傷風

tetrodotoxin poisoning　テトロドトキシン中毒

thalassemia　サラセミア

thanatology　死生学

Thematic Apperception Test：TAT　主題統覚
検査

Theoretical Maximum Daily Intake：TMDI
理論最大一日摂取量

theory　理論

theory of mind：ToM　心の理論

theory of planned behavior：TPB　計画的行動
理論

therapeutic diet　治療食

therapeutic exercise　運動療法

therapeutic relationship　援助関係

therapist　セラピスト

therapy　セラピー

thermal burn　高温やけど

thermal effect　温熱作用

thermal environment　温熱環境

thermal-insulation finish　保温性加工

thermal processing　熱処理

thermography　サーモグラフィー

thermometer　体温計

thermoregulation　体温調節

thermoregulatory disorder　体温調節機能障害

thermoregulatory impairment　体温調節障害

thermotherapy　温熱療法

thiamine deficiency　サイアミン欠乏症；脚気

thickened diet　とろみ食

thickened liquid　濃厚飲料

thickener　とろみ剤；増粘剤；嚥下補助剤

thickener powder　とろみ剤；増粘剤；嚥下補
助剤

thickening agent　とろみ剤；増粘剤；嚥下補
助剤

thoracic spinal cord injury　胸髄損傷

thought blocking　思考途絶

thought disorder　思考障害

three-dimensional gait analysis　三次元歩行
分析

three-dimensional motion analysis　三次元動
作解析

three-jaw chuck pinch　三指つまみ

three-person transfer　三人移乗法

three-point gait　三動作歩行；三点歩行

threshold　閾値；段差

thrombolytic therapy　血栓溶解療法

thrombosis　血栓

thyroid cancer　甲状腺がん

thyroid cartilage　甲状軟骨

thyroid disease　甲状腺疾患

thyroid gland　甲状腺

thyroid hormone　甲状腺ホルモン

thyroid-stimulating hormone：TSH　甲状腺刺
激ホルモン

thyrotropic hormone　甲状腺刺激ホルモン

thyrotropin　甲状腺刺激ホルモン

thyroxine：T4　サイロキシン

tibial plateau fracture　脛骨高原骨折

tic disorder　チック障害

tick　マダニ

Tietze's syndrome　ティーツェ症候群

tilting table　斜面台

Timed Get up and Go Test：TUG　起立・歩行
動作測定法

tinea　白癬（はくせん）

tinea pedis　足白癬

tinea unguium　爪（つめ）白癬

tinnitus　耳鳴（じめい）；耳鳴（みみな）り

toilet bowl　便器

toileting　排泄（はいせつ）

toileting assistance　排泄介護；排泄介助；排泄ケア

toileting schedule　排泄スケジュール

tolerable daily intake　耐容一日摂取量

tolerance　耐性（たいせい）；耐容性

tomography　断層撮影

tonic-clonic seizure　強直間代発作（きょうちょくかんたいほっさ）

tonic neck reflex　緊張性頸反射（きんちょうせいけいはんしゃ）

tonometry　眼圧計

tonsil　扁桃腺（へんとうせん）

tonsillolith　膿栓

tonsil stone　膿栓

tooth brushing　歯磨き

topographical agnosia　地誌的失認

torso　体幹

total aphasia　全失語

total assistance　全介助；全援助

total blindness　全盲

total care　全介護

total cholesterol　総コレステロール

total color blindness　全色盲

total dependence　全面依存

total fertility rate：TFR　合計特殊出生率

total hip replacement：THR　人工股関節全置換術

total parenteral nutrition：TPN　完全静脈栄養

total personal care　全人格的ケア

total quality management：TQM　総合的品質管理活動

touch reading　触読；ブライユ式触読

toxic psychosis　中毒性精神病

trachea　気管

tracheal cannula　気管カニューレ

tracheostomy　気管切開

traction (treatment)　牽引（けんいん）（療法）

trait theory of personality　性格の特性論

tranquilizer　精神安定剤

transdermal：TD　経皮

transfer　トランスファー；移乗；移動；転院

transfer aid　移乗補助具

transfer and mobility　移乗・移動

transfer bar　移動バー

transfer board　トランスファーボード

transference　転移；感情転移

transference neurosis　転移神経症

transfer lift　移動用リフト

transfer trauma　転居ストレス

transient bacteria　通過菌

transient flora　一過性細菌叢（さいきんそう）

transient ischemic attack：TIA　一過性脳虚血発作（ほっさ）

transintestine nutrition　経腸栄養

transitional care　移行期ケア

transitional facility　中間施設

transitional syndrome　通過症候群

transition zone　移行域

transmissible disease　伝染病；伝染性疾病；感染症

transportation　送迎；輸送

trauma　トラウマ；傷害（しょうがい）；損傷

traumatic brain injury：TBI　頭部外傷；外傷性脳損傷；脳外傷

traumatic injury　頭部外傷；外傷性脳損傷；脳外傷

treadmill　トレッドミル

tremor　振戦（しんせん）

Trendelenburg position　トレンデレンブルグ体位

Trendelenburg sign　トレンデレンブルグ徴候

tricuspid valve　三尖弁（さんせんべん）

trigeminal neuralgia：TN　三叉神経痛（さんさ）

trigger　トリガー

triglyceride　トリグリセライド；中性脂肪

triiodothyronine：T3　トリヨードサイロニン

triplegia　三肢麻痺（さんしまひ）

tripod cane　三脚づえ

trochanteric fracture　転子部骨折（てんしぶこっせつ）

true delusion　真正妄想

trunk　体幹

tube feeding　経管栄養法；チューブ栄養

tuberculin reaction　ツベルクリン反応

tuberculin skin test reaction　ツベルクリン反応

tuberculoma　結核腫

tuberculosis　結核

tuberculosis control　結核対策

tumor　腫瘍

tumor necrosis factor：TNF　腫瘍壊死因子

tumor suppressor gene　がん抑制遺伝子

Turner syndrome　ターナー症候群

turnover rate　離職率

twenty-four-hour care　24時間ケア

twenty-four-hour protective oversight　24時間見守り

twilight state　もうろう状態

two-point gait　二動作歩行

tympanic membrane　鼓膜

type 1 diabetes (mellitus)　1型糖尿病；インスリン依存性糖尿病

type 2 diabetes (mellitus)　2型糖尿病

type theory of personality　性格の類型論

U

ulcer　潰瘍

ulceration　潰瘍形成

ulcerative colitis　潰瘍性大腸炎

ulnar deviation　尺屈；尺側偏位

ultrasonography：US　超音波検査

ultrasound　超音波

ultrasound cardiography　心臓超音波検査

ultrasound therapy　超音波療法

ultraviolet disinfection　紫外線殺菌

ultraviolet therapy　紫外線療法

unconditioned response　無条件反応

unconditioned stimulus　無条件刺激

unconsciousness　無意識

underarm crutch　腋窩支持クラッチ

undernutrition　低栄養

underwear　肌着

unemployment　失業；無職

unemployment benefit　失業給付；失業手当

unemployment insurance　失業保険

unemployment rate　失業率

unilateral knee osteoarthritis　変形性膝関節症

unilateral neglect　半側無視

unilateral spatial neglect：USN　半側空間無視

unit　病棟

United Nations：UN　国際連合

United Nations Children's Fund：UNICEF　ユニセフ

United Nations Decade of Disabled Persons　国連・障害者の十年

United Nations Educational, Scientific and Cultural Organization：UNESCO　ユネスコ

Universal Declaration of Human Rights：UDHR　世界人権宣言

universalism　普遍主義

unpaid labor　無償労働

unsaturated fatty acid　不飽和脂肪酸

unstated needs　潜在的ニーズ

upper airway cough syndrome　上気道咳症候群

upper esophageal sphincter：UES　上部食道括約筋

upper esophageal sphincter dysfunction　上部食道括約筋機能障害

upper extremity　上肢

upper extremity lymphedema　上肢リンパ浮腫

upper extremity orthosis　上肢装具

upper gastrointestinal　上部消化管

urea nitrogen　尿素窒素

uremia　尿毒症

uresiesthesia　尿意

ureterocutaneous fistula　尿管皮膚瘻

urethra　尿道

urethral catheterization　導尿；尿道カテーテル（法）

urethrocele　尿道瘤

urge incontinence　切迫性尿失禁

urgency　切迫性

uric acid　尿酸

urinal　尿瓶

urinalysis：UA　尿検査

urinary bottle　尿器

urinary disorder　排尿障害

urinary incontinence　尿失禁

urinary incontinence assessment　失禁アセスメント

urinary management　排尿管理

urinary retention　尿閉

urinary storage disorder　蓄尿障害

urinary tract　尿路

urinary tract infection：UTI　尿路感染症

urination　排尿

urine　尿

urocystitis　膀胱炎

urolithiasis　尿路結石

uropathy　尿路疾患

urosepsis　尿路由来敗血症

urostomy　ウロストミー

useful field of view：UFOV　有効視野

uterine cancer　子宮がん

uterine prolapse　子宮脱

uvula　口蓋垂

V

vaccination　予防接種

vaccine　ワクチン

validation therapy　バリデーション療法

value　価値

value-for-money：VFM　バリューフォーマネー

valvular abnormality　弁膜異常

valvular disease　弁膜症

valvular heart disease　心臓弁膜症

vancomycin-resistant enterococci：VRE　バンコマイシン耐性腸球菌

varicella　水痘

varicella infection　水痘感染

varicella zoster virus：VZV　水痘帯状疱疹ウイルス

varix　静脈瘤

varus　内反

vascular dementia　血管性認知症

vascular imaging　血管造影

vasospastic angina pectoris　冠動脈攣縮性狭心症

vaulting gait　伸び上がり歩行

vegetative patient　植物状態の人間

vegetative state　植物状態

vein　静脈

venous blood　静脈血

ventilation　換気

ventricular fibrillation　心室細動

ventricular septal defect：VSD　心室中隔欠損

verbal aggression　言語的攻撃

verbal apraxia　発語失行

verbal communication　言語的コミュニケーション；口話

verbal IQ：VIQ　言語性IQ

verbal memory　言語性記憶

vertebral artery　椎骨動脈

vertebral column　脊柱

vertebral compression fracture　脊椎圧迫骨折

vertical disease transmission　垂直感染

vertical relationship　上下関係

vertigo　めまい

vestibular dysfunction　前庭障害

vestibulo-ocular reflex：VOR　前庭動眼反射

vibration　振動

vibration massage　振戦法

Vibrio parahaemolyticus　腸炎ビブリオ

videofluorography：VF　嚥下造影検査

violence　暴力

viral hepatitis　ウイルス性肝炎

viral infection　ウイルス感染症

virus　ウイルス

vision　視力

vision substitution　視覚代行

visitation rights　面接権

visual acuity　視力

visual agnosia　視覚失認

visual deficit　視覚障害

visual disorder　視覚障害

visual disturbance　視力障害

visual field defect　視野障害

visual field restriction　視野狭窄

visual hallucination　幻視

visual impairment　視覚障害；視力障害

visual perception　視知覚

visual spatial agnosia　視空間失認

vital capacity　肺活量

vital signs　バイタルサイン；生命徴候

vitamin　ビタミン

vitamin deficiency　ビタミン欠乏症

vocational ability evaluation　職業能力評価

vocational counseling　職業カウンセリング

vocational education　職業教育

vocational evaluation　職業評価

vocational rehabilitation　職業リハビリテーション

voice generator　人工喉頭（こうとう）

voice output communication aid：VOCA　携帯用会話補助装置

volitional disorder　意欲障害

Volkmann's contracture　フォルクマン拘縮（こうしゅく）

voluntarism　ボランティアリズム

voluntary bankruptcy　自己破産

voluntary contraction　随意収縮

voluntary guardianship system　任意後見制度

voluntary hospitalization　任意入院

voluntary movement　随意運動

volunteer　ボランティア

volunteering　ボランティア活動

vomiting　嘔吐

W

waddling gait　動揺性歩行

wage　賃金

wage gap　賃金格差

waiting list　待機者リスト

waiting period　待機期間

walker　歩行器；固定式歩行器

walking cane　歩行補助つえ

walking cycle　歩行周期

walking stick　ステッキ型つえ

wander alarm　徘徊感知器（はいかいかんちき）

wandering　徘徊

wandering alarm　徘徊感知器

waste disposal　廃棄物処理

waterborne infection　水系感染

water-soluble vitamin　水溶性ビタミン

water vapor permeability　透湿性

weak eye sight　弱視

wearing-off phenomenon　ウェアリングオフ現象

Wechsler Adult Intelligence Scale：WAIS　ウェクスラー成人知能検査

Wechsler-Bellevue Intelligence Scale　ウェクスラー・ベルビュー知能検査

Wechsler Intelligence Scale　ウェクスラー知能検査

Wechsler Intelligence Scale for Children：WISC　ウェクスラー児童知能検査；ウイスク

Wechsler Intelligence Scale for Children-Revised：WISC-R　ウェクスラー児童知能検査改訂版

Wechsler Preschool and Primary Scale of Intelligence：WPPSI　ウェスクラー幼児知能検査

weekly care plan　週間ケア計画

Weimar Constitution　ワイマール憲法

welfare　福祉；厚生

welfare policy　福祉政策

welfare society　福祉社会

welfare state　福祉国家

well-being　ウェルビーイング

Werner syndrome：WS　ウェルナー症候群

Wernicke-Korsakoff syndrome　ウェルニッケ・コルサコフ症候群

Wernicke's aphasia　ウェルニッケ失語

Wernicke's area　ウェルニッケ野

Wernicke's encephalopathy　ウェルニッケ脳症

Western Aphasia Battery：WAB　WAB失語症検査

western medicine　西洋医学

wheelchair　車いす

wheezing　喘鳴（ぜんめい）

whiplash　むち打ち症

white blood cells：WBC　白血球

white cane　白杖（はくじょう）

white tongue　舌苔（ぜったい）

widow　寡婦（かふ）；未亡人

widow benefit　寡婦給付

widower　寡夫（かふ）

widowerhood　寡夫期

widowhood　寡婦期（かふ）

widow's pension　寡婦年金

width　幅員（ふくいん）

will　遺言（いごん）；遺言書（ゆいごん）

Wilson's disease　ウイルソン病

withdrawal symptom　離脱症状；禁断症状

word finding difficulty　喚語困難

word finding disorder　喚語障害

word-for-word reflection　逐語反射

workability　ワーカビリティ

Work Ability Index：WAI　労働適応能力指標

work absence　欠勤

work accident　労働災害

workaholic　ワーカーホリック；仕事中毒

work environment　労働環境

workers' accident compensation insurance　労災保険

workers' compensation insurance　労働保険

work hours　労働時間

working-age dementia　若年性認知症；早発性痴呆

working-age population　生産年齢人口；労働力人口

working memory　作業記憶

working poor　ワーキングプア

working population　就業人口

work-life balance　ワークライフバランス

work sharing　ワークシェアリング

workshop　ワークショップ

work tolerance　作業耐性

World Health Organization：WHO　世界保健機関

World Leisure and Recreation Association：WLRA　世界レジャー・レクリエーション協会

wound　創傷

wound care　ウンドケア；創傷ケア

wound classification　創分類

wound dressing　創傷被覆材

wound infection　創感染

writing exercise　書字訓練

written communication　筆談

X

xanthogranulomatous pyelonephritis：XGP　黄色肉芽腫性腎盂腎炎

xerosis　乾燥症

xerostomia　口腔乾燥症

X-linked dominant inheritance　Ｘ連鎖優性遺伝

X-linked recessive disorder　Ｘ連鎖劣性遺伝

x-ray　Ｘ線；レントゲン線検査

Y

Yatabe-Guilford Personality Test　矢田部 - ギルフォード性格検査

younger-onset dementia　若年性認知症；早発性痴呆

Young Men's Christian Association：YMCA　キリスト教青年会

young-old　ヤングオールド；65 ～ 74歳の高齢者

young population　年少人口

Young Women's Christian Association：YWCA　キリスト教女子青年会

youth population　年少人口

Z

zero position　ゼロ肢位

zinc　亜鉛

zoning　ゾーニング；平面計画；区域分け

zoonosis　人獣共通感染症

zoonotic disease　人獣共通感染症

Zung Self-Rating Anxiety Scale：SAS　ツング自己評価式不安尺度

Zung Self-Rating Depression Scale：SDS　ツング自己評価式抑うつ性尺度

Zutphen Elderly Study　ズトフェン高齢者研究

第3部 ─ 英文用語解説

あ

アクティビティ　activity
A term that refers to recreation, action or movement as well as a thing that a person or group does or has done.

アセスメント　assessment
A careful evaluation of the needs, preferences and abilities of an individual based on his or her subjective report and the examiner's objective findings, including physical examination, health history and information obtained from family members and other team members.

アテトーゼ　athetosis
A symptom that is characterized by slow, involuntary, convoluted writhing and continuous movements of the fingers, hands, toes, and feet, typically caused by lesions in the corpus striatum of the brain.

アドボカシー　advocacy
An activity by an individual or organization that advocates on behalf of others to influence decisions within organizations, governments or societies.

アルツハイマー型認知症　dementia of the Alzheimer's type : DAT
A type of dementia that typically occurs in old age, resulting from the formation of plaques or nerve tangles in the brain of Alzheimer's patients.

アルツハイマー病　Alzheimer's disease
A progressive and degenerative disease of the brain which causes the irreversible loss of neurons; reported by Alois Alzheimer in 1907.

あん法　fomentation
The application of warm or cold liquids, moist substances, or medications to the body to relieve inflammation and pain.

い

意識障害　disturbance of consciousness
A term that refers to changes in cognition or perceptual disturbances that cause a lack of awareness about the environment.

移乗動作　transfer motion
An individual moving from one object such as beds and wheelchairs to another.

遺族基礎年金　Survivors' Basic Pension
Pension benefits that are paid to eligible dependents upon the death of a person who had been enrolled in the National Pension Insurance or Old-Age Pension.

移動介助　assistance with mobility
A movement undertaken by an immobile or partially immobile individual, with the help of caregivers.

衣料障害　clothing-related skin irritation
A physical imperfection caused by the abrasiveness of the fabric against the skin, or by allergic reactions to the fabric.

医療ソーシャルワーカー　medical social worker : MSW

A person from the health care field who usually works in a hospital or clinic and delivers psychosocial, emotional and counseling support to individuals and/or their families with multiple problems in their daily life.

医療保険　medical insurance

A system in which the insurer provides insurance benefits to beneficiaries for medical treatment of diseases, injuries, and defects.

インスリン(インシュリン)　insulin

A natural hormone secreted by the islets of Langerhans in the pancreas that reduces the levels of blood sugar.

インテーク　intake

An initial casework screening interview that takes place on entry to a facility or organization to gather basic information and evaluate the needs of the interviewee.

インフォーマル・ケア　informal care

Also called informal caregiving, is a common form of long-term care given to dependent persons who are either temporarily or permanently unable to function independently outside the framework of organized, paid, professional work.

インペアメント　impairment

According to International Classification of Impairments, Disabilities and Handicaps (ICIDH) created by World Health Organization (WHO) in 1980, it refers to "any loss or abnormality of psychological, physiological, or anatomical structure or function."

う

うつ病　depression

A psychosomatic symptom, mainly a mood disorder resulting in prolonged extreme sadness, despair and anxiousness, which also causes some physical symptoms.

運営適正化委員会　Complaints Resolution Committee

A group or organization that resolves any reported complaints regarding social welfare services.

運動失調症　ataxia

A neurological sign or symptom that results in loss of coordination of the muscle movements.

運動療法　therapeutic exercise

A method of performing therapeutic exercise for motility disorders and lack of exercise.

え

エイジズム　agism

Also spelled ageism, is the stereotyping or discrimination of an individual or group of people based upon their age, especially prejudice against the elderly.

エイズ　acquired immune deficiency syndrome : AIDS

An abbreviation for acquired immune deficiency syndrome, is an infectious disease caused by the human immunodeficiency virus (HIV) that progressively reduces the effectiveness of the immune system.

193

栄養 nutrition

The process of taking or providing nutrients necessary for health and growth, such as proteins, fats, carbohydrates, vitamins and minerals.

栄養士 nutritionist

A qualified practitioner who has met educational qualifications and certified by prefecture government to act as a nutrition specialist, whose job is to help people achieve good health by offering information and advice about health and food choices.

栄養所要量 recommended dietary allowance : RDA

Also abbreviated RDA, is the daily dietary intake levels of an essential nutrient, as a vitamin or mineral, considered necessary to meet the requirements of most healthy people (98%).

栄養素 nutrient

An essential substance taken in from foods that provides nourishment necessary for growth, metabolism, and the maintenance of life.

腋窩検温 axillary temperature measurement

A commonly used method to take a person's surface temperature under the armpit and determine whether it is within a normal range.

壊死 necrosis

The death of body cells or tissues, usually within a localized area, due to injury, disease, or the interruption of blood supply.

嚥下 swallowing

A process of sending alimentary bolus and oropharyngeal cavity juice through the pharynges/throat.

嚥下性肺炎 aspiration pneumonia

An inflammation of the lungs and airways to the lungs caused by inhaling a foreign substance, such as vomit or a piece of food, into the bronchial tree.

エンパワメント empowerment

A process or set of processes that helps to increase the political, social, economic, and/or spiritual strength of people who do not have confidence in their own abilities, so they can increase their capability to make decisions to solve their own problems.

お

応益負担 benefit-received principle

The concept that the cost burden should be proportional to the amount of benefit or number of public services that the individual receives or benefits from, irrespective of income or wealth level.

応急手当 first aid

The initial emergency care or treatment provided to a sick or injured person until definitive medical treatment can be applied.

嘔吐 vomiting

Also known as emesis and throwing up, is the forceful discharge of the stomach contents through the throat and mouth as the result of involuntary muscular contractions of the stomach and esophagus.

応能負担　ability-to-pay principle

The concept that the amount of payment an individual pays should be based on the individual's ability to pay, that is, those with less income or number of services should pay less and those with more income or number of services should pay more.

おむつカバー　diaper cover

A cloth cover used to prevent leaks of bodily waste from a diaper.

か

臥位　lying position

A body position where the body is in a flat or horizontal position.

介護　care

Also called caregiving, is a variety of nursing services provided to aid people when they are unable to care for themselves due to physical and/or mental impairments.

介護過程　process of care

A process of accomplishing a suit of assignments which are necessary to provide nursing care with a focus on an individual's needs.

介護休業制度　family caregiving leave system

A system that permits an employee to be absent from his or her job to take care of a family member who requires care.

介護給付　long-term care insurance benefit

The benefits provided to individuals who are classified into "care-required (level 1 to 5)" based on the results of an on-site assessment of each individual's physical and mental status under the long-term care insurance system.

介護サービス計画　care plan

A set of actions the care services providers will implement to aid an individual to meet his or her medical and non-medical needs.

介護支援専門員　care manager

A professional who is responsible for the assessment, development, coordination and implementation of care plans for elderly and disabled persons.

介護従事者　direct care personnel

A nursing staff member who provides appropriate basic care to seniors and patients with physical and mental needs, as well as assisting them with activities of daily living they may have trouble doing on their own.

介護認定審査会　Long-Term Care Certification Committee

A group of health care experts officially delegated to review the applications to determine whether the applicant qualifies for long-term care insurance benefits by taking into account the result of physical, psychological and social assessments and a report from the applicant's doctor, and if so, how much and what kind of benefits are to be provided.

介護福祉士　certified care worker : CCW

A person who has gone through the proper training and acquired a national certification to carry out basic routine tasks in the care of patients with physical and/or mental disabilities, such as bathing, feeding and serving meals, and transporting patients.

介護福祉士国家試験 National Certification Examination for Care Workers

A national objective test provided to assess and evaluate the knowledge and skills of the applicant as a certified care worker.

介護福祉士登録証 care worker certificate

A written document that is official proof issued to any individual who has successfully completed a curriculum of training as a care worker, passed a certification exam, and registered with the Center of Social Welfare Promotion and National Examination.

介護報酬 long-term care insurance reimbursement

A term that refers to the payments that long-term care providers, such as day care, home care and home health agencies, and residential care facilities, receive for services rendered to patients or clients who are covered under the Long-Term Care Insurance program; Long-Term Care Insurance will pay 80 to 90% and the patient will pay the 10 to 20% co-payment.

介護保険 Long-Term Care Insurance : LTCI

A national insurance that covers certain health care costs and expenses, and provides services for those individuals who may require constant care to support their daily living due to being bedridden and/or who are afflicted with dementia.

介護保険事業計画 long-term care insurance planning

As per Long-Term Care Insurance Act, it is the 5-year action plan for long-term care insurance that must be reviewed every three years by both municipal and prefectural governments in Japan.

介護保険審査会 Review Committee on Long-Term Care Insurance

A committee formed in each prefecture whose purpose is to monitor the use, delivery and cost effectiveness of long-term care services provided to long-term care insurance beneficiaries and to review the appeal of the decision of the committee.

介護保険法 Long-Term Care Insurance Act

A law that established the provision of long-term care services for the elderly who require assistance or care because of age, physical, mental and/or developmental disabilities.

介護目標 goal of care

A goal that will give direction for the care plan.

介護予防 disability prevention services for long-term care insurance beneficiaries

A system of health care which provides services designed to help prevent individuals from being care- or assistance-required under long-term care insurance.

介護療養型医療施設 designated long-term care hospital

A type of long-term care insurance-covered health care facility designed for people who require regular medical attention and nursing supervision and/or care.

介護老人福祉施設 welfare facility for the elderly

An inclusive term for a certified long-term care insurance facility that provides nursing and social welfare services for the elderly.

介護老人保健施設 health facility for the elderly

A type of long-term care insurance-covered health care facility designed for elderly people whose health condition is in a stable stage and who require regular medical attention and rehabilitation.

介助 assistance

The supplemental or alternative help supplied by individuals such as nursing care workers and family members to the elderly, sick and disabled, based on their daily needs.

疥癬 scabies

A contagious skin disease caused by tiny invisible parasites called Sarcoptes scabiei that burrow under the host's skin, causing severe allergic itching.

回想法 reminiscence therapy

One of the psychotherapeutic techniques which reviews, discusses and assesses the experience or events of the individual's life.

回復期リハビリテーション recovery-phase rehabilitation

Rehabilitation provided approximately six months following the time of the onset of problems and acute phase of rehabilitation.

潰瘍 ulcer

A sore on an external or internal surface of the body with the disintegration of tissues caused by a partial break in the skin or mucous membrane.

かかりつけ医 primary doctor

A medical doctor who offers both the first contact for and health consultation to a person with an undiagnosed health concern, and orders medical care and treatments as necessary.

核家族 nuclear family

A basic unit of family that consists of two married parents and their unmarried children.

家計 household budget

A term that refers to household economy.

家政婦 housekeeper

A woman who is employed to perform the domestic work and is responsible for the maintenance and cleaning of the household on behalf of her employers, mainly housewives.

家族 family

A small group of individuals of common ancestry; composed of relatives who are related by marriage or blood, such as a husband and wife, siblings, parents and their children.

片麻痺 hemiplegia

Total or partial paralysis of one side of the body due to brain diseases that are localized to the cerebral hemisphere opposite to the side of weakness, or damage or injury to the parts of the brain responsible for movement or spinal cord.

活動(ICF) activity

A component of the International Classification of Functioning, Disability and Health (ICF) defined as the execution of tasks or actions by a person in the current environment, including general tasks, communication, interpersonal interactions and relationships, mobility, self-care, and learning and applying knowledge.

活動制限(ICF) activity limitations

A component of the International Classification of Functioning, Disability and Health (ICF) defined as difficulties a person may have in executing activities at the person level, varying from minimal to severe in terms of quality and/or quantity or to the extent that is expected of persons without a disability or a medical condition.

合併症　complication

A medical condition in which one or more diseases occur with another at the same time.

寡婦　widow

A bereaved woman who has not married again after the death of her spouse.

加齢　aging

Also spelled ageing, is the gradual, organic process of getting older.

がん　cancer

A group of diseases characterized by uncontrolled cell growth with the potential to invade or spread to one or many parts of the body.

換気　ventilation

The exchange of air or gasses in a room to provide high air quality.

環境因子(ICF)　environmental factors

A component of the International Classification of Functioning, Disability and Health (ICF) defined as the physical, social and attitudinal environment in which people live and function, including products and technology, natural environment and human-made changes to environment, support and relationships, attitudes, and services, systems and policies.

看護　nursing

The profession or practice of providing care for people who are sick, infirm, injured, or old with all aspects of health to help them lead a healthy life.

肝硬変　(liver) cirrhosis

A disease of the liver caused by repeated episodes of inflammation or hardening of the liver, preventing proper function.

看護師　nurse

According to the Public Health Nurses, Midwives and Nurses Act (Article 5), it refers to "a person who has obtained a formal permission from the Minister of Health, Labour and Welfare in Japan, being a professional in providing nursing care and support for medical treatments."

関節可動域　range of motion : ROM

Also abbreviated ROM, is the degree of movement that a joint can move voluntarily or involuntarily.

関節リウマチ　rheumatoid arthritis : RA

A chronic, autoimmune and systemic inflammatory disorder that principally attacks synovial joints that can also affect other internal organs.

感染症　infectious disease

A disease caused by infectious agents such as bacteria, viruses and so forth, causing tissue damage and impairing host function.

感染予防　prevention of infection

An act of preventing infectious agents from entering, settling, or growing in the body.

浣腸　enema

Also known as clyster, is a method of eliminating stool and gas inside the colon by inserting liquids into the rectum and colon.

管理栄養士　dietitian

Also spelled dietician, is an expert in dietetics (food and nutrition) who has fulfilled all the educational and examination requirements as a licensed nutrition specialist, provides dietary advice, and helps promote good health through healthy eating habits and with the therapeutic use of diet in the treatment of illness.

緩和ケア　palliative care

A multidisciplinary approach to specialized care for individuals with life-threatening illness and their families; mainly provides mental and emotional support in addition to relief from pain and other distressing symptoms.

き

記憶障害　memory impairment

A deficit in memory that appears somewhere in encoding information and in the retention of acquired information or in the recall of information.

気管　trachea

Colloquially called the windpipe, is a long tube that connects the pharynx to the lungs, conveying air to and from the lungs.

起座位　sitting leaning-forward position

A sitting position while leaning forward against a support such as a pillow on the overbed table.

義歯　denture

A removable, partial or complete set of artificial teeth used for one or more missing teeth.

義肢装具士　prosthetist and orthotist : PO

A health care professional who has skills and knowledge in making and fitting artificial parts of the human body and is nationally qualified by the Prosthetists and Orthotists Act of 1987.

機能訓練　functional training

A type of exercise provided to individuals with decreased physical ability due to illness or aging, and which involves maintaining and improving health and physical function to independently carry out activities performed in daily life and preventing them from requiring long-term care.

機能障害　impairment

According to International Classification of Impairments, Disabilities and Handicaps (ICIDH) created by World Health Organization (WHO) in 1980, it refers to "any loss or abnormality of psychological, physiological, or anatomical structure or function."

虐待　abuse

A term used to describe improper or inappropriate acts or treatment toward a person.

ギャッチベッド　gatch bed

A bed specially designed for the comfort of the patient and for the convenience of nursing care worker that has special features such as adjustable height for the entire bed, side rails that can be raised or lowered, a frame in three movable jointed sections equipped with mechanical spring parts that permit elevating the head-end, foot-end, or middle as needed.

救急救命士　emergency medical technician : EMT

A professional who is trained to provide emergency medical services in conjunction with a doctor while transporting a critically ill patient to a hospital.

仰臥位　supine position

A lying down position with the face up, upper limbs near the body and lower limbs folded.

共感(共感的理解)　empathy (empathic understanding)

An ability to be aware of, understanding of, and sensitive to others' feelings, emotions, thoughts, and mood without having had the same experience.

共同生活援助　group home

A small community-based facility or supervised home-like residence for impaired people with similar needs who cannot live alone without proper supervision.

起立性低血圧　orthostatic hypotension

A form of decreased blood pressure due to sudden changes in body positions such as the supine to the standing position.

記録　progress notes

The part of a medical record where healthcare professionals such as physicians, nurses, physical therapists, social workers, and other relevant healthcare professionals record details to document the patient's condition and progress, the treatment given or planned, and other healthcare-related information that may be important.

筋萎縮　muscular atrophy

The wasting or loss of skeletal muscle mass in a quantitative manner due to disease or limb immobilization.

金銭給付　cash benefit

A benefit paid by the government to eligible people, in the form of a cash payment, cash transfer, or tax reduction, to reduce some type of burden.

く

苦情解決　grievances and complaints resolution

A process or set of processes to solve complaints and dissatisfaction reported by an individual.

くも膜下出血　subarachnoid hemorrhage : SAH

A life-threatening type of stroke caused by bleeding into the subarachnoid space between the pial and arachnoid membranes.

グループワーク　group work

One of the techniques in social work through which individuals work in groups assisted by a staff member, who guides their interaction in the program.

車いす　wheelchair

A chair with wheels that is used by an individual with a mobility disability for the main purpose of both indoor and outdoor locomotion.

クロックポジション　clock position

The relative direction of an object or item described using the positions shown on the clock face to describe angles and directions.

け

ケア　care

In general, the term refers to helping individuals based on their wishes and needs.

ケアカンファレンス　care conference

A meeting of health care professionals who are involved in the care of patients to discuss appropriate care for the patients.

ケアチーム　care team

A team formed by a variety of health care professionals to provide care to maximize and maintain the highest level of independence.

ケアハウス　care home

One type of residential care setting where a number of elderly people live together with access to on-site care and support services.

ケアプラン　care plan

A plan or sequence of actions undertaken by the caregivers to aid an individual to meet his or her medical and non-medical needs.

ケアマネジメント　care management

A multi-step process which coordinates necessary social services with resource providers on behalf of an individual to resolve and fulfill his or her multiple social needs.

ケアマネジャー　care manager

A professional who is responsible for the assessment, development, coordination and implementation of care plans for elderly and disabled persons.

経管栄養法　tube feeding

A nutrient supply method that gives liquid nutrition to a person who cannot take food or drink through swallowing by inserting a catheter in the opening of the digestive tract.

傾聴　active listening

A communication skill that requires the listener to listen to the emotional undertone of what a person is saying and comprehend, interpret and evaluate what the listener hears.

契約　contract

A written or verbal agreement made by one party to another.

ケースカンファレンス　case conference

A meeting or investigation performed to analyze a case.

ケースワーク　casework

The social work that involves directly and interpersonally working with individuals who need support.

下血　melena

Also spelled melaena, is the discharge of black, tarry, bloody stools containing decomposing blood that is usually associated with a hemorrhage in the upper part of the digestive tract.

血圧　blood pressure

One of the vital signs that the pressure exerted by the flow of blood on the walls of the arteries, and is typically expressed as two numbers: the systolic (upper) number and the diastolic (lower) number.

けっかく
結核　tuberculosis

Also abbreviated TB, is a serious infectious disease that can affect almost any part of the body, especially the lungs, caused by the organism Mycobacterium tuberculosis, and characterized by the growth of nodules (tubercles).

けっかんせいにんちしょう
血管性認知症　vascular dementia

Also known as multi-infarct dementia (MID), is a common form of dementia caused by cerebrovascular disease such as a series of small strokes.

けっとう ち
血糖値　blood sugar level

Also called a blood glucose level, is the amount of glucose in the blood, which is circulated in the blood to provide energy to all cells in the body.

げ り
下痢　diarrhea

A condition in which an individual has frequent and liquid bowel movements.

げんかく
幻覚　hallucination

A sensory experience involving the apparent perception of something that does not exist.

けんこう
健康　health

According to World Health Organization (WHO), it refers to "a state of complete physical, psychological and social well-being and not merely the absence of disease or infirmity."

けんこう ほ けん
健康保険　health insurance

A mandatory insurance that provides health insurance coverage to almost all workers.

げんごしょうがい
言語障害　speech and language disorders

A communication disorder that affects the ability to talk, understand, write and read.

げんごちょうかくし
言語聴覚士　speech-therapist : ST

A professional who provides speech therapy to people who have difficulties with communication caused by speech and hearing impairments.

けんとうしきしょうがい
見当識障害　disorientation

A state where orientation is damaged and the person does not recognize time, location and persons.

げんぶつきゅうふ
現物給付　in-kind benefit

A nonpecuniary benefit, such as an item, service and transaction not involving money, provided to individuals by the government for free or at a reduced rate.

けん り ようご
権利擁護　human rights advocacy

The protection and advocacy of the rights of persons.

こ

こうえきじぎょう
公益事業　public-benefit services

An organization that supplies necessities to the public.

こうおんしょうがい
構音障害　articulation disorder

An inability to pronounce particular sounds correctly due to speech impairments.

こう き こうれいしゃ
後期高齢者　elderly aged 75 and above

One of two categories of old age that refers to a person or persons aged 75 and older in Japan.

口腔ケア　oral health care

Any measures taken to improve or maintain one's oral cavity by brushing, flossing and cleaning.

口腔検温　oral thermometry

A method to take a person's body temperature under the tongue; the normal oral temperature is between 97.6 and 99.3°F (36.4 and 37.4°C) for children, 98.6°F (37°C) for adults, and 98.2°F (36.8°C) for older people.

合計特殊出生率　total fertility rate : TFR

The total number of children the average women in a population would have based on current birth rates in her lifetime.

高血圧（症）　hypertension

Also known as high blood pressure (HBP), is a condition in which the arterial blood pressure is higher than normal.

拘縮　contracture

A condition of shortening or stiffening of the muscles, tendons, ligaments, skin, or tissues that often results in reduced movement and range of motion.

拘束　restraint

An act of restraining: constricted or controlled.

後天性免疫不全症候群　acquired immune deficiency syndrome : AIDS

Often abbreviated AIDS, is an infectious disease caused by the human immunodeficiency virus (HIV) that progressively reduces the effectiveness of the immune system.

更年期　menopause

Also known as the climacteric, is the time during which women stop having menstrual periods due to the natural depletion of ovarian oocytes from aging, and they are no longer able to bear children.

高齢者　elderly person

A term that refers to a person or persons aged 65 and above in most developed countries.

高齢社会　aged society

A society with more than 14% of the population aged 65 and above.

高齢者虐待　elder abuse

Also called elder mistreatment and senior abuse, is a single or repeated physical, emotional, financial or sexual mistreatment, or neglect, occurring within any relationship where an expectation of trust exists, which harms or causes distress to older people.

高齢者虐待防止法　Elder Abuse Prevention Act

A law established in 2005 calling for increased national responsibility in protecting the elderly from abuse and neglect, and also relieving caregiver stress.

高齢者世帯　elder household

A household consisting entirely of persons above the age of 65.

誤嚥　pulmonary aspiration

A situation in which material such as food or liquid, saliva, or stomach contents accidentally enters into the airways instead of the esophagus.

誤嚥性肺炎　aspiration pneumonia

An inflammation of the lungs and airways to the lungs caused by inhaling a foreign substance, such as vomit or a piece of food, into the bronchial tree.

呼吸　breathing

The physical act or chemical process of exchanging oxygen and carbon dioxide between the atmosphere and the body cells to supply its cells and tissues with oxygen required for metabolism and relieve them of the carbon dioxide formed in energy-producing reactions.

呼吸器機能障害　respiratory dysfunction

A disability of function in exchanging oxygen and carbon dioxide caused by a respiratory disease.

国際疾病分類　International Classification of Diseases : ICD

The international classification codes concerning disease or cause of death issued by the World Health Organization (WHO).

国際障害分類　International Classification of Impairments, Disabilities and Handicaps : ICIDH

A common framework for classifying the consequences of disease issued by World Health Organization (WHO) in 1980.

国際生活機能分類　International Classification of Functioning, Disability and Health : ICF

A comprehensive classification of health and health-related conditions approved and published by World Health Organization (WHO) in 2001 that helps to explain changes in body functions and structures, and what an individual can do in a standard environment and in their usual environment.

個人因子(ICF)　personal factors

The background of a person's life and living, including variables such as age, gender, race, lifestyle, habits, education, profession, coping styles, upbringing, and past and current experience.

骨折　fracture

A medical term for a complete or incomplete break in a bone due to an excessive external force.

骨粗鬆症　osteoporosis

A progressive, age-related health condition of reduced bone mass in which bones become prone to fracture due to a reduction in bone density.

個別援助計画　individualized care plan

A set of actions the nursing staff will implement to aid an individual to meet his or her medical and non-medical needs.

個別ケア　individualized care

A form of customized, person-centered care that is planned to meet the needs, wants and demands of individual patients.

コミュニケーション　communication

An act of transmitting or exchanging information such as thoughts, messages and feelings as by gestures, signals and language.

コミュニケーションエイド　communication aid

An instrument or tool used as an aid or alternative medium for communication when verbalization is difficult.

コレステロール　cholesterol

A lipid that is used to produce essential substances such as cell membrane, bile acids and hormones.

昏睡　coma

A state of profound unconsciousness in which a person fails to respond normally to base stimuli such as pain, light or sound, exhibits no voluntary movement, and cannot be awakened for a significant length of time.

献立作成　menu planning

A process of generating an optimal menu content ahead of time that includes applying the knowledge of food and nutrients to meet the dietary goals.

昏眠　sopor

A condition of abnormally deep sleep or unusually profound sleep from which a person can be roused only with difficulty.

昏迷　stupor

A state of near-unconsciousness or insensibility in which a person is almost unconscious and shows a marked decrease in response to the environment.

さ

サービス担当者会議　service providers meeting

A meeting of health care professionals held at the time of creating or changing care plans.

座位　sitting position

A body position where the upper half of the body is in the standing position with the upper limbs hanging parallel and the body weight is put on the rear of the hips and thighs, which are used as a supporting surface.

再アセスメント　reassessment

A re-evaluation for confirming whether the services are provided as previously planned and creating a care plan for new issues.

在宅介護　home care

A form of health and supportive care provided in the patient's home by health care professionals from medical and welfare perspectives so that the patient could continue to live at home and maintain the same quality of life.

作業療法　occupational therapy : OT

A type of rehabilitation therapy that improves health and independence by enabling individuals with physical and mental disability to perform purposeful activities.

作業療法士　occupational therapist : OT

According to the Physical Therapists and Occupational Therapists Act (established in 1965), it refers to a health professional who provides therapy, primarily handcraft, under the direction of the doctor for individuals with physical and mental disabilities to promote the recovery of social skills and adaptive behavior skills.

参加(ICF)　participation

A component of the International Classification of Functioning, Disability and Health (ICF) that brings in the concept of involvement and is defined as involvement in a life situation, including general tasks, communication, interpersonal interactions and relationships, mobility, self-care, and learning and applying knowledge.

参加制約（ICF） participation restrictions

A component of the International Classification of Functioning, Disability and Health (ICF) defined as problems a person may experience in involvement in life situations at the societal level, determined by comparing to that which is expected of persons without a disability or a medical condition in that culture or society.

残存能力 residual functional capacity : RFC

The remaining abilities of a person who has a physical or mental disability, after taking the disability into account.

し

歯科衛生士 dental hygienist

A specialist in oral hygiene with a national qualification to provide dental services such as teeth cleaning, applying medication and educating patients on oral hygiene under the supervision of a dentist.

視覚障害 visual impairment

Any chronic visual deficit, ranging from low vision to total blindness, that impairs an individual's ability to function adequately in everyday life and is not correctable by ordinary eyeglasses or contact lenses.

止血 hemostasis

Also spelled haemostasis and abbreviated Hb or Hgb, is the natural or surgical stoppage of bleeding or hemorrhage that keeps blood within a damaged blood vessel.

思考障害 thought disorder : TD

A term that refers to a symptom of several psychotic mental illnesses that result in incoherent or disordered thinking, as evidenced by disorganized speech and writing.

自己覚知 self-awareness

An awareness of oneself including one's value, judgment standard, feelings and behaviors.

自己決定 self-determination

An act or process of deciding what to do or think without external compulsion and to be responsible for that decision.

自己実現 self-actualization

A concept that was originally introduced by Kurt Goldstein and later used by Abraham Maslow that refers to the process of realizing one's full potential and life goals.

脂質異常症 dyslipidemia

A disorder of lipoprotein metabolism that results in abnormal, either decreased or increased, amounts of lipids and/or lipoproteins in the blood.

四肢麻痺 quadriplegia

Also known as tetraplegia, is paralysis of all four limbs that results from disease of or injury to the brain or the spinal cord.

自傷行為 self-harm : SH

Also known as self-injury or self-mutilation, is the intentional, non-suicidal act of injuring one's own body.

自助具 self-help device

Also called adaptive equipment and assistive device, is a collective term for any instrument, equipment, or tool that enables people with a disability to function independently.

自助グループ self-help group : SHG

A group or organization formed by people or families having a common problem or situation and where activities are conducted to overcome and resolve problems by helping each other.

死生観 view of life and death

An approach or attitude toward life and death.

施設サービス institutional care services

A type of facility-based care provided to adults or children who reside in an institutional setting rather than in their own home.

肢体不自由 orthopedic impairment

A functional damage to the bone, joint, nerve, muscle, blood vessel and/or central nerve system that regulates motor function, caused by injury or illness.

失禁 incontinence

An involuntary excretion of urine or passage of stool because of the inability to control bladder or bowel movements.

失語 aphasia

A partial or total loss of the ability to produce and comprehend language, due to disease or injury to the related part of the brain.

実支出 actual expenditure

The sum of expenditures of an individual, group or nation on consumption and non-consumption expenses for daily life.

実収入 actual income

The income of an individual, group or nation after paying income taxes and adjusting for inflation.

失認（症） agnosia

A neuropsychological disorder that causes an inability to recognize common objects, persons, sounds, shapes or odor while the major senses of sight, hearing, smell, touch and taste are not defective nor is there any significant memory loss.

自動運動 active movement

The movements of intended parts of the body with one's own will and strength.

自閉症 autism

A disorder in the neural development that can lead to impaired social interaction and communication and is a term used to describe a diagnostic category called pervasive developmental disorders (PDD).

社会資源 social resources

A generic term for the facilities, equipment, capital, products or skills used to fulfill the needs of the social life of an individual or group.

社会的不利 handicap

A disadvantage experienced by a person due to functional disabilities or impairments, which limit the person's life abilities and opportunities.

社会福祉　social welfare

The various social services and assistance provided to people with social difficulties after determining and confirming the needs for every aspect of daily life.

社会福祉士　social worker : SW

A person with the expertise and techniques to provide advice, education, referrals to other professionals, such as physicians and health care personnel who provide health and welfare services, and coordinate those services (Article 2 of the Social Workers and Care Workers Act).

社会福祉事業　social welfare services

A field which includes the planning and implementation of activities aimed at improving the quality of life for individuals, groups and communities.

社会保険　social insurance

A mandatory insurance program that aims to materialize social policies.

社会保障　social security

A system that aims to provide social protection based on the state's responsibility so that all Japanese can enjoy the decent minimum standard of living.

社会保障審議会　Advisory Council on Social Security

The affiliated organization of the Ministry of Health, Labour and Welfare that has the power or duty to advise on the Social Security system.

収益事業　profit-making business

A term that refers to the business that aims to make a profit.

従属人口　dependent population

A group of people who do not work and rely on others.

住宅改修　home modification

An act of reforming one's house in response to disorders, impairments or increasing age, with the aim of improving independent living, preventing accidents and reducing the burden of care.

周辺症状　behavioral and psychological symptoms of dementia : BPSD

Also known as neuropsychiatric symptoms, are a group of symptoms of disturbed perception, thought content, mood, and behavior that occur in parsons with dementia, often difficult to manage and impact the quality of life of both the persons with such symptoms and their caregivers.

終末期　end-of-life

A period in one's life when the end of life is close.

終末期の介護　end-of-life care

A term that refers to the multidimensional and multidisciplinary supportive care of people who are terminally ill and/or nearing the end of life.

主治医　primary doctor

A medical doctor who takes the main responsibility for a patient's health and provides diagnosis, medical advice and treatments for the patient.

主治医意見書　physician's report

A descriptive written report created by the applicant's doctor, used to determine the eligibility for long-term care insurance benefits.

手段的ADL　instrumental activities of daily living：IADL

Also abbreviated IADL or IADLs, are a series of life functions necessary for independent living in a community setting such as preparing meals, taking medications, shopping for groceries, using the telephone and managing money.

守秘義務　duty of confidentiality

An ethical obligation imposed on all health care professionals such as doctors and nurses to respect the confidentiality of their patients and not to divulge any information obtained during the course of consultation or treatment.

手浴　hand bath

An act of washing one's hands by putting them in warm water.

手話　sign language

The important means of communication employing signs made with hands, arms and other movements such as facial expressions and postures of the body, used usually by individuals with hearing impairments.

障害　disability

According to the Persons with Disabilities Basic Act, it refers to any people who suffer from a substantial limitation in daily or social life.

障害基礎年金　Basic Disability Pension

A form of pension provided when people who are enrollees of the Basic Pension program or enrollees of the National Pension Insurance program aged between 60 and 64 become disabled and are unable to work due to an illness or disability.

小規模多機能型居宅介護　small-scale multi-functional home-based care services

A type of community-based day care facility that is small but provides a wide range of services such as day care, home care and short-term institutional care for up to 25 elderly people who live at home.

少子化　depopulation

A reduction in the number and percentage of children in society.

少子・高齢化　depopulation and aging

A condition where the number of children decreases and the number of elderly increases every year.

ショートステイ　short-term stay

A term that refers to the provision of short-term or temporary care provided at a nursing facility for those who are sick or disabled and live at home.

職業リハビリテーション　vocational rehabilitation

Any programs or services designed to restore disabled individuals to their optimal physical, mental, and vocational ability, and prepare for, obtain, and maintain employment.

食事療法　medical nutrition therapy：MNT

A therapeutic approach that includes individualized assessment, intervention, monitoring, and follow-up of nutrition interventions that aim to manage and treat certain kinds of illness, such as diabetes, and malnutrition.

褥瘡　pressure ulcer

Also called a pressure sore, bedsore, or decubitus ulcer, is a localized wound or skin breakdown due to prolonged pressure applied to the skin and/or underlying tissue.

食中毒　food poisoning

A generic term for health problems caused by eating improperly stored, prepared or managed food that may be contaminated by a harmful pathogen.

植物状態　vegetative state

Also known as unresponsive wakefulness syndrome, is a wakeful unconscious state where the brainstem function is maintained but the larger brain functions have stopped so that the patient's consciousness is impaired and he or she becomes bedridden.

食欲　appetite

An instinctive physical desire to eat or drink.

初老期認知症　presenile dementia

A form of dementia caused by organic deterioration in the brain, occurring between the ages of 40 and 64.

自立　independence

The fact or state of being independent; mainly not depending on others.

自立支援　independent living support

Any support given by health care professionals to individuals who cannot live independently.

事例検討　case study

An investigation of an individual or an event to determine causes and solutions for a positive outcome.

心気症　illness anxiety disorder : IAD

A recent term for what used to be called hypochondria or hypochondriasis, is a mental disorder or health anxiety characterized by excessive preoccupation or repetitive complaints about having a serious illness, even when there is no medical evidence to prove the presence of an illness.

人工呼吸　rescue breathing

An act of assisting, stimulating or supporting respiration in emergency cases to individuals who cannot breathe on their own.

心疾患　heart disease

A general term for a wide range of diseases, disorders and conditions that affect the heart and impair its normal functioning.

身上監護　personal guardianship

A legal support service for those who lack the mental capacity to make decisions to carry out the activities of daily living.

心身機能(ICF)　body functions

A component of the International Classification of Functioning, Disability and Health (ICF) defined as the physiological and psychological functions of the human body, including mental functions, sensory functions and pain, voice and speech functions, functions of the cardiovascular, hematological, immunological and respiratory systems, functions of the digestive, metabolic and endocrine systems, genitourinary and reproductive functions, neuromusculoskeletal and movement related functions, and functions of the skin and related structures.

心身症　psychosomatic disorder : PSD

Also called psychophysiologic disorder, is a mental disorder in which physiological changes are facilitated by psychological stresses.

しんせん
振戦　tremor

An involuntary, repetitive and rhythmical alternating movement of one or more parts of the body caused by disease, anxiety, fear or weakness.

しんぞうべんまくしょう
心臓弁膜症　valvular heart disease

Any heart disease that is characterized by damage or a defect in one or more of the four valves of the heart.

しんたいかいご
身体介護　physical care

An act of providing direct care and assistance to aged or impaired people who have difficulties with activities of daily living.

しんたいこうぞう
身体構造(ICF)　body structures

A component of the International Classification of Functioning, Disability and Health (ICF) defined as anatomical parts of the human body, including structures of the nervous system, the eye, ear and related structures, structures involved in voice and speech, structures of the cardiovascular, immunological and respiratory systems, structures related to the digestive, metabolic and endocrine systems, structures related to the genitourinary and reproductive system, structures related to movement, and skin and related structures.

しんたいこうそく
身体拘束　physical restraint

Also called a body restraint, is an act or instance of limiting the movements of an individual forcefully in order to avoid fall incidents, rollover or to avoid removal of tubes used for intravenous drips or feeding.

しんらいかんけい
信頼関係　rapport

A trusting and intimate relationship between the care provider and the care recipient.

す

すいぶんほきゅう
水分補給　rehydration

A process of restoring lost moisture or fluid to the body tissues.

すいみんしょうがい
睡眠障害　sleep disorder

Also called somnipathy, is a group of medical disorders that includes trouble falling or staying asleep, falling asleep at the wrong times, and too much sleep.

スーパーバイザー　supervisor

An individual who supervises, oversees, directs and evaluates the performance and activities of a supervisee.

スーパーバイジー　supervisee

An individual who is supervised by a supervisor or who works under a supervisor.

スーパービジョン　supervision

An action or process of directing and overseeing the performance and activity of an individual or a group of individuals.

ずつう
頭痛　headache

A continuous pain in the head area, especially above the eyes or the ears, behind the head, or in the back of the upper neck.

ストレス　stress

An intense physical and/or psychological type of tension caused by strong external stimuli, both physiological and psychological.

ストレッチャー　stretcher

A medical cart used for moving injured or immobile people from one place to another.

ストレングス視点　strengths perspective

A method which helps individuals recognize their strengths and abilities to cope or overcome their personal issues and challenges.

せ

生活援助　home help services

An act of assisting people living in the community to maintain their physical, mental and emotional health by helping with their clothing, nutritional and housing issues.

生活習慣病　lifestyle disease

A disease deeply related to one's lifestyle and which worsens with age.

生活の質　quality of life : QOL

A concept used to measure the general well-being of individuals, including physical and mental status; often used at a time when health care professionals are attempting to comprehend the impact of an illness or disability.

生活保護　public assistance

A government assistance program which includes the following categories: (1) living aid or general relief, (2) education aid, (3) housing aid, (4) medical aid, (5) long-term care aid, (6) maternity aid, (7) occupational aid, and (8) funeral aid.

生活歴　personal life history

Records of the series of events that have happened in the past and still affect a person's life.

清拭　sponge bath

An act of washing the body with a wet cloth or sponge using warm water and soap to maintain the cleanliness of the body for those who cannot take a bath.

精神科ソーシャルワーカー　psychiatric social worker : PSW

Also referred to as a clinical social worker or mental social worker, is a qualified person who works and helps people with mental disorders and their families deal with their problems.

精神障害　mental illness

A generic term for any pattern of psychological symptoms that causes a disruption and abnormality in an individual's thinking, feeling, moods and so forth.

精神障害者　person with mental illness

According to Mental Health and Welfare of Persons with Mental Disabilities Act (Article 5), it refers to a person with schizophrenia or a person who suffers from acute poisoning by psychotropic agents or addiction, mental retardation, intellectual disabilities and/or other related conditions.

精神保健福祉士　psychiatric social worker : PSW

Also referred to as a clinical social worker or mental social worker, is a qualified person who works and helps people with mental disorders and their families deal with their problems.

成年後見制度 adult guardianship system

A system that protects and supports judgment-impaired adults who have some difficulty in protecting their rights.

整容 personal hygiene

A set of practices such as washing face and hair, brushing teeth or shaving, associated with ensuring good health and cleanliness.

世界保健機関 World Health Organization : WHO

One of the specialized organizations of the United Nations, established in 1948 with headquarters in Geneva, that acts as an authority on international public health.

脊髄損傷 spinal cord injury : SCI

The occurrence of a traumatic damage to the spinal cord that results in a loss of function such as mobility.

世帯 household

A basic residential unit consisting of the members of a family who live together and share the same living accommodation.

摂食障害 eating disorder

Any of various psychological disorders such as anorexia nervosa or bulimia, characterized by significant disturbances in eating habits.

セルフケア self-care

A term basically refers to any personal health maintenance activities performed by a person with the intention of maintaining health, protecting life and becoming independent.

繊維 fiber

A thin, elongated filament; threadlike structure.

全介助 total assistance

A state where an individual is totally dependent due to physical and/or mental disabilities.

洗剤 detergent

A chemical substance or a mixture of substances with cleaning properties in the form of a powder or liquid that remove the dirt and stains from clothes or dishes.

染色体異常 chromosomal abnormality

A genetic abnormality in the number of chromosomes and/or its structure such as missing or extra pieces.

尖足 foot drop

A condition where a person has difficulty pointing their toes upward.

せん妄 delirium

Also known as acute confusional state, is a medical condition where an individual suffers from drowsiness, disorientation and hallucination.

そ

躁うつ病 bipolar disorder

Also sometimes called manic-depressive illness or manic depression, is a mental disorder characterized by repeated episodes of mania and depression.

装具　orthosis

An orthopedic device designed to support and improve movement of an injured or weak part of the body.

喪失体験　experiences of loss

A psychological experience of losing important things and a reaction to the destruction of attachments.

ソーシャルワーカー　social worker : SW

A person with education, training, values, knowledge, theories and skills in social work; works for the social services or for a private organization.

側臥位　lateral recumbent position

A lying position in which a person lies on one side with both legs straight.

足浴　foot bath

An act of washing one's feet by putting them in hot water.

咀嚼　mastication

A medical term for chewing and is the first step of digestion in which food is crushed and ground by teeth, mixed with digestive enzymes and then sent down the throat.

措置制度　patient allocation system

A system of assigning each patient to a particular facility or service for all their needs according to the regulations.

た

ターミナルケア　terminal care

Supportive care services provided to individuals with a terminal illness during the terminal phase.

体位変換　position change

An act of changing the orientation of a person's body posture.

体温　body temperature

The internal temperature of a living organism, normally 98.6°F or 37°C in humans.

体格指数（BMI）　body mass index : BMI

Often abbreviated BMI, is a measurement for assessing overweight and underweight, calculated by dividing body weight in kilograms by height in meters squared.

退行　regression

One of the defense mechanisms identified by Sigmund Freud, that is characterized by the reversion to earlier patterns of feeling or behavior, or stages of mental and physiological functioning.

退行期うつ病　involutional depression

Also known as involutional melancholia, is a psychiatric disorder that usually develops between the ages of 50-60 years and is often accompanied with anxiety, agitation, restlessness, and paranoia.

帯状疱疹　herpes zoster

Commonly called shingles, zona, and zoster, is a viral disease caused by the varicella-zoster virus, characterized by a painful blistering skin rash in a localized area.

大腸がん colorectal cancer
A disease characterized by uncontrolled growth of malignant cells in the lining or epithelium of the longest portion of the large intestine.

ダウン症候群 Down's syndrome
Often abbreviated DS or DNS and also known as trisomy 21, is a congenital disorder caused by the inheritance of three #21 chromosomes, which results in intellectual disability, a flattened face, widely spaced and slanted eyes, and hypotonia.

脱臼 luxation
A displacement or misalignment of a joint due to some external cause.

脱水症 dehydration
An excessive loss of fluids, especially extracellular fluids, and salt from the body.

他動運動 passive exercise
A method of physical fitness performed with the assistance of a person or equipment which moves a part of the body.

短下肢装具 ankle-foot orthosis : AFO
An appliance used for the lower leg and foot to support the ankle.

短期記憶 short-term memory
A part of the memory system that holds up to 7 pieces of information at the same time only for roughly 30 seconds unless they are rehearsed in that timeframe.

端座位 sitting posture at the edge of the seat
A body position with both lower legs hanging over the edge of the bed or seat.

ち

チアノーゼ cyanosis
A bluish or purplish discoloration of skin and mucous membranes usually resulting from inadequate oxygenation of the blood.

地域包括支援センター comprehensive community support center
A community-based organization implementing comprehensive support operations.

チームアプローチ team-based approach
An approach made by a team composed of members with varied qualifications, skills and experiences that contribute to the improvement of a patient's care.

チームケア team-based care
The provision of health and long-term care services to individuals, families, and/or their communities by health and long-term care professionals who work collaboratively with patients and their caregivers.

チェーンストークス呼吸 Cheyne-Stokes respiration
An abnormal breathing pattern marked by alternating periods of decreased and increased breathing.

窒息 suffocation
Also called asphyxiation, is the state or condition caused by severely deficient supply of oxygen and excess of carbon dioxide in the blood, produced by interference with respiration or insufficient oxygen in the air, which can result in unconsciousness or death.

知的障害　intellectual disability
A term used for significant limitations in cognitive functioning and adaptive behavior that have occurred during the development stage and requires some kind of assistance in daily living activities.

知能　intelligence
Usually said to involve general mental abilities such as the ability to reason, plan, solve problems, perceive relationships and analogies, think abstractly, understand complex ideas, use language fluently, store and retrieve information, learn quickly and learn from experience, and to adapt effectively to the environment.

知能指数　intelligence quotient : IQ
Often abbreviated IQ, is an index derived from the results of an intelligence test, expressed as the ratio of the mental age in months to chronological age, multiplied by 100.

聴覚障害　hearing impairment
Also known as hearing loss and auditory impairment, is a reduction in the ability to hear and perceive sound; may range from mild to profound hearing loss.

長期記憶　long-term memory
A part of the memory system that holds unlimited amounts of information over long periods of time, ranging from a few hours to a lifetime.

調整交付金　adjustment grant
A federal governmental subsidy paid to municipal governments to support the provision and delivery of a steady long-term care service.

重複障害　multiple disabilities
A combination of various disabilities resulting in significant movement difficulties, sensory loss, intellectual, and/or behavior and emotional problems.

腸閉塞　ileus
An abnormal condition caused by a partial or complete non-mechanical blockage of the small and/or large intestine and resulting in the failure of intestinal contents to pass through properly.

直接援助技術　direct social work practice
A method of delivering direct support and therapy though a worker-client relationship based on bonding.

つ

対麻痺　paraplegia
An impairment in motor or sensory function of the legs and lower part of the body because of severe damage to the nervous system.

通所介護　adult day care
A community-based center that provides care, supervision and transportation to persons who require assistance with daily living activities.

通所リハビリテーション　outpatient rehabilitation
A type of home-based care service in which individuals travel to a clinic, hospital, or day care center to attend rehabilitation sessions and then return home the same day.

つえ　cane

A slender walking aid which has a hand grip on the support bar.

て

手洗い　hand washing

An act or process of washing hands using soap and running water.

低血圧　hypotension

Also known as low blood pressure (LBP), is a condition where the arterial blood pressure is abnormally low, causing decreased cardiac output.

低血糖症状　hypoglycemia

Also called low blood glucose or low blood sugar, is a condition in which the blood sugar (blood glucose) levels drop below normal, usually less than 70 mg/dl.

ディスアビリティ　disability

An umbrella term for physical, mental, cognitive, or developmental conditions (such as chronic illnesses or injuries) that damage, impair, interfere with, or limit a person's ability to engage in certain tasks or actions or participate in daily living activities and interactions.

摘便　digital removal of feces : DRF

Also spelled digital removal of "feces" and called digital removal of stools, digital stool removal and digital evacuation of stool, is a method of using fingers to dislodge impacted stool or mass of hardened stool lodged in the lower rectum or a bowel management technique for patients who have sustained a spinal cord injury or have chronic neurological conditions such as multiple sclerosis.

手すり　handrail

A narrow rail, attached to the wall or placed on the side of a stairway or walkway, used to prevent slip and fall incidents while providing stability and support.

手引歩行　assisted ambulation

One of the methods used for guiding impaired people by using a hand.

伝音性難聴　conductive hearing loss

A hearing impairment caused by a defect in the part of the ear that conducts sound, specifically the area between the eardrum and middle ear.

点字　Braille

A special reading and writing tool for the blind that is made up of tactile dots and can be read only with the sense of touch.

電動車いす　electric wheelchair

Also known as a powerchair or electric-powered wheelchair (EPW), is a wheelchair specially designed for aged and physically challenged people that is propelled by means of an electric motor.

電動ベッド　electric bed

A bed specially designed for people in need of some form of care that has electric height, head and foot adjustment features that can be controlled by a remote control.

と

動悸 palpitation

A sensation in which a person is aware of a rapid, forceful, pounding, or irregular heartbeat.

統合失調症 schizophrenia

A psychological disorder characterized by abnormal social behavior and cognitive impairment where information obtained from one's surroundings cannot be synthesized properly, occurring as fantasies and delusions, and can affect interpersonal contacts.

透析 dialysis

One of the medical practices that removes the waste and excess water from the blood of a patient suffering from renal (kidney) failure.

疼痛 pain

An unpleasant sensation occurring in the body.

糖尿病 diabetes mellitus : DM

Commonly referred to as diabetes, is a group of metabolic diseases in which the pancreas fails to produce enough insulin that is essential for survival or cells stop responding to the insulin, so that glucose in the blood cannot be absorbed into the cells of the body and gets discharged in the urine.

動脈硬化（症） arteriosclerosis

A chronic disease in which thickening, hardening or changing in the shape of the artery walls result in impaired blood circulation.

特殊寝台 hospital bed

A bed specially designed for the comfort of the patient and for the convenience of nursing care worker that has special features such as adjustable height for the entire bed, side rails that can be raised or lowered, a frame in three movable jointed sections equipped with mechanical spring parts that permit elevating the head-end, foot-end, or middle as needed.

特別養護老人ホーム welfare facility for the elderly

An institutional care facility which provides a wide range of care to people aged 65 and above, who have physical, mental and cognitive disorders and require continuous care but cannot be cared for at home or in the community.

読話 speechreading

Also called lipreading, is a method used by people with hearing impairment to understand the speech of others by visually interpreting the facial expression and movements of the lips and mouth.

吐血 hematemesis

Also spelled haematemesis, is the vomiting of blood or coffee-ground material due to hemorrhage in the gastrointestinal system.

徒手筋力テスト Manual Muscle Testing : MMT

A method of examining muscle power by using an electronic device developed by Robert Lovett.

閉じられた質問 closed-ended question

A question format which can be answered with a simple "yes" or "no," a specific piece of information, one- or two-word response, or with a selection from multiple choices.

な

内部（機能）障害　visceral impairment

A term that, while the International Classification of Impairments, Disabilities, and Handicaps (ICIDH) defines as impairments of internal organs that include mechanical and motor impairment of internal organs, impairment of cardiorespiratory, gastrointestinal, urinary and reproductive function, and deficiency of internal organs, refers to impairment of cardiac, respiratory, kidney (renal), bladder or rectal, small intestinal and liver function, and human immunodeficiency virus (HIV) induced impairment of immune function in Japan under the Welfare of Physically Disabled Persons Act.

難聴　hearing loss : HL

A wide range of hearing difficulties in determining the sounds and conversations in one's surroundings.

難病　intractable disease

A Japanese-specific term for diseases that result from unknown causes, have no known cure or standard treatment, and require long-term medical attention.

に

ニーズ　needs

A term that refers to necessity, requirement and demand.

日常生活活動（動作）　activities of daily living : ADL

Also abbreviated ADL or ADLs, are the basic, routine tasks of everyday life that most individuals perform such as eating, toileting, bathing, dressing and transferring.

日内変動　circadian variation

The biochemical and physiological or behavioral processes that occur during a 24-hour cycle.

入眠　falling asleep

Being in a state of sleep to relieve fatigue and gain energy.

尿　urine

A liquid byproduct of the body after the body fluids have been filtered through the kidneys.

尿失禁　urinary incontinence

Involuntary urination from one's body due to the loss of bladder control.

尿路感染症　urinary tract infection : UTI

Abbreviated UTI, is an infection of any part of the urinary system, including urethra, bladder, ureters, and kidney, usually caused by a bacterium, and often resulting in a frequent urge to urinate and pain or burning when urinating.

認知症　dementia

A general term that refers to a category of brain disorders that causes loss of memory and cognitive/intellectual functions such as language, judgment, reasoning, recognizing, or identifying people or objects.

認知症高齢者　elderly with dementia

An elderly person or persons suffering from dementia.

認知症高齢者の日常生活自立度判定基準 criteria for determining the independence level of elderly with dementia

The criteria for determining the independent level of daily living of elderly people suffering from dementia, established by the Ministry of Welfare (currently known as the Ministry of Health, Labour and welfare) in 1993.

認知症対応型共同生活介護 group home for people with dementia

A community-based residential care facility that provides supervision and care for people who suffer from dementia.

認知症対応型通所介護 day care services for people with dementia

A community-based care service for people with dementia who require care and mentally stimulating activities.

ね

ネグレクト neglect

One type of abuse, and is a deficit in meeting a person's basic needs, including the failure to provide adequate health care, supervision, nutrition as well as their physical, mental, social and safety needs.

寝たきり高齢者 bedridden elderly person

An old person who cannot leave the bed due to severe impairment or illness.

熱傷 burn

Injuries to skin due to liquids, gases or solids that come into contact with the skin and or mucosa.

年金保険制度 pension insurance system

An insurance benefit paid to people or their family members, which is paid throughout their lives to safeguard their income.

の

脳血管障害 cerebrovascular disease : CVD

An inclusive term for a group of brain dysfunctions caused by blockage or the bursting of blood vessels in the brain, which may cause paralysis, impaired consciousness, speech impairment and so forth depending on the parts of the brain damaged.

脳血管性認知症 cerebrovascular dementia

Also known as multi-infarct dementia (MID), is a common form of dementia caused by cerebrovascular disease such as a series of small strokes.

脳血栓(症) cerebral thrombosis

A medical condition in which a foreign body slowly adheres to the inner wall of a blood vessel in the brain, eventually blocks the vessel, and prevents the circulation of blood in the blocked area of brain tissue.

脳梗塞 cerebral infarction

A medical condition in which the blood vessel in the brain is narrowed (stenosed) or blocked, causing a disturbance in blood supply to the brain.

脳死　brain death

The irreversible loss of all functions of the entire brain, including the brainstem, as evidenced by absence of electrical activity of the brain on an electroencephalogram.

脳性麻痺　cerebral palsy : CP

An inclusive term for a group of conditions that can cause the development of an immature brain and produce non-progressive lesions, which can result in a permanent central impairment of motions.

脳塞栓(症)　cerebral embolism

An obstruction of the cerebral artery by an embolus such as a blood clot formed inside a blood vessel, that is carried by the bloodstream to the brain where it blocks the artery.

脳(内)出血　brain hemorrhage

Also known as cerebral hemorrhage or intracerebral hemorrhage (ICH), is a potentially life-threatening condition in which a ruptured artery causes bleeding into the brain or into the space between the membranes surrounding the brain.

能力障害　disability

An umbrella term for physical, mental, cognitive, or developmental conditions (such as chronic illnesses or injuries) that damage, impair, interfere with, or limit a person's ability to engage in certain tasks or actions or participate in daily living activities and interactions.

ノーマライゼーション　normalization

A principle that aims to build a society where all children, disabled and elderly people will be respected as individual human beings, their rights as citizens will be safeguarded and they would be able to lead independent lives in society.

ノロウイルス　norovirus

Previously known as Norwalk or Norwalk-like viruses, is a very contagious virus that causes acute gastroenteritis (stomach flu) and makes people vomit and have diarrhea.

ノンレム睡眠　non-rapid eye movement sleep

Often abbreviated NREM or non-REM sleep, is a recurring state of sleep during which quick, random movements of the eyes and dreaming do not occur.

は

パーキンソン病　Parkinson's disease : PD

A degenerative disease that affects the central nervous system impairing motor skills and is characterized by the three cardinal motor symptoms of tremors, rigidity and akinesia.

肺炎　pneumonia

An inclusive term for an inflammatory condition of the lung caused by organisms such as viruses and bacteria and can result in the alveolar filling with fluid.

徘徊　wandering

A state of walking around without any purpose.

肺がん　lung cancer

Also known as lung carcinoma, is a malignant lung tumor that forms in one or both of the lungs.

肺気腫　pulmonary emphysema

A chronic lung condition in which the alveoli in the lung may be over-inflated and stretched and making it difficult to exhale air.

背景因子(ICF)　contextual factors

The complete background of a person's life and living, including both environmental and personal factors that may affect people with a disability or a medical condition.

肺結核　pulmonary tuberculosis

A potentially fatal contagious, inflammatory, reportable lung disease caused by the bacterium Mycobacterium tuberculosis.

バイステックの七つの原則　Biestek's seven principles of the social work relationship

Seven principles of the casework relationship between workers and clients conceptualized by an American priest and social work professor, Felix Biestek, which include individualization, purposeful expression of feeling, controlled emotional involvement, acceptance, nonjudgmental attitude, self-determination, and confidentiality.

排泄　excretion

Also called toileting, is an act or process of eliminating waste from the body.

バイタルサイン　vital signs

Signs that include heart rate (pulse), blood pressure, temperature and breathing (respiration) rate that show sustainment of life.

排尿障害　urinary disorder

A disorder characterized by frequent urination, difficult urination or incontinence.

排便障害　defecation disorder

A disorder in defecation such as constipation or diarrhea.

ハイムリッヒ法　Heimlich maneuver

An emergency procedure for removing a foreign object lodged in the airway that is preventing a person from breathing, performed by putting a sudden strong pressure on the person's abdomen, between the navel and the rib cage.

廃用症候群　disuse syndrome

A general term for various types of mental and physical functional decline resulting from prolonged physical inactivity or immobilization.

廃用性萎縮　disuse atrophy

A wasting or diminution in the size of bones or muscles occurring as a result of low activity.

白杖　white cane

Also known as a blind cane, is a lightweight sturdy cane specially developed for individuals who are blind or visually impaired that makes it easier for those people to feel obstacles such as stairs, curbs and steep hills, and alerts others that they are visually impaired.

白内障　cataract

A clouding of the lens in the eye due to the breakdown of tissue and protein clumping which leads to a decrease in vision.

長谷川式認知症スケール(改訂版)　Hasegawa's Dementia Scale-Revised : HDS-R

A rating scale for dementia: a set of items developed by Kazuo Hasegawa in 1974 for assessing the cognitive status of the elderly.

発達障害　developmental disability

A group of disorders that usually occur during childhood, including intellectual disability, autism, learning disability, cerebral palsy and epilepsy.

バリアフリー　barrier free

A term that refers to the elimination of not only the structural and architectural boundaries found in public and transportation facilities, but also the political, cultural, informational and emotional biases found in various situations.

バルーンカテーテル　balloon catheter

A tube with an inflatable balloon at its tip which is inserted in the urinary bladder to enlarge a narrow opening or passage within the body in order to withdraw or introduce fluid.

ハンディキャップ　handicap

According to International Classification of Impairments, Disabilities and Handicaps (ICIDH) created by World Health Organization (WHO) in 1980, it refers to "a disadvantage for a given individual that limits or prevents the fulfillment of a role that is normal."

ひ

BPSD　behavioral and psychological symptoms of dementia

Also known as neuropsychiatric symptoms, are a group of symptoms of disturbed perception, thought content, mood, and behavior that occur in parsons with dementia, often difficult to manage and impact the quality of life of both the persons with such symptoms and their caregivers.

被害妄想　persecutory delusion

A false belief and thought of being hurt by others that is maintained despite evidence against it.

非言語的コミュニケーション　nonverbal communication

A process of exchanging information such as opinions, thoughts and emotions with others through eye contact, facial expressions, attitudes and gestures.

ビタミン　vitamin

Any of a group of organic components required in minute amounts for maintaining good health, growth and reproduction of the human body.

被保険者　insured person

Also called insuree, is a person having rights to receive benefits from the insurance provider due to paying insurance premiums.

肥満　obesity

A medical condition caused by excessive accumulation of body fat causing one's weight to exceed his or her ideal body weight.

秘密保持　confidentiality

An ethical principle associated with professionals, of maintaining information of the client by not disclosing it to anyone who is not authorized to have access.

氷のう　ice bag

A thin waterproof rubber bag to hold ice and water.

日和見感染症　opportunistic infection

An infection caused by pathogens that do not normally infect a healthy host.

開かれた質問　open-ended question

A question format which allows individuals to answer with sentences and stories so that they can answer in as much detail as they like in their own words.

貧血　anemia

A state where a number of red blood cells or quantity of hemoglobin measured in unit volume is reduced below normal levels.

ふ

ファーラー位　Fowler's position

A body posture in which the upper half of the body is elevated approximately 45 degrees above the level, with the knees sometimes also raised.

不安障害　anxiety disorder

A group of psychological disorders characterized by anxiety as the primary symptom, including panic disorder, obsessive compulsive disorder and agoraphobia.

フェイス・シート　face sheet

A document that contains information about the client such as name, gender, age, occupation and highest education level.

フォーマル・ケア　formal care

A form of care that is supplied by the health- and social-care systems or given by those in health and social care professions.

フォロー・アップ　follow-up

An act of confirming and evaluating whether health care services provided based on the care goals and plan created by health care professionals along with clients and their family are appropriate.

腹臥位　prone position

A body position in which one lies on the chest with face down, puts the upper extremities on the trunk and extends the lower extremities.

副作用　side effect

An undesirable secondary effect of a drug, treatment, or therapy in addition to the intended effects.

福祉　welfare

The good health, happiness, prosperity, and fortunes of, the provision of well-being and social support for, or the government aid that provides financial support to a person or a group of people who cannot support themselves.

福祉機器　adaptive equipment

A general device made for supporting the life of a person in need of nursing care.

腹式呼吸　abdominal breathing

Also known as diaphragmatic or belly breathing, is a breathing pattern that occurs primarily by the contraction of the diaphragm (inspiration) and abdominal pressure (expiration).

福祉事務所　welfare office

A central organization of social welfare policies.

福祉用具　adaptive equipment

Also called technical aid, assistive device and assistive technology, is a device which assists and makes daily life activities convenient for those whose physical and mental functions are reduced and face difficulties in performing daily life activities.

福祉用具貸与　adaptive equipment rental services

A social service that allows people to rent and lease assistive technology items for daily life activities at the government's expense.

浮腫　edema

An abnormal and excessive accumulation of fluid in the cells, tissues, or cavities of the body, resulting in swelling or distention of the affected areas.

プライバシー　privacy

An area or condition which is separated or secured from the presence or view of other people; personal things; personal secrets.

プライマリ・ケア　primary care

According to the Ministry of Health, Labour and Welfare, it refers to a health care system by medical doctors/physicians who help maintain good health and provide the first consultation for a person or a group of people with a health concern as well as diagnosing, providing appropriate orders and emergency medical treatments, referring to specialists or providing continuous treatments and rehabilitation.

平均寿命　average life span

The length of time a new born is expected to live between birth and death, assuming mortality trends stay constant.

平均余命　life expectancy

An indicator which shows how long an individual in each age group will live on average.

ペースメーカー　pacemaker

A small electric medical device that is surgically implanted in the chest or abdomen to regulate irregular or abnormal beating of the heart (arrhythmia).

便器　toilet bowl

A bowl-shaped part of a toilet that collects excreted urine and stool in a sanitary manner.

便失禁　fecal incontinence : FI

The inability to control the passage of stools through the anus; unconscious, accidental leakage of solid or liquid stool.

便秘　constipation

A state of discomfort or pain occurring due to feces accumulating inside the intestine and difficulties occurring with defecation.

訪問介護　home care
A form of care service provided in the individual's home by home helpers or certified care workers; provides assistance related to activities of daily living, such as toileting, bathing and eating, and instrumental activities of daily living, such as shopping, cooking, washing and cleaning.

訪問看護　home health
Health care or supportive care provided in the patient's home by licensed nurses when his or her attending physician believes the patient requires care and orders those services.

訪問看護ステーション　home visiting nursing station
An area or station where nursing staff congregate and carry out their administrative duties.

訪問入浴介護　in-home bathing services
A service whereby a nurse will visit the home of clients with a bathtub and provide bathing assistance to maintain the cleanliness of the body.

訪問リハビリテーション　home-based rehabilitation
A service whereby physical, occupational and speech therapists will go to an individual's home and provide rehabilitation and education.

ポータブルトイレ　commode
A chair-like movable and portable toilet with a container below the toilet bowl.

ホームヘルパー　home helper
A care professional who visits the home of elderly and disabled people in need of care; offers support for patients with incurable or difficult-to-treat diseases, provides assistance with activities of daily living, such as toileting, bathing, and eating, and with instrumental activities of daily living, such as shopping, cooking, washing, and cleaning, and also provides consultation related to their overall daily lifestyle.

保健師　public health nurse : PHN
A specialized professional who has a special national qualification for offering health guidance for citizens. They are usually employees of public health centers, hospitals, private or sector organizations.

保険者　insurer
A person running an insurance system, collecting insurance premiums and providing the insurance benefits to the insured in case of an accident.

保健所　public health center
A public agency aimed to prevent disease and promote and improve public health in the community.

保険料　insurance premium
The periodic payment made by the insured to the insurer in order to cover the expenses required for carrying out insurance business.

歩行器　walker
A three-sided walking tool configured of left and right frames joined by a middle pipe that allows the user to stand and walk in the center of the frame.

補聴器　hearing aid

A small electric device designed to amplify sound waves and is usually place in or behind the ear to compensate for impaired hearing.

発疹　skin rash

An eruption of the skin causing symptoms such as decreased blood flow, loss of or decreased pigment deposition, skin cancer, inflammation and hyperplasia of the epidermis.

発赤　erythema

Red spots on the skin that disappear when pressure is applied and reappear when pressure is relieved.

ボディメカニクス　body mechanics

Also known as biomechanics, is the study of posture and movement of bones, muscle and internal organs and the relationship between them.

ボランティア　volunteer

Any type of activity where a person provides services to benefit another person, group or organization without being promised any remuneration.

ホルモン　hormones

Chemical substances secreted directly into the blood and lymph nodes from the endocrine glands and have effects on special target organs.

ま

松葉づえ　crutch

A long stick, either wooden or aluminum with a padded piece at the top that fits under a person's arm, used by people with a leg injury as an aid in ambulation.

麻痺　paralysis

A loss of voluntary movement and/or sensory perception in a body part caused by injury or disease of the nerves, brain, or spinal cord.

み

ミキサー食　blenderized diet : BD

A type of diet in which foods have been blended into a smooth consistency.

ミニメンタルステート検査　Mini-Mental State Examination : MMSE

Also abbreviated MMSE, is a brief, structured written assessment instrument that evaluates and assesses cognitive function and mental status including memory and orientation; introduced by Folstein, S. E., et al. in 1975.

ミネラル(無機質)　mineral (inorganic solid)

A naturally occurring inorganic nutrient that is necessary for the health and maintenance of bodily functions such as calcium, magnesium, potassium, and iron.

脈拍　pulse

A rhythmical throbbing of the arteries caused by the regular contractions of the heart, typically as felt in the wrists or neck.

め

メタボリックシンドローム　metabolic syndrome
A set of any two or more of the following signs in the same person meet the criteria for the metabolic syndrome: abdominal obesity, high blood sugar, high blood pressure and dyslipidemia.

メチシリン耐性黄色ブドウ球菌　methicillin-resistant Staphylococcus aureus : MRSA
Often abbreviated MRSA, is a type of staph bacteria called Staphylococcus aureus that is resistant to the antibiotic methicillin and causes several infections that are difficult to treat.

滅菌　sterilization
An act of removing or killing all living pathogenic organisms from the surface of instruments, body and food.

免疫　immunity
The ability of an organism to resist a particular infection, disease or toxin through the action of specific antibodies or blood cells produced by them in response to the presence of an antigen, as from natural exposure or vaccination (active immunity) or the transfer of antibodies from another person, as through injection, placental transfer or through breast milk (passive immunity).

も

妄想　delusion
A false personal belief or thought that is either false, fanciful or derived from deception, and has no evidence in fact.

燃えつき症候群　burnout syndrome
An experience of exhaustion that principally involves extreme physical and mental fatigue and depletion of emotions, often caused by involvement in situations that are demanding.

モニタリング　monitoring
A stage of carefully observing whether a patient's difficulties are being resolved.

問題行動　problem behavior
An action or reaction of a person that is destructive, antisocial or against the common good.

や

夜間せん妄　nighttime delirium
A confused state during the night due to clouded consciousness accompanied by hallucination and delusion.

薬剤師　pharmacist
A health care professional in medicine with a national qualification to assist people with understanding what and how the medications they are taking will work.

薬物療法　pharmacotherapy
Also referred to as drug therapy, is the medical treatment of a disease or disorder by means of medications, in contrast to such methods as psychotherapy, surgical therapy, radiation therapy, physical therapy, or other alternative therapies.

ゆ

有料老人ホーム private elderly care home

A facility aiming at providing some help with activities of daily living such as bathing, as well as instrumental activities of daily living such as preparing meals. It is different from a geriatric welfare facility that provides continuous nursing care.

ユニットケア unit-based care

An act or process of providing care in small groups for people in need of care in long-term care facilities.

ユニバーサルファッション universal fashion

An idea that means to provide functional and fashionable items such as clothing and foot wear to as many individuals as possible regardless of age, body shape, size and ability.

よ

要介護者 care-required

A person aged 65 or older with significant health needs, or a person aged 40 to 64 with one or more of the 15 specified diseases such as terminal cancer and cerebrovascular disease, and is classified into one of five care-required levels based on the results of assessments of each individual's physical and mental status under the long-term care insurance system.

要介護度 classification of level of care-required

The classification levels of benefits under long-term care insurance.

要介護認定 certification of long-term care insurance care-required benefits

An act of equally and objectively assessing and classifying an applicant into one of five care-required levels for long-term care benefits under long-term care insurance.

養護老人ホーム adult foster care facility

A facility which provides supportive care to people aged 65 and above and require continuous care, but can not be cared for at home or in the community due to some environmental and financial issues (Article 11 of the Welfare Law for the Elderly).

要支援者 assistance-required

A person aged 65 or older with significant health needs, or a person aged 40 to 64 with one or more of the 15 specified diseases such as terminal cancer and cerebrovascular disease, and is classified into one of two assistance-required levels based on the results of assessments of each individual's physical and mental status under the long-term care insurance system.

要支援認定 certification of long-term care insurance assistance-required benefits

An act of equally and objectively assessing and classifying an applicant into either assistance-required level 1 or 2 for preventive care benefits under long-term care insurance.

腰痛 low back pain

Also called lumbago, is a condition where pain is experienced in the lower back and surrounding parts of the body.

腰痛予防 prevention of low back pain

An act of reducing the risk of developing lower back pain.

予防給付 preventive benefit

The benefits provided to individuals who are classified into one of two assistance-required levels based on the results of assessments of each individual's physical and mental status under the long-term care insurance system.

ら

ライフレビュー life review

A reminiscing process characterized by the progressive return of consciousness of past experiences and unresolved past conflicts for reevaluation and resolution that may help individuals to make meaning of their own lives.

ラポール（ラポート） rapport

A trusting and intimate relationship between the care provider and the care recipient.

り

理学療法士 physical therapist : PT

A health care professional who provides physical therapy under the supervision of a medical doctor.

立位 standing position

A body position in which the body is raised upright on the feet.

リハビリテーション rehabilitation

A process, or set of processes which aims to restore the skills and abilities of an individual who has had an illness or injury so they can attain maximum self-sufficiency and function as normal as possible.

リハビリテーション医学 rehabilitation medicine

Rehabilitation in the medical field that aims to maintain or restore the body function that was lost through injury or illness.

リビング・ウィル living will

A written document that allows a person to state which medical treatment he or she does or does not want to receive in the event of becoming mentally incompetent during the course of a terminal illness or becoming permanently comatose and is unable to declare his or her intentions.

留置カテーテル indwelling catheter

A flexible plastic tube inserted from the urethra into the bladder to withdraw urine.

流動食 liquid diet

A diet of foods served in liquid or strained form that has no residue and is easy to swallow and digest.

流動性知能 fluid intelligence

A general ability of humans to learn and recognize new things, and reason in an abstract way and solve problems independent of previously acquired knowledge and experience.

緑内障 glaucoma

A disease of the eyes, in which abnormally high fluid pressure within the eyeball damages the optic disc, often resulting in partial or complete loss of vision.

れ

レクリエーション　recreation

An inclusive term for various activities for getting comfort, peace and enjoyment in one's life.

レム睡眠　rapid eye movement sleep : REM sleep

A state of sleep during which quick, random movements of the eyes and dreaming occur.

ろ

老化　aging

Also spelled ageing, is the progressive physiological and biological changes that occur in humans after they reach the age of maturity.

老眼　presbyopia

A visual condition which becomes apparent especially in middle age and in which the lens of the eye becomes progressively unable to focus clearly on close objects.

老人性難聴　presbycusis

Also known as an age-related hearing loss, is the loss of the ability to hear high frequencies, followed by a loss in ability to hear mid and low frequencies due to aging.

老年痴呆　senile dementia : SD

A disease caused by the degeneration of brain cells, often associated with old age and is the predominant symptom of progressive dementia.

老齢基礎年金　Basic Old-Age Pension

A national pension program in which the government provides money to people who are age 65 and older with at least 25 years of contributions.

ロールプレイ　role play

Also known as role playing, is a technique in which several individuals or a small group of participants act out roles to explore a particular scenario or situation, often used to develop and practice interpersonal skills such as communication, conflict resolution, and group decision making.

参考文献一覧

一般社団法人国際交流&日本語支援Y編著『介護の言葉と漢字ハンドブック　英語版』一般社団法人
　　国際交流&日本語支援Y, 2015.

井部俊子・開原成允・京極高宣・前沢政次編『在宅医療辞典』中央法規出版, 2009.

大森正英編『改訂　介護職・福祉職のための医学用語辞典』中央法規出版, 2014.

京極高宣『社会福祉学小辞典(第2版)』ミネルヴァ書房, 2000.

公益社団法人国際厚生事業団『介護導入研修テキスト　日英版(第5版)』公益社団法人国際厚生事業団,
　　2014.

小山剛監『介護支援専門員基本用語辞典(第2版)』エクスナレッジ, 2008.

「シリーズ・21世紀の社会福祉」編集委員会編『社会福祉基本用語集(七訂版)』ミネルヴァ書房, 2009.

杉本敏夫・東野義之・南武志・和田謙一郎編著『ケアマネジメント用語辞典(改訂版)』ミネルヴァ書房, 2007.

武久洋三監『早わかり リハビリテーション用語・略語・英和辞典』ナツメ社, 2011.

田中雅子監『介護福祉士基本用語辞典』エクスナレッジ, 2007.

中央法規出版編集部編『七訂　介護福祉用語辞典』中央法規出版, 2015.

独立行政法人国際交流基金関西国際センター『外国人のための看護・介護用語集—日本語でケアナビ
　　英語版』凡人社, 2009.

日本在宅ケア学会監『在宅ケア事典』中央法規出版, 2007.

日本地域福祉学会編『新版 地域福祉事典』中央法規出版, 2006.

山縣文治・柏女霊峰編『社会福祉用語辞典(第7版)』ミネルヴァ書房, 2009.

古川孝順・白澤政和・川村佐和子編『社会福祉士・介護福祉士のための用語辞典(第2版)』誠信書房,
　　2006.

吉田聡編著『福祉・介護・リハビリ英語小事典』英光社, 2008.

吉田宏岳監『介護福祉学習事典(第2版)』医歯薬出版, 2007.

小松真監『介護・福祉・医療用語集(改訂版)』エルゼビア・ジャパン, 2008.

Barker, R. L., The Social Work Dictionary: 5th Edition. NASW Press 2003.

Birren, J. E. and Schaie K.W., Handbook of the Psychology of Aging. Academic Press
　　Limited 1996.

Colman, A. M., Dictionary of Psychology. Oxford University Press 2009.

Davies, M., The Blackwell Encyclopedia of Social Work. Blackwell Publishing Ltd
　　2000.

Kandel, J., The Encyclopedia of Elder Care. Facts on File 2009.

World Health Organization, International Classification of Impairments, Disabilities
　　and Handicaps. World Health Organization 1980.

著者紹介

澤田　如（Yuki Sawada）

1996年	南カリフォルニア大学心理学部卒業
2000年	南カリフォルニア大学老年学スクール修士課程修了（老年学修士）,
	Keiro Senior HealthCare, ICF, Social Services Dept. Manager
2006年	日本福祉大学COE研究員
2010年	日本福祉大学大学院社会福祉学研究科社会福祉学専攻博士後期課程修了（社会福祉学博士）
現在	日本福祉大学健康社会研究センター　客員研究員

主要著書

『アメリカ高齢者ケアの光と陰―ケアの質向上のためのマネジメントシステム』大学教育出版, 2012年, 『国際介護保険用語辞典―介護保険の国際化』共編, 大学教育出版, 2012年, 『Achievements and Future Directions of the Long-Term Care Insurance System in Japan』大学教育出版, 2014年ほか.

住居　広士（Hiroshi Sumii）

1982年	鳥取大学医学部卒業
1987年	岡山大学大学院医学研究科修了（医学博士）
1993年	岡山県立大学短期大学部助教授
1998年	ミシガン大学老年医学センター（文部省在外研究員）
2000年	広島県立保健福祉大学教授
2005年	県立広島大学保健福祉学部人間福祉学科教授
現在	県立広島大学大学院保健福祉学専攻教授, 医師, 社会福祉士, 介護福祉士

主要著書

『介護福祉用語辞典』編集代表, ミネルヴァ書房, 2009年, 『国際介護保険用語辞典―介護保険の国際化』共編, 大学教育出版, 2012年, 『Achievements and Future Directions of the Long-Term Care Insurance System in Japan』大学教育出版, 2014年ほか.

介護福祉用語和英・英和辞典
Dictionary of Long-Term Care and Related Terms

2017年 10月10日 発行

著　　者	澤田 如・住居広士
発 行 者	荘村明彦
発 行 所	中央法規出版株式会社
	(Chuohoki Publishing Co., Ltd.)
	〒110-0016　東京都台東区台東 3-29-1 中央法規ビル
	営　　業　TEL 03-3834-5817　FAX 03-3837-8037
	書店窓口　TEL 03-3834-5815　FAX 03-3837-8035
	編　　集　TEL 03-3834-5812　FAX 03-3837-8032
	https://www.chuohoki.co.jp/

印刷・製本	株式会社ジャパンマテリアル
装幀・本文デザイン	大下賢一郎

Copyright © 2017 by Yuki Sawada and Hiroshi Sumii.
All rights reserved.
ISBN978-4-8058-5573-7

本書のコピー，スキャン，デジタル化等の無断複製は，著作権法上での例外を除き禁じられています．また，本書を代行業者等の第三者に依頼してコピー，スキャン，デジタル化することは，たとえ個人や家庭内での利用であっても著作権法違反です．

No part of this book protected by this copyright notice may be reproduced or transmitted in any form or by any means, electronic or mechanical, including photocopying, recording, or by any information storage and retrieval system, without the written permission from the copyright holder.

定価はカバーに表示してあります．
落丁本・乱丁本はお取替えいたします．